Reading the Fascicles of Emily Dickinson

Reading the Fascicles of Emily Dickinson
Dwelling in Possibilities

Eleanor Elson Heginbotham

The Ohio State University Press

Columbus

Copyright © 2003 by The Ohio State University.
All rights reserved.

Library of Congress Cataloging-in-Publication Data

Heginbotham, Eleanor Elson.
　Reading the fascicles of Emily Dickinson : dwelling in possibilities / Eleanor Elson Heginbotham.
　　p. cm.
　Includes bibliographical references (p.　) and index.
　　ISBN 081420922X (hardcover : alk. paper)—ISBN 0-8142-9004-3 (CD-ROM)
　　1. Dickinson, Emily, 1830–1886—Criticism, Textual. 2. Dickinson, Emily, 1830–1886—Manuscripts. 3. Dickinson, Emily, 1830–1886—Technique. 4. Manuscripts, American—Editing. 5. Poetry—Editing. I. Title.

PS1541.Z5H44 2003
811'.4—dc21
　　　　　　　　　　　　　　　　　　　2002154492

Cover design by Dan O'Dair.

Poems reprinted by permission of the publishers and the Trustees of Amherst College from THE POEMS OF EMILY DICKINSON, Thomas H. Johnson, ed., Cambridge, Mass.: The Belknap Press of Harvard University Press, Copyright © 1951, 1955, 1979 by the President and Fellows of Harvard College; and by permission from THE LETTERS OF EMILY DICKINSON edited by Thomas H. Johnson, Cambridge, Mass.: The Belknap Press of Harvard University Press, Copyright © 1958, 1986 by the President and Fellows of Harvard College.

Manuscripts are printed by permission of The Houghton Library, Harvard University. © The President and Fellows of Harvard College, and by permis-sion of Amherst College.

Contents

Acknowledgments	vi
Introduction Reading Dickinson Contextually	viii
1 Dickinson's Aesthetics and Fascicle 21	5
2 Owning the Gold: The Surge of Fascicle 21	23
3 Inferring from "Duplicates": Fascicle 8's Magic	44
4 "Alabaster Chambers": Two Versions of Dwellings of the Dead	70
5 "Whatever it is—she has tried it": Exploring the How and Why of the Fascicle Project	103
6 Asking/Giving Uncommon Alms from Fascicle 1 to 40	116
7 "Only [Our] Inferences Therefrom!"	143
Appendix A Contemporary Poets Consulted	151
Appendix B Duplicate Poems	155
Notes	156
Bibliography	169
Index to Poems and Letters	179
Index to Names and Subjects	182

Acknowledgments

To the many who nourished my fascination with Emily Dickinson, her words: "Thank you tenderly—I was breathlessly interested" (L 979). Many of those people will not know the debt I owe them; I cannot adequately thank them nor include by name all those who since a childhood steeped in potent language, including Dickinson's, have enabled the writing of this book.

First, to my father, "Preceptor of the whole" (J1556, Fr1586) and mother, who encouraged and modeled reading and writing poetry; to a dozen teachers of whom I will only name two: Dorothy Mateer at the College of Wooster and Martha Nell Smith at the University of Maryland, both of whom modeled scholarship and insisted on Dickinson-style discipline. With warmth and wit they inspired the work: "Luck is not chance—/it's toil" (J 1350, Fr1360); to Betty Day, the late Mary Alice Delia, and other cohorts in interpretation, who supported the initial writing of much of this book; to beloved colleagues at Stone Ridge Country Day School, Bethesda, Maryland, especially Frances Gimber, RSJC, and at Concordia University Saint Paul, of whom I single out the entire Reineck family; to Dickinson friends and scholars, many of whom are cited within this text and most of whom are fellow travelers (literally) in the Emily Dickinson International Society; and particularly to Jane Eberwein, who read this study in a previous, much longer form, offering helpful suggestions and priceless encouragement; and, most profoundly, to Erland, Robin, Eric, Katsue, and Naoki: "I scarcely know where to begin, but love is always a safe place" (L 1034). These dear people, and those not named, cannot imagine how much their spirit, wisdom, and patience contributed to my ability to write this book.

Most recently, thanks to Connie Heginbotham and John Solensten for help on the early manuscript; to Leslie Morris at the Houghton Library; Daria D'Arienzo at Amherst University; and to the thoughtful, skilled, clear-eyed, and tactful editors at Ohio State University Press: Emily Rogers, who began the process; Heather Lee Miller, who furthered and encouraged it; Karie Kirkpatrick and Carol Hoke, who labored to correct its errors, clarify its obscurities, and polish its presentation. Any blotches that survive are, of course, my own.

Thanks also to generations of Dickinson friends, scholars, and fellow readers, many more than are listed in the bibliography and some of whom are students. To all the poets, whose experience and wisdom, quoted within and listed in Appendix A, and whose support of this project helped it from the moment, almost five years ago, when they answered my questions about their practices and their educated hunches about Dickinson's, deep thanks. Especially, of course, thanks to Ralph Franklin, whose monument is the beautifully re-composed *Manuscript Books* on which this book depends.

Emily Dickinson's manuscripts are quoted by permissions of the Trustees of Amherst College and by permission of the Houghton Library of Harvard University. Emily Dickinson's poetry is reprinted by permission of the publishers and the Trustees of Amherst College from *The Poems of Emily Dickinson: Variorum Edition,* R. W. Franklin, ed. Cambridge, Mass.: The Belknap Press of Harvard University Press, 1998; and *The Poems of Emily Dickinson,* Thomas H. Johnson, ed., Cambridge, Mass.: The Belknap Press of Harvard University Press, copyright © 1951, 1955, 1979, 1983 by the President and Fellows of Harvard College. Emily Dickinson's letters are reprinted by permission of the publishers from *The Letters of Emily Dickinson,* Thomas H. Johnson and Theodora Ward, eds. Cambridge, Mass: The Belknap Press of Harvard University Press, Copyright © 1958, 1986 by the President and Fellows of Harvard College. A fuller version of some material from contemporary poets quoted appears in *Emily Dickinson at Home,* ed. Gudrun M. Grabher and Martina Antretter. Trier, Austria: WVT Wissenschaftlicher Verlag Trier, 2001.

Introduction:
Reading Dickinson Contextually

> They ask but our Delight—
> The Darlings of the Soil
> And grant us all their Countenance
> For a penurious smile—
> (J868, Fr908)[1]

Whatever else Dickinson intended in leaving at least forty hand-bound books for our "delight" (and we must begin with the qualification that we cannot *know* what she intended them to be), they are quite simply the most important clue she provided for reading the poems within them. They are Dickinson's own context. Outside of this context for over one hundred years the individual flowers, the lyrics of Emily Dickinson, have been quoted, queried, quarreled with, used for sermon fodder, and analyzed for psychological, philosophical, cultural, historical, and, most temptingly, autobiographical import. They have been "improved" upon by early editors and even altered by later experts who shifted original idiosyncratic lineations and sifted individual lyrics from their earliest appearances on into categories.

The 1890s categories favored "Love," "Death," "Nature," and so on, and those that reach into the twenty-first century continue to be organized into the slots that fit the scholar's interests: into various strategies for surviving nineteenth-century womanhood, for example, or those reflecting agoraphobia, or those reflecting Puritanism, or those reflecting Zen thought. Essays and books showing the influence of George Herbert, of Emerson, of contemporary popular literature, of Shakespeare, and even of Milton have blossomed like those flowers Dickinson so often privileged. And, of course, from an author rich in reading, thought, imagination, passion, and skill such studies are entirely appropriate. Few, however, have allowed Dickinson's own groupings to guide them.

Until 1981 that would have been difficult in any case. Scholars needed special permissions to use the holdings at Harvard's Houghton Library, Amherst, and elsewhere. In that year, however, an event occurred that has the potential—to this point not quite realized—of revolutionizing the way any reader armed with two heavy, amazingly revealing books might read Emily Dickinson. In the words of Suzanne Juhasz, one of the few to take sufficiently appreciative note of the publication of Ralph Franklin's *Manuscript Books of Emily Dickinson*, these books are most valuable for "the sense of her poems as hers, as belonging to and issuing from her specific and particularly personal character and lifestyle." Juhasz borrows from one of the earliest biographers, the poet's niece, in this next assessment of the publication: "Face to face with her *own* poems, presented to us by means of the bibliographic care of Franklin's work, I come closer to their artistic and biographical presence" (1983b, 60).

I am more interested in the artistic presence in this study than in the biographical presence, though, of course, the two can hardly be separated. To put it more bluntly, I would feel most uncomfortable deducing from the forty books called fascicles (I explain the term in chapter 1) that Dickinson was or was not wildly in love with any individual, far less the identity of that person; that she was or was not an unwavering believer in the God handed her by her Puritan/Congregational forebears; that she did or did not have political leanings, whatever the prominence of Squire Dickinson; or that she was obsessed with disappointment, illness, the grave, or similarly dark subjects about which she, as a human being living between 1830 and 1886, knew so much. Reflections of all the preceding seep into the poems she gathered into the fascicles and those she did not.

What interests me the most is the canny, intriguing, and, I must conclude—in spite of the weighty and persuasive arguments by some of the most influential Dickinson scholars (including the distinguished Dr. Franklin himself)—*intentional* artistry she used to compile these books. In fact, in light of some earlier studies based on the fascicles, one has reason to be wary.[2] Although I do not shy from suggesting various possibilities for interpretation based on fascicle context, what I want to share in this study is not any single interpretation but rather my own excitement at the glimpse the fascicle groupings provide into the playful and inventive mind of Emily Dickinson at her workshop; there, as others have put it, she self-published roughly half of her extant poems (almost nine hundred) between 1858 and 1864.

I see the forty books, then, not so much as composing one large finished architectural structure as offering delight in discovering the poet/editor's play within individual books. These, I grant, are far from finished. What David Porter says of "Dickinson's Unrevised Poems" must be heeded—especially considering that the source was one of Dickinson's wisest explorers: "Dickinson's glorious ricketiness, more authentic to her than finish, was part of a manifest, if unstated poetics in which the word, coming into being, was made not semantic flesh but sensation. . . . Her poems participate in an incomplete universe, exploiting the virtues of nonclosure" (1984, 27). That said, the fact of the fascicles deserves attention. Regardless of whether they were complete or finished or intended as prepublication studies, as self-publishing artifacts, as gifts, as scrapbooks, or as workbooks, they *exist*. That Dickinson, as far as we know, did not ask that they be destroyed; that she compiled them as she was reaching out to the publishing community most vigorously; mostly that she gave each the care and wit that I as well as others have discovered in them argues for taking them seriously. Margaret Freeman's clever creation of a so-far unpublished "Fake Fascicle 41" may show that other groupings are possible and that they, too, may be studied for internal unity and tricky patterns—but they are not Dickinson's.

Meeting Dickinson here on her own ground can be, as Randy Blythe said in the *South Atlantic Review* of Sharon Cameron's highly respected study of the fascicles, "a life's work." Blythe makes clear that the work must engage many scholars and many years "to determine and make suppositions about all of the fascicles, their inner subtleties of arrangements, and their interrelatedness" (1994, 156). Not quite a life's work yet, this study, which stakes out particular territory, will, I hope, move the discussion about the nature of the collection as a whole and of the place of individual poems within the whole further along in a positive direction. If it spurs readers to select a fascicle or two for their own discoveries, so much the better; if students from high school to graduate school use fascicle groupings as beginning points for Dickinson studies, they will be richly rewarded.

When Ralph Franklin published the *Manuscript Books of Emily Dickinson* in 1981, he offered the closest thing to the unmediated mind of the artist Emily Dickinson that all but those fortunate few who use the carefully guarded library holdings will ever encounter. Within the two fat volumes of crisply copied manuscripts, admittedly conveying a different effect from the actual thin sheets of paper, the reader may encounter forty extant fascicles that show Dickinson's skills as an *editor* as well as the creator of individual poems that have been variously called metaphysical, lyric, pastoral, romantic, modern, and more. Each book, holding between eleven and twenty-nine poems, was composed of four to seven stationery sheets, folded, stacked (not nested), and sewn together with twine.

These books are among the treasures Lavinia Dickinson discovered in what has variously been described as a "rosewood" or a "mahogany" chest. All Dickinsonians know the story: how Dickinson's sister and executor Lavinia took her recently deceased sister's poems to sister-in-law Sue and then to family "friend," Mabel Loomis Todd, precipitating not only a battle between the house of Dickinson/Bianchi and that of Todd/Bingham but also a series of competing publications, beginning in 1890. None of these early publications followed Emily Dickinson's words and prosody—far less her own groupings—adequately. Although the fascicles are threaded together both literally and figuratively, they have been ignored or belittled as part of any project with an aesthetic plan.

Healthy skepticism about some details is entirely appropriate, and an even healthier curiosity keeps us wondering whether there were more than these forty books. Did Dickinson give any to friends, for example? Might some turn up as the Evergreens are more thoroughly archived? Most important of all, obviously, are the probably unanswerable questions about *why* Emily Dickinson composed them. Absent answers to such tantalizing questions, we have quite enough work to explore the forty we know. They point the way toward the *how* of the project, though that, too, will remain unknown unless a diary or letter turns up miraculously to document the enterprise. It is the *what* that amazes and delights us.

Previous fascicle studies have taken various approaches. Dissertations by Paul Gallipeo (1984) and Robyn Bell (1988) attempt an overview of all forty books, as did the privately printed work of Martha O'Keefe and the first book on the subject by William Shurr. More recent studies—those by Sharon Cameron and Dorothy Oberhaus—have focused on specific individual groupings. Cameron's *Choosing Not Choosing* (1992), in addition to looking closely at several of the middle cluster of fascicles, considers the theoretical assumptions behind Dickinson's increasing use of variants in her manuscripts. Oberhaus (somewhat as did O'Keefe) offers a more theological and thematic reading of Fascicle 40 particularly, though she also touches on earlier books. Shorter studies by John Gerlach and William Doreski use specific books as demonstrations of ways to read Dickinson's self-publications.

This book, influenced by several of these, began before half of them had been published. Central to its thesis is that context shapes interpretation. Conscious always of the dangers of stepping onto the shaky grounds of the "intentional fallacy," I posit that it is not illogical to see what proximate poems can tell us about each other and what the selections—for they are that, it seems to me, rather than repositories—suggest about the concerns of their author at the moment she bound them together. Neil Fraistat's collection of essays, *Poems in Their Places* (1986), reinforced such a thesis, making this reader wonder why so few had attempted to put Dickinson's back in *their* places. Although Fraistat's book involved mainly British canonical poets, this notion, iterated within the essays, became central to my study; returning to the original publication's groupings of individual lyrics or narratives may tip us off to possible meanings not obvious when a poem is isolated. But what would provide a testing ground for such a thesis? How could one use these books to make responsible guesses to interpretive possibilities (I use the plural emphatically).

In other words, *what* poems and *what* places? When I discovered, through Franklin, that eleven of Dickinson's poems had been "repeated" (he posits that she "forgot" she had already used one) in a second fascicle, I looked closely at the surrounding contexts for the repeated poems. The result is this book. Nothing, it seems to me, shows so dramatically the effects of the pressures of the surrounding work—the contiguous poems, the shape of a book, the "thumbprint," for want of a better word to describe the peculiar tone of each book, than comparing the way a single poem operates in two different settings.

At first I determined to look at all eleven repetitions—at about twenty-two fascicles, though that is a tricky number because, as you will see, some fascicles contain more than one repeated poem, and one fascicle (Fascicle 8, included in this study) contains two versions of the same one. So rich was the mine in which I had chosen to delve that it seemed better to look closely at a representative sample than to attempt a more superficial survey of all of the repetitions. I chose four pairs; those have been more than sufficiently challenging and rewarding. Perhaps the discoveries I have made within these eight fascicles will move others to read the books in their own ways.

The four pairs encompass the beginning and end (Fascicles 1 and 40) of the six-year project that must have taken up so much midnight weaving time for the thirty-something-year-old poet at the height of her powers. They include, too, Fascicles 6 and 10, in which Dickinson placed the poem (in quite different versions) that is perhaps most discussed in terms of the editorial collaboration between Sue and Emily, "Safe in Their Alabaster Chambers—" (J216, Fr124). They also include Fascicles 14 and 3, which house the same poems as those in Fascicles 1 and 40 respectively. And my choices include the remarkable Fascicle 21, with which I begin this study, for the most stunning of the paired poems, a pairing that reveals (albeit slant) Dickinson's aesthetic principles, and Fascicle 8, which includes a duplicate of an important poem within Fascicle 21.

Reading what Jerome McGann calls Dickinson's "Visible Voice" increases exponentially one's appreciation for the deliberate care of the person whom Richard Sewall has no trouble labeling a "genius." Convinced as I was by the startling surprises revealed in the "visible voice" of the fascicles that the order of the little books that I compared with each other represented editorial choices, I was not daunted by the history of negative responses to fascicle reading, which I discuss later. Simply reading the fascicles for years was enough to convince me. Although I find Michael Riffaterre's theories on the *Semiotics of Poetry* (1978) (which do not, of course, include Dickinson) helpful descriptions of the enterprise of reading poetry, this study is not indebted to any particular theoretical school. It is, however, bolstered by practicing poets, Dickinson's inheritors. Acting on Dickinson's boldness, I began conversations with about a dozen working poets, some of whom are among America's "laureates" (literally). I asked them not about individual poems or theories of poetry but about their own (often agonizing) editorial choices. Knowing that twelve poets will have twelve different ways to select previously written works for a small publication, I nevertheless thought that their practices and their hunches about those of Dickinson would form an appropriate support for this examination of an extraordinary self-publishing enterprise. In telling their own stories about attempting to order the wildness of the poems, they hauntingly evoked images of the woman who elected to give her life to writing poetry in that big house on Main Street in Amherst; perhaps she, too, spread poems out on the floor, considering them one by one, riffling through piles of copies for the perfect match; filling a gap here or chuckling at herself at the punning possibilities in putting one poem near another. No one *knows* how or why she undertook the fascicle project, but we do know the effect they may have on an alert reader.

The fascicles have the wildness of bottled genies. It is true they are not particularly great in extent or size although few contemporary poets can claim to have edited more than eight hundred poems into forty volumes, each of which produces the surprise in the reader of which Frost spoke ("No surprise for the writer, no surprise for the reader"). Spending time with the fascicles convinces the reader that Dickinson is not only one of the great poets in the English language but one of the craftiest editors as well. When Johnson's variorum appeared in 1955, Louise Bogan said of "this new text" what the fascicles, the oldest text, reveal in even greater measure: "To read Emily Dickinson in this new text, in which every idiosyncratic habit of spelling, punctuation, diction, and localism is reproduced, is to read her in a slightly different language. . . . We come upon a woman of timeless genius . . . and an artist who more often than not was right the first time" (96). It is time to return to that "first time" once more—this time with minds open not only to Dickinson's different and wholly absorbing language but also to her visual tricks.

Knowing that most readers will not be armed with Franklin's volumes, although we can hope for a readers' edition someday, I must ask the reader to trust this much about the chapters that follow: whenever I quote a poem from a fascicle, it will appear in a form as close to the manuscript as print can render it (and my eye distinguish it). That means that lineation (and sometimes capitalization) will differ from that in the two most dependable current readers' volumes: that edited by Johnson, which has been the variorum from the 1950s to 1998, and that edited (and newly numbered) by Franklin. Although it seems awkward, there is no way around the thicket of numbers that follows each poem: J = Johnson's number; Fr = Franklin's number; F = fascicle number. Whenever all of the poems within a discussion are clearly from one fascicle, the last number will not appear. Missing from this thicket of signs is another contextual clue that would open up an entirely different study, but that is one in which scholars such as Martha Nell Smith, Ellen Hart, Erika Scheurer, and others are engaged: the study of the letters in which many of these poems were also embedded. Such settings provide yet another ground of contextual study of poems in their places, one we hope will increase as Dickinson scholarship progresses in the twenty-first century. Let us hope that it is a century in which someone will discover in some long-lost "ebon box" a bundle of dusty pages that we can hold to the light as Dickinson said she held a letter (J169, Fr180, F8). After all, she said, "I keep bringing These— / Just as the Night keeps / fetching stars" (J224, Fr254, F10). However tantalizing it is to think that such a discovery might solve some of the riddles a study such as this one raises, let me begin to share the surprises currently visible to one reader.

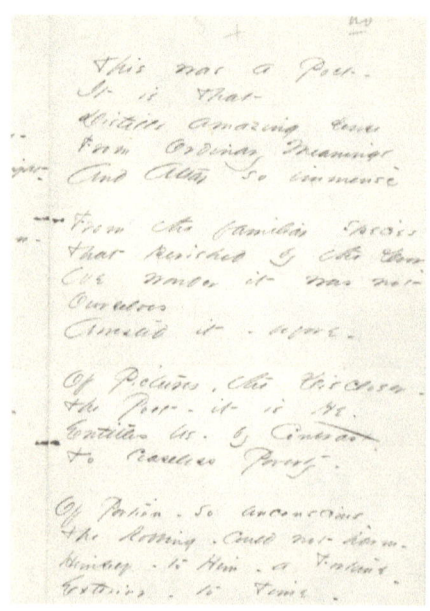

About midway through her fascicle project (numbers six and seven in Fascicle 21) Dickinson placed "They shut me up in Prose—" (J613, Fr445) opposite to "This was a Poet—" (J448, Fr446). Franklin describes the fascicle as dating from about 1862. The paper is "embossed laid, cream, and blue-ruled." The word "No" and the "X" on the top of the second page were jotted by one of Dickinson's early editors, probably Mabel Loomis Todd. Dickinson stacked folded sheets of paper and sewed them into her booklets/fascicles. "They shut me up" is on the back of one folded sheet, and "This was a Poet" is the front of the next folded sheet. These appear in The Manuscript Books I, 464–65. Printed by permission of the Houghton Library, Harvard University. Transcriptions appear on the following page

They shut me up in Prose—
As when a little Girl
They put me in the Closet—
Because they liked me 'still'—

Still! Could themself have peeped—
And seen my Brain—go round—
They might as wise have lodged
a Bird
For Treason—in the Pound—

Himself has but to will
And easy as a Star
+Look down opon Captivity—
And laugh—no more have I—
+Abolish his—

J613, Fr445

This was a Poet—
It is That—
Distills amazing sense
From Ordinary Meanings
And Attar so immense

From the familiar Species
That perished by the Door
We wonder it was not
Ourselves
Arrested it—before—

Of pictures, the Discloser—
The Poet it is He—
Entitles us—by Contrast
To Ceaseless Poverty—

Of Portion—so unconscious,
The Robbing—could not harm—
Himself—to Him—a Fortune
Exterior to Time—
                J448, Fr446

Sixth and seventh poems in Fascicle 21.
Franklin's variorum differs in lineation. As
the manuscript shows, print cannot replicate the way poem balances poem as hand-
written on the opposing pages.

CHAPTER 1

Dickinson's Aesthetics and Fascicle 21

Midway through a fascicle that is midway through her entire self-publishing project Emily Dickinson declared her aesthetic principles. In Fascicle 21 she copied, facing each other, two poems that, as far as we know, she had never sent to any correspondent and that were not published—and then separately—until more than thirty years after Dickinson's death: "They shut me up in Prose—" (J613, Fr445) and "This was a Poet—" (J448, Fr446).[1] Fifty years and generations of commentaries on the poems in isolation from each other passed before Ralph W. Franklin's *Manuscript Books* (1981) allowed us to see Dickinson's own settings for the poems in what she must have thought of as a matched set. Read together, in this the only "published" context she provided for them (Fascicle 21), the poems reveal the full scope of Dickinson's claim for the ultimate possibilities of her art.

As happens again and again in reading Dickinson's "poems in their places," a term I borrow from Neil Fraistat, the two poems speak to each other across the page, each opening up interpretive possibilities for the other. Although they come from the middle of her opus, they provide a suitable beginning, a test case for a revolutionary way to read Emily Dickinson and an opening to a discussion that I hope offers new ways to teach her. Here are two poems, both of them familiar to Dickinson readers as disparate entities; when explored together, however, as they concatenate against each other, as they echo and speak to each other across the page, they become new artifacts by virtue of their proximity. On the left, sixth in a series of seventeen poems, is the image of the speaker who resists being "shut me up in Prose—"; on the right, seventh in the series, is a triumphant response to that resistance in the exploration of why "This was a Poet—." On these pages "Prose," visually, almost viscerally, confronts "Poetry."

"Prose," a word that occurs only one other place in Dickinson's poetry, and that, tellingly, in "I dwell in Possibility— / A fairer house than Prose" (J657, Fr466, F22),[2] is the subject of a poem in which the speaker is a Houdini-bird. Later in this chapter I discuss the ways in which this poem also gathers images from previous poems within Fascicle 21; for now, let me focus on the ways it plays against the poem it confronts in the opened fascicle.

> They shut me up in Prose—
> As when a little Girl
> They put me in the Closet—
> Because they liked me 'still'—

recalls the speaker of the poem on the left. Across the page the speaker applauds:

> This was a Poet—
> It is That—
> Distills amazing sense
> From ordinary Meanings—
> And Attar so immense

The poet is also, as the encomium (perhaps to Elizabeth Barrett Browning)[3] suggests, one who "Arrests" the "familiar species / That perished by the Door"; one who "Discloses" the Picture; one who is "Entitled" to "a Fortune." Each poem (almost always read without the other) is rich enough to sustain many an essay—and each has. For example, although Sewall cautions against reading the first poem as a "complaint against repression" (1980, 322), others, notably Karl Keller (1979, 186–87) and Maryanne Garbowsky (1989, 86), link the fear of criticism implied in "They shut me up in Prose" to the poet's relationship with her family and her fear of entrapment. Reading the first verse of this poem as it faces the first verse of "This was a Poet" confirms Sewall's point that literal incarceration and deprivation are less important to Dickinson than her sense of "herself as a poet." The onomatopoeic snap of that first line—"They shut me up in Prose"—offers a thesis; the image of the poet (in the poem on the opposite page) as the "Discloser," opening the door of that closet, offers the antithesis. The fact that the "they"s liked the "little Girl" to be "still" is the thesis; that the poet "distills" is the homophonic antithesis.

To be "shut up in Prose," to be "still" has horrifying Dickinsonian resonances. It is to be dead or dead-in-life. The poet had suggested that meaning in the punning end to "Some things that fly" (J89, Fr68, F3): "How still the Riddle lies!" This stillness is eerier and more oppressive than physical death;

it is the claustrophobia of trying to live with stolid minds, with "the stultifying prosaic, the leaden" (Bell 1988, 152), with "stasis, finality and absence of affective energy" (Stonum 1990, 120). It is a tremendous feat that the poet can "Distill." Along with the literal meanings of the line—to distill is to produce a heady liquor or a heavenly perfume (the Attar from the Rose)—and along with the way the use of the word echoes Emerson's "The Poet"[4]—the word "Distill" is also clearly a pun in this, Dickinson's own context. Emphasizing the speaker's repugnance at an imposed stillness—a state far from the dreamlike suspension of personality and prejudice associated with Negative Capability—the speaker of J613, Fr445 repeats defiantly:

> Still! Could themselves have peeped—
> And seen my Brain—go round—
> They might as wise have lodged
> a Bird
> For Treason—in the Pound—

The impossibility of doing so, of confining the Nightingale's apparently treasonous brain and voice by capturing it in a "Pound," defined in Dickinson's lexicon[5] as a place for cattle or the beasts "taken in trespassing, or going at large in violation of the law," is made both more clear and more ironic by its placement and resulting play with words. In this context the poet is the de-stiller, the de-stabilizer, the defiant.

Read thus, the crisp and ambiguous "That" in the poem on the right ("It is That") is less mysterious. An asexual reference to the poet who is the subject of its own poem, it is also a further discussion of the bird that can escape the stultifying house of prose—and that can allow those of us who follow the mental gymnastics to do so as well. Read in the context of the fascicle in which it appears, the "treason" in "They shut me up in Prose—" faces one of Dickinson's synonyms for the poet, as one who "arrested" meaning. The closeted would-be-poet/bird in the poem on the left removes herself farther and farther as poet/bird segues into bird/star, looking down from vast heights. As bird, she—or rather—"Himself" laughs at the misguided audacity of the "they"s to contain her. As did Whitman, this poet declares active, timeless, spaceless, eternal existence.

Discovering and Naming the Fascicles

As Whitman, too, but with less self-congratulation (and less of a coterie), this poet published herself. I will return to the effect Emily Dickinson's self-publication project has on the way we read the two poems in Fascicle 21 that declare her artistic purposes. First, let me set the scene for their appearance on these two pages. When she died in 1886, Emily Dickinson left in "the old mahogany bureau . . . her friends' letters marked to be burned unread, and her own manuscript poems," reports her niece and future biographer and editor, Martha Dickinson Bianchi (1924, 102). Most interesting among the latter were the little volumes Bianchi describes as "slender packages [tied up] with a single thread." We may balk at the devoted niece's description of the Amherst poet as "another Lady of Shalott [working] at her subtler tapestries that were to amaze her readers when her little boat had drifted down to Camelot forever" (ibid., 86) but not at Bianchi's notion of these little books as subtle tapestries, tied literally and figuratively with, if not "a single thread," then with discrete and discoverable threads. Tracing these threads enables a bracing and perhaps more grounded (in Dickinson's own choices) way of reading the poet than had been available before the books were reconstituted by Ralph Franklin and presented to Dickinson readers in 1981.

Whitman called his gatherings—all five versions of them—"Leaves of Grass." What Dickinson herself called the (at least) forty little books, each made of four to seven prefolded (not nested) stationery sheets bound with thick string, we do not know. References to "my books," "a little manuscript volume," "portfolios of verses," and "the little pamphlet" (L444a, L937a, L193) tantalize, but the name her first editor, Mabel Loomis Todd, gave them links them etymologically with Whitman's "leaves." Todd's daughter, Millicent Todd Bingham, simplified her mother's term "fascicules" to "fascicles." According to the *OED* a fascicle is "a bunch, bundle . . . a cluster of leaves or flowers . . . a tuft . . . a bunch of roots growing from one point" and, of course, "a part, number, livraison (of a work published by instalments)." These books, then, are Dickinson's own leaves of grass. As Whitman bids us "read these leaves . . . every year of your life," Dickinson also admonished her "Sweet—countrymen—" to read her "Letters to the World" and "Judge tenderly—of Me" (J441, Fr519, F24). The poet who punned would have appreciated the possibilities in a related word, "fasces": "a bundle of rods bound up with an axe in the middle [with] its blade projecting. These rods were carried by lictors before the superior magistrates at Rome as emblem of their power." Todd's word for Dickinson's manuscript books, then, is more appropriate than she or her daughter probably realized. The term, not an unusual one for writers in the "portfolio tradition," relates both to a nourishing, beautiful, and organic unit (grass, flowers) and to a sharp, sometimes cutting, symbol for power.

As was Whitman (about whom she famously claimed not to know—"I never read his Book—but was told that he was disgraceful" (L261)—Dickinson is self-consciously representative of and speaking directly to us, her "Sweet—countrymen," to whom she pleads for a "tender" judgment. As the fascicle study reaches a new stage, how to judge her in her own context is the problem this book poses. What Amy Lowell said about the challenge of reading Dickinson long before the Franklin reconstitution project was imagined is multiplied by reading her in this, the only context she provided for her work with the important and now much discussed exception of the inclusion of poems in letters:[6] "I think she'd be exacting, / Without intention possibly, and ask / A thousand tight-rope tricks of understanding." As Lowell imagines the visit with Emily Dickinson, she anticipates the energy and alertness readers need for reading Dickinson in her fascicles: "But, bless you," she says, "I would somersault all day / If by so doing I might stay with her."[7] Although for years Dickinson was read in imperfect editions,[8] her work invited readers to do what Lowell implies in her "tight-rope tricks," her somersaulting. Now the delights of the game—if you will—are even more difficult and delightful. Now Dickinson's own choice of placement for lyrics into "fascicles," available in reconstituted form in Ralph Franklin's 1981 *Manuscript Books,* invites current readers to discover and accompany Dickinson on the mental gymnastic feats they reveal.

Describing the fascicles, the only unmediated way of reading the poet, Richard Sewall calls them "her private substitute for publication or, most important for us, her notion of the way her poems should be presented to the world" (1980, 538); Maryanne Garbowsky speaks of them as "private acts of publication . . . a lens through which a more focused angle of vision is possible" (1989, 77–78); and Martha Nell Smith speaks of them as one of the strategies by which Dickinson controls the gender and political limitations of print and "expos[es] the ideological presumptions driving insistence on textual 'resolution.'" They are, says Smith from her vantage point as specialist in the letter manuscripts (and most recently as director of the Dickinson hypermedia-text project)," works that call all our modes of textual regulation into question" (1985, 57) and that force readers "to rethink . . . critical methods" (ibid., 56).

Those who have been interested enough to read Dickinson through these private substitutes for publication (these acts and performances) struggle with questions of intentionality. Although Jerome Loving declared the Franklin publication "the event for this year," noting that *The Manuscript Books* may also change the way we look at individual poems" (1981, 84–85), they immediately created controversy. For example, not everyone agrees with Willis Buckingham, who, in his review of the then-new *Manuscript Books,* proposed that each fascicle "may well constitute an intended sequence of interrelated poems" (1984, 614), or with Rosenthal and Gall, who went even further, discussing them as precursors of "the modern poetic sequence" (1983, 56).[9] Such proclamations were challenged before they were even uttered.

Franklin himself calls the fascicles "simply, poems copied onto sheets of stationery and, without elaboration, bound together. . . . They served

Dickinson as her workshop" (1983, 16–17). Robert Weisbuch concurs. In his 1983 review of the early reception of Franklin's work he slams Rosenthal and Gall for reading them as more than that: "Nearly every poem they treat," he declares, "is misread. More importantly, their fascicle narrative shows not a jot more coherence than one could derive from any random grouping of any of Dickinson's poems" (1983, 94).[10] David Porter follows the skeptical line of Franklin and Weisbuch. Although he says that Dickinson assembled her books "quite deliberately" and that the fascicles are the "sole repository of Dickinson's publications and thus take us closer to the poet's intention than we have ever been before," Porter also believes that Dickinson's motive was, simply, "to reduce disorder in her manuscripts" and that she "placed poems on the fascicle sheets according to the space available" (1983, 85). I do not lightly flaunt these daunting doubts—nor have others.

Although—or because—there is no consensus about the purpose of, significance of, or most appropriate way to read the *Manuscript Books,* studying Dickinson through her fascicles "promises to be one of the great voyages of discovery in modern criticism" (Rosenthal and Gall 1983, 73). The discovery has gotten off to a slow and somewhat rocky start. In the 1980s, in spite of incrementally proliferating studies of Dickinson's psyche and poetic methods, the possibilities inherent in the newly published *Manuscript Books* seem remarkably underobserved. Evaluations such as those by Porter, Weisbuch, and Buckingham were rare. Rummaging through issues of some seventeen journals that carry Dickinson-related articles uncovers little mention of the epoch-making event other than, in some, the publisher's advertisement.[11] Nevertheless, a few articles and two full-length studies—radically different from each other—were on the way.

In 1983 William Shurr offered the first full-length study in his version of what he saw as evidence in the fascicle sequence of the "marriage" between Dickinson and the Reverend Wadsworth; in 1986 Martha Lindblom O'Keefe identified the entire sequence as religious reflections following the Catholic tradition of St. John of the Cross; in 1993 Sharon Cameron reversed the tone of fascicle studies by selecting fascicles (primarily 13, 14, 15, 16, and 20) to shed light on what is more interesting to her than personal or religious sources, the ontological implications of the variants within individual poems; and in 1995 Dorothy Oberhaus found Fascicle 40 to be the culmination of a conversion narrative. At least four dissertations and a half-dozen articles have offered substantial discussions of the value of reading Dickinson in the context she provided, the fascicles.

Vigorous, even occasionally contentious, discussion about what the fascicles represent is in keeping with the entire publishing history of the poet. Complex and often baffling ("All men say 'What' to me," as she told the powerful editor Thomas Wentworth Higginson [L271]), Dickinson herself set the tone. On the one hand, she initiated a lifelong correspondence with Higginson in response to his famous challenge to women poets; on the other hand, this New Englander, an aristocrat deeply influenced at an early age both by the eleemosynary teachings of Mary Lyon and by the transcendentalists' abhorrence of the marketplace, staunchly decreed that "Publication— is the Auction / Of the Mind of Man—" (J709, Fr788 F37). Her own self-contradictory statements about publication are reflected in the cautionary words of major scholars: Weisbuch, Franklin, Porter, and others. There are reasons to be cautious about manuscript studies (though the one or two scholars who call it a "fetish" seem unduly wary). Perhaps they are thinking of some of the few studies that have begun the "great voyage" of fascicle reading, variously freighted with assumptions and theories of the readers themselves. Unavoidable and appropriate as this is, as Stanley Fish has convinced us, some of these readings tend to limit the possibilities that make the difference, as Dickinson implies in those paired poems, between prose and poetry. Anything as reductive as a single story seems to shut the little girl up again in that closet.

Stories are tempting, however, and those few that have been offered have persuaded many. William Shurr, the first to offer a reading after Franklin made fascicle study possible, finds a provocative one. Shurr's *Marriage of Emily Dickinson* (1983) posits that the entire forty-fascicle sequence is a narrative of a frustrated passion, but one that spurred the narrator's (in Shurr's view, that of the poet herself) explosion of writing. To make his claim, one widely quoted, even in the space of a major book, Shurr, of course, had to be selective, picking those lyrics that supported his narrative of a life-changing meeting with a clergyman; an erotic, anguished attachment, especially on a particular day "at Summer's full"; a painful separation; and more—all suggested as literal. Radically different in her conclusions but similar to Shurr in assuming a unifying narrative voice in the forty fascicles is Dorothy Oberhaus, who posits that Fascicle 40 is the culmination of the narrator's spiritual quest, that in the final fascicle the poetic "I" is "the meditator," who is represented as addressing Christ and herself" (1995, 29). Oberhaus says that "until one sees that the fascicles are the account of a long spiritual and poetic pilgrimage," one will not understand "the Christian nature of her mind and art" (187).

Shurr and Oberhaus reflect major lines of autobiographical inquiry: one involves Dickinson's romantic/sexual life, the other her spiritual quest. Both are debated vigorously. Almost every critical biography, including the newest by Alfred Habegger (2001), offers candidates for the "Master," for example. Just as much print has been devoted to the debate between those who discover heterodox beliefs (Dickinson stamps her foot at God), on the one hand, and those who have found devotional messages for sermons on the other.[12]

Readers might differ on how appropriate such discussions are to the poet who said "I hide myself / within my flower" (J903, Fr80, F3, and F40) but who also cautioned Higginson not to confuse her with the "I" who is the "supposed person" (L268).

Readings such as those of Shurr and Oberhaus (different as they are from each other) form one approach to the fascicles thus far: to follow what the reader sees as something approaching a narrative. Another has been to sample the fascicles and apply to them principles of contemporary literary theory. In a sense that original work of Rosenthal and Gall, the subject of Weisbuch's scorn, a study of Fascicles 15 and 16 that likened them not to narratives but rather to the "modern poetic sequence," was such a study. Although it used different critical premises, another theoretical discussion was Paul Gallipeo's 1984 dissertation, which likened Fascicle 17 to a "unified structured link-poem" and to "a magnet or electrical field . . . created by its component parts and transformed by those same parts" (101).

The most notable example, however, a stunning model of the application of theory to simple observations, is Sharon Cameron's *Choosing Not Choosing* (1992). Cameron admits that Dickinson's work is not "sceneless" when taken in fascicle context and that "scenes and subjects can be said to unfold between and among the poems as well as within them" (4); she argues forcefully that the fascicles are witness to Dickinson's resistance to closure. Far from unlocking a secret or telling a story, the fascicles, says Cameron, "*embody* the problem of identity," particularly in the variants that indicate intentional resistance to closure. The fascicles are indications not of "leanness" but of an "excess of meaning" (43).

Cameron's focus on the variants is an example of a growing interest in the *how* of Dickinson's presentations over the *what*. Susan Howe, Paula Bennett, Martha Nell Smith, Ellen Hart, and Jerome McGann have pointed increasingly to the look of the poem or letter, to what Bennett (1992) calls the "Spectral Presence in Dickinson's Letters" and what McGann calls "Emily Dickinson's Visible Language" (1993). Such interest in the appearance of the texts, an interest that predates the reconstitution of the fascicles (see, for example, James Miller's discussion of Dickinson's "Bright Orthography" [1967]) and is not limited in applicability to the fascicles (see Paul Crumbley's *Inflections of the Pen* [1996]), informs my readings of the texts. With such readers, I am almost as interested in the play of black on white, on the uses of space, on the nonverbal marks, as in the diction and imagery themselves. Margaret Dickie ends an instructive review of such scholarship with an invitation: "Known as the author of her poetry, Dickinson must now be studied as its editor and publisher" (1995, 332).

I come to this study with neither a conviction that the fascicles tell a unified story of passion (whether of spirit or of body, although traces of narrative wind through single "books") nor a willingness to attribute to Dickinson a prophetic sympathy for postmodern critical theory, although her poetry and her aesthetic principles anticipate, for example, Michael Riffaterre's semiotic theory.[13] My study owes much to the scholarship of hundreds of others, but it is primarily the result of simply looking long enough at the fascicles, armed with Dickinson's dictionary and my own open mind. As Ruth Miller suggested readers do when she made a first foray into fascicle studies even before the corrected version was reproduced, I have tried to "let Dickinson's voice guide" me (1968, 8)—rather, to let her *voices* guide, for, as Cameron insists, the fascicles as an entire project and as single entities are as resistant to closure as the individual poems that compose them. My readings will no doubt be as challenged as have those of Shurr, Oberhaus, and others. Such a dialogue, entirely appropriate in textual studies, particularly those dealing with the self-contradictory Dickinson, will be healthy. I hope that the *method* of looking at the poems—as they present themselves on the page—closely and with an open mind provides another model for the reading and teaching of the Bird freed from the Pound.

My reading, then, joins the fray that Dickinson anticipated when she said that her "Wars are laid away in Books" (J1549, Fr1579). The wars did not begin with Franklin's work on the fascicles. Few poets have created such feisty publication battles. If they began when Dickinson uttered nearly opposite proclamations about publishing, they were fully joined shortly after her sister Lavinia, who had discovered the forty little volumes in that "mahogany bureau,"[14] took them to sister-in-law and intimate friend Sue, then retrieved them in a huff at Sue's apparent inaction, and took them to the wife of an Amherst professor, a woman with her own literary ambitions and intimate ties to the Dickinson family. The related struggles between the families over property, literary and landed, are vividly recreated in Polly Longsworth's *Austin and Mabel* (1984). They continued as the house of Todd (Mabel and daughter) and the house of Dickinson (Sue and daughter) produced competing editions of the poems and interpretations of the remarkable poet, as their holdings were distributed between two libraries (Amherst and Harvard), and even as Thomas Johnson's epochal (for Dickinson readers) variorum (1958) met a critical public in the 1950s. Just so, the wars of interpretation over the intentionality of Dickinson in creating her books continue in more subtle forms.

Franklin and the Fascicles

Although more and more people have, in Martha Nell Smith's words, "been interested enough to take the time" to explore the fascicles, they have not been particularly encouraged by the scholar whose work alone makes fascicle study possible. Ralph Franklin's position on the revolution his *Manuscript Books* (1981) makes possible is itself somewhat ambiguous. In his introduction he implies that Dickinson's fascicles were her method of facing the chaos of life and art (ix), but he seems in one sentence to allow for two opposing interpretations. On the one hand, he argues that she may have stopped binding in 1864 after six years of the practice because she had "survived the crisis and drive of 1861–63" (her need); on the other hand, he says that with her survival from whatever crisis claimed her, "the desire to leave an organized legacy to the world" (her vocation) declined (xii). In the two phrases he offers the scenario, first, that the collection was a frantic attempt at survival and perhaps somewhat inchoate; later, that it was a distinct form of self-direction.

Two years later, answering some preliminary fascicle studies, he followed up his long introduction to the book with an article in *Studies in Bibliography*. This article offers provisional answers to important questions, questions on which this study and all others depend: Can we know that Dickinson actually did the compiling (yes); were there other fascicles at the time of Dickinson's death besides those Franklin compiled? (probably not); who mutilated the few poems that have been cut or scratched out? (he thinks Todd, although Todd herself said it was Austin Dickinson); what was Dickinson's purpose in her compilation work? Here he repeats his view that "the fascicles are, simply, poems copied onto sheets of stationery and, without elaboration, bound together" (4), that "they were private documents copied for her own uses" (16), and that they served Dickinson as her workshop" (17).

Finally, in the last two pages of the article he addresses those who find a pattern in the sequences, saying that "the thematic, narrative, or dramatic structure discerned according to such possibilities, if any, would be looser than criticism has often assumed or perhaps would find attractive." Admitting a fraction of the evidence that there *is* some structure (the contrapuntal nature of the two poems in Fascicle 21 is his one example), he insists that "order can be apparent even in randomness. The tune, as Dickinson reminds us," he says, "may not be in the tree but in ourselves." The magnitude of Franklin's contribution and his status have made this view almost a commonplace.[15]

In the spirit of Franklin's resistance to taking seriously attempts to find patterns, David Porter contends that proof of Dickinson's motive "to reduce disorder in her manuscripts" was that "she placed poems on the fascicle sheets according to the space available [and that] short poems are usually used as fillers" (1983). A close reading of the poems in their places, however, ratifies Willis Buckingham's observation (countering that of Porter) that "there remains a likelihood that several poems on each sheet represent a significant grouping" (1984, 614). That likelihood indeed seems corroborated by close reading of, for example, Fascicle 8, in which several small poems, poems *not* included, I suspect, merely to use the space, speak to each other across the pages as much as do the two prose/poetry poems I have selected for the opening of this chapter and by the fact that Dickinson was apparently not resistant to leaving spaces when it suited her purpose. She does so, in fact, at a significant stage of Fascicle 21.

If one does not select the four or five or six poems of a fascicle—or from many fascicles that suit a thesis (see Scholl, for example)—one is more likely to see that patterns exist everywhere and that Dickinson has slyly left not only the doublings such as in the prose/poetry pair but also a number of other "tight-rope tricks" as well. For example, at times a poem in the center of a fascicle acts as a sort of stile, up toward and away from which the fascicle moves. Elsewhere Dickinson seems to have compiled her poems as her niece and nephews must have played dominoes, ending one poem with an image that will begin the next. She may end a fascicle with a poem that seems both a culmination of the fascicle and a precursor to the first poem so that, as is true in Fascicle 1, the opened book provides the visual trick of leading the reader back to the first poem from that on the back cover. In addition to the mirroring of poems on opposing pages of the opened book as in the prose/poetry confrontation, Dickinson has chosen poems to place on neighboring leaves that are at once reprises and revisions of earlier poems. She has made poems (or speakers in poems) address each other dialogically. She has spilled lines from certain poems and used them on the next page as titles for adjacent poems. She has used verses separated from previous verses on their new page to bridge proximate poems. She has often privileged clusters of images in each fascicle, giving each what, for want of a better word, seems its own "thumbprint" or maybe its "DNA": that network of design that differentiates it from the others.

Looking for and finding such tricks, somersaulting with Dickinson as I do, is the only "story" this book provides. Because this volume is limited to a sample (of eight) fascicles, it invites others to turn classrooms into laboratories for similar observations of the remaining books. How many of the tricks did Dickinson intend? That question, insistently and sometimes querulously posed by students, is unanswerably absent of any miraculous attic discoveries of letters or interviews. Without such a miracle, however, one may guess by way of parallels. In choosing from her poems those for each book, Dickinson was probably as balanced between willful planning and serendipity as her less verbal sisters who stitched intricate patchworks out of the fabrics of their lives.

In literary terms she followed a tradition that Neil Fraistat's "literary history for contextual poetics" (1986, 13) shows is as old as Horace and as familiar to Dickinson as Milton, Herbert, and Browning. Most of these subjects of the essays in Fraistat's book worked collaboratively with editors.

Dickinson, working alone (with the important exception of her communications with Sue), has left even more interesting studies in the trickiness of contextuality. Perhaps she wove her individual poems together as Frost says he composed single poems, with intentional self-conscious craftsmanship balanced with an openness to surprises: "No surprise for the writer," Frost said, "no surprise for the reader" (1972, 394). Reading Dickinson's "tight-rope tricks" recalls Frost's delight in "remembering something I didn't know I knew. I am in a place, in a situation, as if I had materialized from cloud or risen out of the ground. There is a glad recognition of the long lost and the rest follows. Step by step the wonder of the unexpected supply keeps growing" (ibid., 394–95).

Perhaps, too, contemporary poets can help as we imagine Dickinson's bookmaking project. In a later chapter a number of working poets tell us how they put together their collections; some stress careful choice, whereas others claim to surprise themselves. No doubt, careful craftsman though she was, Dickinson, who said "Trust in the Unexpected—" (J555, Fr561, F27), surprised herself, both with the poem and also with the new thing the poem became in the booklet in which she placed it. The fascicles, evidence of craftsmanship and serendipity, of the willed and the wild, are the products of the process Frost and others describe. Was it a surprise, we wonder, to discover that the stillness of the little girl shut up in prose could be de-stilled by a poem that—Franklin's revision of Johnson's numbering notwithstanding—might have been written earlier? Such mysteries of the creative process will not be solved, and such mysteries contribute to my skepticism that the entire forty contain a *single* story.

When one takes the time to read the poems in their fascicle settings, however, it is difficult not to believe that Dickinson must have planted or at least recognized most of the surprises that await the reader. The poems exist on the page. Emily Dickinson placed them there. Unlike any other major poet except perhaps Blake and Whitman, the arrangement has been unmediated by any other mind. Intentionality is irrecoverable; what exists on the page, thanks to Franklin, is recoverable and readable.

The Paired Poems: "Familiar Species"?

What is recoverable and readable, for example, are the two poems of Fascicle 21 with which this chapter begins. Placed opposite to the remembered resistance to enclosure—exemplified by the laugh of the bird that cannot be kept in the pound ("They shut me up in Prose")—is "This was a Poet's" certainty that "Himself—to Him—a Fortune [is] / Exterior to Time" (J448, Fr446). From first line to last the two poems about the poet speak across as well as down the pages. Curiously the first, "They shut me up in Prose," never uses the word "poem" or "poet," and the second, "This was a Poet," defines the poet (Dickinsonianly slantwise) by negatives, in vocabulary dotted with prefixes "de-," "a-," and "un-." There is that pun on "Distill," for example. The poet unsettles us and also presses and imprints the ordinary into the thoughtful and beautiful, as the two possibilities for sense/incense suggest.

Such sense is amazing, another word with punning possibilities, as in a/maze. "Amazing sense" is almost oxymoronic. The adjective is a word that, in its primary, unpunning form implies wonder. In her own culture, as Cynthia Griffin Wolff points out, "amazing sense" evokes John Newton's hymn to Grace (1986, 216). Thus subliminally suggested, "grace" echoes elsewhere in the fascicle. The substantive "sense" on the other hand, for its long list of meanings in the 1828 Webster's,[16] is most commonly associated with common (ordinary) sense, practicality, or reasoned judgment. "Sense" is subverted by the epithet of which it is part, especially when one plays with its adjective as with "distills" and "disclose." To be in a maze is to be confused, confounded, puzzled, unsettled. Hawthorne's minister, for example, is "in a maze" as he emerges from his visit with Hester in the woods; having become aware of more possibilities for escape than he had thought possible, he responds in manic manner. Little girls who are confined in stillness to a closed closet are discouraged from such a state. The reader of the paired poems might add that, because the last line of the matching poem presents the bird/star/poet laughing, the poet may also a/muse us.

The poet in the poem on the right ("This was a Poet") arrests the familiar species, suggesting both that she is empowered to stop the world for her artistic purposes as Keats does with the youths chasing maidens around the Grecian urn and that she a/rests as she de/stills—that she troubles (in one reading) that "familiar species / That perished by the Door." The reader is back to the little Girl in the Closet, put there by the "they"s who liked her "still" or at rest. The power of poetry is oppositely to stop (arrest) time and to stir things up, to a/rest as he or she de/stills. What she a/rests is "the familiar species." This word ("species"), too, acquires new meaning when read in its fascicle setting. Without that setting, we may suppose that the poem is divided into two parts, the first part offering a botanical metaphor. Its first two verses propose the poet as a kind of chemist transforming through distillation the ordinary (familiar species) into the extraordinary (Attar so immense). Read as a scientific analogy (involving botany, chemistry, and perhaps even alchemy), the familiar species are botanical specimens—perishable but recoverable if pressed into lovely Attar (the "Essential Oils" of J675, Fr772, F34 that are "expressed" by Suns and Screws to enhance the "Lady's Drawer"), but the reader of the poems paired would also think of the human species, in this case, perhaps ordinary humans, the "they"s pent up in the House of Prose, the kind about whom Dickinson spoke to Higginson as people "without any thoughts . . . (you must have noticed them in the street)," she remarked. "How do they live. How do they get the strength to put on their clothes in the morning" (L342). Dickinson's dictionary has another meaning for "species," as well, one to which I will return with a suggestion of a corroborating source: It is a "Representation to the mind. Wit— the faculty of imagination in the writer which searches over all the memory for the *species* or ideas which it designs to represent." A simple botanical metaphor is densely complicated by the writer who read her lexicon closely and who arranged her poems carefully.

The second half of the "This was a Poet" also gathers meaning by its proximity to "They shut me up in Prose." That on the left suggests that the poet, the Little Girl who would not be closeted, has boundless powers if "Himself" but "wills" his (her) own freedom to "Abolish his Captivity." To "will" has legal implications that remind the reader of the entitlement of the poet and reader in the answering poem's next two verses. Switching from botanical to economic language, the poet becomes, apparently, a wealthy philanthropist who allows glimpses into his or her "Fortune— / Exterior to Time," but the poem ends on another page, where the final verse both serves as an introduction to the next poem and the summation of the paired poems. What the poet, uncloseted, has "to will" is "so much that "Robbing—could not harm." This is Emerson's finale to his essay on the poet: The poet, in Emerson's words, is "the owner of all land, tax free." The vast holdings of the poet's imagination is a theme to which Dickinson often turned, of course ("My basket holds—just— / Firmaments" [J352, Fr358, F17]; "To make a prairie" [J1755, Fr1779], and "The Brain is Wider than the / Sky" [J632, Fr598, F26], for example). That all that universe to which the poet by dint of imagination is entitled may be given away without any diminishment to the poet and that there is so much that even the poet is "unconscious" of it is the point of both poems. As she would say later, "A word is dead / When it is said, / Some say. / I say it just / Begins to live / That day (J1212, Fr278).

Kamesian Poetics: An Unlikely Source?

Dickinson's emphasis in the paired poems on the subversive and affective possibilities of poetry situates her aesthetic principles far from those of her contemporary "fireside poets," whose more strictly metered, true-rhyming, nationalistic, and inspirational verse was rarely de-stilling or unsettling. It is not so far, however, from that of Emerson or, as Gary Stonum vividly describes, from that of Emerson's inspiration, Carlyle. What Stonum tells us about "Tell all the Truth but tell it slant—" (J1129, Fr1263) fits the paired poems and the fascicle that frames them, the way one reads each fascicle, in fact: "The hermeneutic zigzag of truth and error, blindness and enlightenment, or affirmation and insinuation may itself be a little dazzling. Indeed, the razzle-dazzle may be the point, and the zigzag is certainly the method. Dickinson's double writing *differs* itself, always actively and often flagrantly from any singularity it has itself signified" (64–65). Dickinson's own famous description of the razzle-dazzle of genuine poetry, the subject of the paired poems, privileges the affective nature of poetry: "If I read a book [and] it makes my whole body so cold no fire ever can warm me I know *that* is poetry. If I feel physically as if the top of my head were taken off, I know *that* is poetry. These are the only way I know it. Is there any other way" (L342a). Although early readers discounted that statements such as this or poems such as the paired ones in Fascicle 21 might be based on any particular aesthetic background or convictions, many readers have since noted Dickinson's profound debts to Emerson,[17] and Gary Stonum's book thoroughly articulates the influence of Carlyle.

Few, however, have followed up on Carlton Lowenberg's suggestion of another possible influence, Henry Home, Lord Kames. According to Lowenberg, Kames was taught at Amherst Academy between 1835 and 1849 (Dickinson studied there from 1840 to 1847).[18] Although Christine Ross has recently traced the effect of that study on Dickinson's prosody (particularly her meter), she does not discuss this poem's heretofore (I believe) unnoted echo. One of the Scottish Associationists, Kames contributed to many of the familiar tenets of English romantic poets and critics. Both indirectly and directly, he also affected nineteenth-century American writers.[19] Particularly when he devotes chapters to answering his own question, "By what mark does the ear distinguish verse from prose?" (308), and cites the effects of harmony that make the reader say "this is poetry" (307),[20] his words seem an influence on Dickinson; she repeats, paraphrases, and improves on him, most notably in Fascicle 21's "This was a Poet." Although she may have eschewed his pedantry on grammar, syntax, and even syllabication (her questioning of whether "syllable" differs from "sound" in "The Brain is Wider than the / Sky—" [J632, Fr598, F26] seems an oblique reference to such passages), her keen ear and her knowledge of poets from Shakespeare on may have led her to pay attention to Kames's view of poetry as "strictly the language of the imagination . . . the most vivid form of expression that can be given to anything . . . the perfect coincidence of the image and the words with the feeling we have, and of which we cannot get rid in any other way" (342). ["Is there any other way?"] That is what Fascicle 21, particularly the pair of poems at their center, is all about: the exhilaration of self-identification, a sense of belonging in the company of those "elevated above common nature" (Kames 1761, 308), those who are free from the house of prose. When Dickinson tells us that the poet is "so unconscious" of the vastness that is his entitlement that "The Robbing—could not harm," she comes close to

Kames, who—distinguishing between perception, sensation, conception, imagination, feeling, and memory—said: "I transport myself ideally to the place where I saw the tree and river yesterday . . . and in this recollection, I am *not conscious* of a *picture* or representative image, more than in the original surveys" (ibid., 10–11). Melinda Ponder, who has written on Hawthorne's use of Kames (Hawthorne studied Kames at Bowdoin), explains that Kames's "theory of ideal presence" insisted on an interpretation of imagination that pervaded romantic literature. "Imagination," explains Ponder, was "a complex faculty that could store and recall" (1990), not simply recreate images for didactic purposes.

Kames, a profound influence on Keats, begins his study with a discussion that may have informed the witty fullness, the astounding, penetrating quality of Dickinson's lines. Although Kames deplores puns, he praises wit as "joining things by distant and fanciful relations, which surprise because they are unexpected"; solid judgment neglects "trivial relations." Just so, "Memory and wit are often conjoined, but seldom with solid judgment" (1761, 22). Dickinson says as much in a more dazzling way in the paired poems that differentiate the stultifying house of prose (solid judgment) from the poet's house of possibilities in which memory and wit are conjoined, sometimes (seldom) with common sense, more often with "amazing sense."

Later in his study Kames employs Addison and Locke to explore the nature of wit, calling it the "most elegant recreation. . . . Wit gently elevates without straining, raises mirth without dissoluteness, and relaxes while it entertains" (ibid., 208). Dickinson's whole poetic enterprise is directed away from relaxing readers, but, as Amy Lowell's somersaulting suggests, it is, among much else, "entertaining" as it amazes, de/stills, and puzzles.

Without overly determining that Dickinson's vivid, eye-blink-brief aesthetic statement—the paired poems imbedded in and radiating through Fascicle 21—is indebted, consciously or not, to a rather turgid eighteenth-century critic, it is nevertheless worth noting that she had two centuries of theory behind these two pages. In them she seems to have distilled the essence, the "amazing sense" in the poetic impulse. Kames, part of that layering of influences, offers his distinction between verse and prose by saying that one difference is in the effect on the ear (ibid., 309). He begins his long list of such effects—lists of meters—by saying that "different *species* of verse are governed by different rules peculiar to each *species*" (312). Adept at memorizing, Dickinson may have harbored this use of a relatively odd word to apply to poetry from her academy reading to add to her notion of the poet as one whose Attar is formed from "familiar species," one who is the discloser of pictures, unconscious of the difference between the actual and the remembered, therefore perpetually rich, immune from theft—"Exterior—to—Time."

Reading Contextually

Discovering "rules" peculiar to the species of books Dickinson compiled is reductive of the permeable, plastic, varied, and idiosyncratic nature of each. Nevertheless, taking the time to study tricks such as those imbedded in the paired poems in the middle of Fascicle 21 yields the surprise for the reader Frost talked about. Reading poems closely in their fascicle context, that "great voyage of discovery," is both an inward journey into the heart of individual poems and an outward one into the possibilities inherent in the new entity the collected mass becomes.

First, consider the inward journey, one that occupies much of this book. Separated from their intended repositories and pigeonholed into "topics" ("love" and "death," for example), the poems have been read for one hundred years in synthetic isolation/combination. Even modern and postmodern editions and critical commentaries have imposed the order of the compiler (is the subject, say, agoraphobia or thirst or monastic devotion?). Reading a single poem in the context of its fascicle cannot cancel out the contextual possibilities, particularly those by versions that the poems in letters suggest. Each poem had an originating impulse that was probably quite separate in time, space, and condition from the editor's (Dickinson's) determination to include the poem in the new context. Reading the individual lyrics in and out of fascicle context might be compared to reading Henry James, say, in his notebooks, then in the first edition of novels, and then in the 1910 New York edition, complete with hindsight prefaces. On the other hand, close reading of these books must certainly be attempted by anyone wishing to move closer to the poet who said, "Good to hide, and hear 'em hunt!" and who ends that poem with, "Can one find the rare Ear / Not too dull—" (J842, Fr945). Reading individual lyrics through the prism that their contextuality provides engages the reader in a process closer to Dickinson's own deliberations—at least those of the moment of the fascicle binding—than any of the reader's own devising, no matter how schooled in Dickinson's life and work or the prosody of the nineteenth and twentieth centuries that critic might be. More than half of her extant poems written in or before the six busy years Dickinson apparently created the fascicles (1858–1864) are imbedded in the forty books that, as far as we know, she did not mandate be burned.

Reading individual lyrics in their fascicle places, as this study shows, turns one of the "slight" early poems, "The Gentian weaves her fringes—" (J18, Fr21, F1) into an invocation, an opening blessing. The process makes mutual mirrors not only of the two poems I have discussed in this chapter but also of eight poems (no fewer than four pairs) in Fascicle 14. It transforms "As if some little Arctic flower" (J180, Fr177, F8) into a self-reflexive text, punctuated with a suggestion of how to read the poems and the books those poems made: how to discover the possibilities by "your inference therefrom."

Along with opening up individual poems for revision, close reading of the fascicles reveals that Dickinson engineered structural surprises within the groups. Without reducing these surprises to rules or formulas (à la Kames) or claiming that any one of these is common to each fascicle, the tricks of arrangement provide a structure far more complicated than a house of prose. Contextual reading through the fascicles challenges what Denis Donoghue said twenty years before the *Manuscript Books* proved otherwise: "Shall we say that the values of the long poem are those of interview—adjustment of measure, addition, and subtraction, the modulation of perspective, the massive deployment of force. And image is the short poem, the single glance. If it requires adjustment there will be time—we hope—for another glance, in another poem" (1965, 123). Donoghue follows this differentiation with his conclusion that "Emily Dickinson is one of the greatest masters of image. There is no reason to think that she had any talent at all for interview" (ibid.).

But the fascicles show that Dickinson's talent for "the image, . . . the single glance" is, in fact, melded with that "of interview." The sharply aphoristic dazzlers for which Dickinson is famed[21] have a context, and our involvement in both the line and context increases the reader's respect for the multiplicities of potential discoveries in and between even the apparently simple poems. William Doreski's study of Fascicle 27 maintains that reading contextually in the fascicles "offers an alternative way of understanding some poems that have until now seemed fairly transparent in their thematic content, and others that have been largely ignored by critics because of their obdurate opacity" (1986, 64). As Doreski demonstrates, such contextual reading increases or changes appreciation for canonical Dickinson poems and alerts us to the hitherto hidden interest of those that have never been part of the dialogue on the canon, whether because of "obdurate opacity" or because of their apparent insignificance.

Reading contextually is an established practice as Fraistat's collection of essays demonstrates. Included in that collection is Stuart Curran's highly relevant discussion of Wordsworth's groupings: "To remove poems from the context in which Wordsworth intended them to be read at the very least leads to a narrowing of their meaning," says Curran. "In a few cases it may wholly alter it" (1986, 236). In chapter 2, I explore the context for the paired poems in Fascicle 21, in which movement surges from the terrified speaker of the first poem to the bold and wealthy speaker, at last identified: the poet.

CHAPTER 2

Owning the Gold:
The Surge of Fascicle 21

F	J	Fr	
1	609	440	I—Years had been—from / Home—
2	610	441	You'll find—it when you / try to die—
3	611	442	I see thee better—in the Dark—
4	447	443	Could—I do more— for Thee—
5	612	444	It would have starved a Gnat—
6	613	445	They shut me up in Prose—
7	448	446	This was a Poet—/ It is That
8	614	447	In falling Timbers buried—
9	449	448	I died for Beauty—but / was scarce
10	450	449	Dreams—are well—but / Waking's better
11	451	450	The Outer—from the Inner
**12	174	172	At last—to be identified—
13	452	451	The Malay—took the Pearl—
14	453	452	Love—thou art high—

(another sheet for completion of J453, Fr452)

15	615	453	Our journey had advanced—
16	616	454	I rose—because He sank—
17	454	455	It was given to me by the Gods—

(another sheet for completion of J454, Fr455)

**Poem repeated from Fascicle 8

23

Without discounting other possibilities for interpretation, this chapter begins with a contextualizing of the poems that surround those paired poems in Fascicle 21, compiled in that annus mirabilis 1862. As the two poems in its center suggest, Fascicle 21 revolves around images of the working poet. This chapter explores the larger context for those two poems, showing how way leads on to (and sometimes contrasts with) way and how it may reveal networks of possibilities for interpreting the aesthetics those paired poems imply. If the paired poems indicate an aesthetic stance, the entire fascicle reflects the "business" of the working poet. The fascicle begins with a poem that states this subject. "My Business—just a Life / I left—" declares the terror-stricken persona of the opening poem, "I—Years had been—from / Home—" (J609, Fr440). Reading this poem in isolation bewilders one. Whose eyes might "Stare vacant into mine— / And ask my Business there—"? By the time we reach the paired poems, numbers six and seven in the sequence, we have grounds for an educated guess. These eyes belong to the inhabitants of the house of prose, those who might catch and closet the applicant at the door, still timid in this first poem in the sequence. Remembering my own cautionary warnings not to limit any poem or fascicle to a single story, let me posit that, although there is no consistent narrative, there seems to be a surge of movement in this fascicle from the speaker as returning victim of some psychic shock, so frightened even to knock that, not unlike Munch's figured screamer, she flies from the door, to the confident speaker of the last poem ("It was given to me by / the Gods—" [J454, Fr455]), who crows, "The Difference—made me / bold—" This chapter, then, demonstrates, I hope, the rewards of reading contextually.

From the fascicle's first poem on the speaker finds herself positioned in relation to doors, closed or unclosed, as in this first, almost Kafkaesque, sad story. "Doors," repeated three times in the first poem, are emblematic of oppositional figures in the fascicle: enclosure inside or exclusion from a house of prose, on the one hand, or open gates to multiple possibilities on the other. As the paired poems discussed in the previous chapter suggest, it is the poet's "business" to dis/close the doors. It is serious business. Along with its marketplace meaning, the word "Business" appears in Dickinson's lexicon (her 1828 *Webster's* dictionary) in variants that would make it impossible to think of the poet as one who writes verses as others make antimacassars.[1] Here are some of those secondary, but no doubt significant, meanings to the poet who tells us in Fascicle 8, the one that, significantly, shares a poem with Fascicle 21, that her "business" is "to find" (J178, Fr175) and also that her "business" is valuable and "so dear" (J179, Fr176):

> 3. That which engages the care and attention. 'You are so much the business of our souls.' Dryden. 4. Serious . . . important occupation, in distinction from

trivial affairs. 'It should be the main business of life to serve God and obey his commands.' 5. Concern; right of action . . . 'What business has a man with the disputes of others?' 6. A point; a matter of question; something to be examined . . . 'Fitness to govern is a perplexed business.' Bacon.

In the first poem of the fascicle the speaker and the evidently small-minded doorkeeper are on different cognitive, ethical planes. For the doorkeeper with his or her "vacant" stare ("stolid" in the 1872 version as—implicitly—in this), "my business" signifies only the market/pragmatic primary meaning. On the other hand, the speaker, who has faced "Danger and the Dead" (which sums up the subject of other poems in the fascicle), rejects this small-minded enclosedness. What might remain in the house of prose she left is too "awful" in both senses for the poet who thinks of her business of life in the largest sense as something of great importance.

She is worried that life in that house she left might be "*still* dwelling there": limited, claustrophobic, flat, turgid, stale, sour, and leaden—not yet de/stilled. She "fumbles at her nerves." That's serious, too. In the next fascicle (22) Dickinson tells us that God "fumbles at your soul," which is to say not only at her "organ of sensation and motion" but also at her "strength, fortitude, firmness of mind, courage and authority"—all synonyms for "soul" in Dickinson's lexicon. That strength fails her. In a synaesthesiac manner she looks ("scanned the Windows o'er") and hears nothing ("The Silence—like an Ocean / rolled— / And broke against my Ear—"). The silence of that prosy house and the vacancy of the doorkeeper's face, the nothingness there, causes the speaker to hold her ears as "like a Thief / [she] Stole [Fled]—gasping—from the House." This speaker has long to go before she discovers the birdlike freedom from the physical captivity she seems to fear in the first poem.

Having just alluded to her courage (failed in the first poem) of facing "Danger—and the Dead," she places across from those lines the first words of the second poem, words of advice from one who has "faced" the grave:

> You'll find it when you
> try to die
> The easier to let go—
> For recollecting such as went—
> You could not spare—you know— (J610, Fr441)

This speaker, perhaps the same as that in the fascicle's first, also mentally occupies a distant time. These memories of loved ones are so old that their marble names have been covered with moss, an image that recurs almost verbatim in "I died for Beauty" later in the fascicle. Were the speaker as vacant as the doorkeeper of the first poem, a dweller in prose, these names might have been "superseded" with those of more recent friends. "Supersede" does not mean simply to replace; it is "literally, to set above; hence to make void . . . or useless by superior power"; it is also "to come or be placed in [to sit in—*supersede*] the room of." This speaker seems acutely aware of its range of meaning as she observes that as

>this World—sets
>further back—
>as Dying—say it does—
>The former love—distincter grows—
>And supersedes the first—

Whatever panic causes the speaker of the first poem to fear opening a door to the past is either answered by a new speaker or changed to a new time perspective, for the speaker of the second privileges that past; he or she views death as the synthesis of old and new, a reunion with the long-dead and a future of new relationships. To insist on life with "newer names," not to hold on but rather to let go, is "too Tawdry Grace"; the new names are just "toys / we bought—to ease their / place." The odd junction of words, reinforced by rhyme, reminds the reader of Dickinson's revisions of "Grace." Although the child of Edward Dickinson and student of Mary Lyon often uses the word, a word hinted at in the central poem's "Amazing sense," attended by its Puritan theological baggage,[2] just as often she conveys its secular sense: The summer day has "a shimmering grace" ("A something in a summer's Day" [J122, Fr104, F5]), for example. In the setting of Fascicle 21's second poem, the tawdry grace of new toys "bought to ease their [empty] place" suggests the deep dichotomy of the entire fascicle: that between the temporal, the tawdry of the new, on the one hand, and, on the other, the graven grace of the ancient and venerable—old names grown "distincter," both because of their intrinsic worth and because of the love invested in them by those who remember, especially those like poets who can make permanent that remembrance.

Such love needs no tawdry ("fine and showy in colors without taste or elegance," says her lexicon, adding, "without grace") light, for, continues the speaker (or answers another), "I see thee better—in the Dark" (J611, Fr442). So the third poem of the sequence begins. Dickinson has left a generous half page between her elegy for the long-dead, the reverence for whom obliterates the need for tawdry new "toys," and the fascicle's third poem. The gap, like the empty space in the speaker's life (of which she has just spoken), seems anything but accidental. As does a "rest" in music, it replicates and calls to mind the absent friends of the second poem. Absence is presence, in other words, a phrase Shurr uses (1983, 85) in a literal autobiographical sense in relation to the fascicle's third poem. If the second poem's focus was the dead, that of the third is the dark moss-covered marble crypt itself. Here "the former love" of the second poem "distincter / grows." Now the speaker declares that her love or the power of her imagination illuminates, replaces, and makes habitable the darkness as well as or better than the three disparate metaphors she uses.

First, her love is a prism. The three-sided glass Dickinson's dictionary describes sifts, intensifies, and rearranges colors as the imagination might act on that which comes within its planes. In Dickinson's words, the prism, like love, is superior to "Violet," a word full of Dickinsonian possibilities.[3]

Second, it is like a Miner's Lamp, suggesting that the dark is both a grave and a mine, a place for extracting the kind of riches she speaks of later in the fascicle. Riches in mines, as poems from poets, accrue with time and are condensed and layered in the geological process that parallels the distillation of roses to attar. Such a geological link is suggested in the speaker's reference to "the years / That hunch themselves between—," an image that simultaneously suggests the long, long time that literally hunches slabs of marble into strange shapes and often into beauty as love and insight deepen through years, not through reason and logic, but—to use another meaning—through hunches, intuition, and the insight in the dark. The long time recurs in "At last! to be identified," a later, small, significant poem in the fascicle. Similarly, the dark recurs in the fascicle's eighth and ninth poems, and it is equally essential to the creative process. So says Wendy Barker in her study of *The Lunacy of Light* (1987).

Finally, in a third metaphor, the speaker calls her love "ruddy" with the light of a "surpassing Sun," suggesting the vividness of a summer's noon. Imagined or self-created continual "Meridian," that last line in the third poem, spills over into the next page, where it almost becomes a title for the four lines that bridge the radiant, relieved darkness of the grave or mine in the third poem and the fifth. Between them is this little verse that, isolated, seems to have nothing at all to do with the dark of death (present in both third and fifth poems). Here is the fourth poem, complete in its four lines:

> Could—I do more—for Thee—
> Wert thou a Bumble Bee—
> Since for the Queen, have I—
> Nought but Boquet? (J447, Fr443)

One way to read these lines is as part of the "love relationship" suggested in the third poem. Of course, in the context of this fascicle, one in which the self-conscious writer offers an aesthetic statement, the "Boquet" might also be a cluster of poems.

Lest the reader relax with that easy figure, almost a truism, she is jolted to attention with the strange imagery of the fifth poem, "It would have starved a Gnat—" (J612, Fr444). It is a leap from the Bumble Bee to this strange creature: a bug with clawlike, leechlike, and weirdly dragonlike qualities. The lyric poet has yielded to the metaphysical: Barrett-Browning collides with Donne. Riffling back through the fascicle, the reader discovers that the gnat image is not inappropriate. The speaker has parallels to the first poem's constricted, pained, and alienated child returning home. What "would have starved a Gnat," says this speaker, would be "to live so small as I," suggesting the little girl who soon shows up in the closet in the poem chapter 1 discusses. If the mood of the first poem in this sequence was panic, the mood of this fifth poem is bitterly resentful at the pittances offered. If in the first poem the speaker had the ability to fly away—albeit gasping—in this one she lacks that privilege. She lacks even the ability to manage her own death: She lacks "the Art / Opon the Window Pane / To gad my little Being out— / And not begin—again—."

Even the proximity of such an oddly disquieting poem with the two central, famous paired poems is de/stilling and unsettling as the notion that the speaker would prefer to be a Bumble Bee capable of receiving a Bouquet or a bug capable of squashing out his life than someone forced into the closet of prose. So go the fourth, fifth, and sixth poems of this fascicle. Contemplations on a gnat thus provide an introduction to the pair of poems in which Dickinson discusses her art. The little poem has been read as a solipsistic reflection on a frustrated suicide,[4] Yes, but it is also an intriguing link to the Little Girl in the next poem, shut up in Prose. That, in Dickinson's aesthetic world, is to live "Small."

And so, the two poems with which I began in chapter 1 follow, picking up some of the imagery in the preceding poems and introducing other images that continue, in that dazzling zigzag way (Stonum 1990), to reflect the values she places on her art—and herself as artist. In "This was a Poet," Dickinson has said that in distilling attar the "poet arrests the flux of our perishable existence" and thus "achieves the ontological status of being exterior to time like the 'Artist in the City of Kooroo'" (Kher 1974, 118). She has implied that the "Lyric is immortal . . . it is complex and completed in and of itself, transcending mortal limits. . . . Thus it withstands, stands adjacent to the very temporal scheme out of which it has been lifted" (Cameron 1979, 197). Seen in that light, the progression is a natural one to "In falling Timbers buried—" (J614, Fr447). In this, the eighth poem, the speaker takes the point of view of a spectator at a disaster in which a man is literally "Exterior to Time."

Whether Dickinson witnessed or read of such an accident[5] is less important than the way she merges with both spectator and victim. The poem borrows from and extends the "This was a Poet's" suggestion of "Negative Capability," the notion of the poet as so "unconscious" of self and so "Exterior—to Time" that he or she may be imprinted or impressed with others. Dickinson's staccato, breathless, irregular lines replicate the panic of victim, would-be-rescuer and story-telling bystander in much the same way that on the previous page's matched set she had snapped out and thus conveyed the impatience of the trapped child. Also, as with "They shut me up," the shifting angle of vision follows a similar pattern: The first stanza of both begins with the claustrophobic consciousness of the one buried alive; the second stanza in both poems moves to those outside who cannot know the true situation of the one within. Both poems are framed in subjunctive language ("Could themselves have peeped" in the sixth poem and "Could He—know—they sought / Him—Could they—know—He breathed—" in the eighth). And both poems end with an overview from beyond the living or literal death. The poet/bird/star looks down and laughs at captivity in the earlier poem; in this one the speaker finishes the story of the man in the Horrid Sand Partition by agreeing with the notion that death is "Reward of Anguish." The phrase, set within Dickinson's quotation marks, suggests that its speaker regards the assurance as a cultural commonplace, but one she shares as we just read in the yearning of the gnat to "gad" its being out. Finally, the speaker sums up "In Falling Timbers" with a stanza that links the eighth to the fascicle's earlier poems:

> Many Things—are fruitless—
> 'Tis a Baffling Earth—
> But there is no Gratitude
> Like the Grace—of Death—

As grisly in mood as the opening premise of the poem may be compared with those that precede it, "In falling Timbers buried—" is tightly linked to other poems in the fascicle: It conveys the panic of the first ("I—Years had been"), the fascination with death of the second ("You'll find—it when you try to die"), the privileging of darkness of the third ("I see thee better—in the Dark"), the deprivation of life and desire for death of the fifth ("It would have starved a Gnat"), and the structure and movement of the sixth poem ("They shut me up in Prose"). Both sixth and eighth poems occupy the west side of the opened book. "In falling Timbers" also has a paired poem, an antithesis (which contains a synthesis) to its thesis. Both "answers" to the poems with which they are paired ("They shut me up" and "This was a Poet"; "In falling Timbers" and "I died for Beauty") are quieter and more meditative in tone than the first. They move from the particular situation to a universal declaration. In this the speaker carefully prepares for the shift, as she says that "Things" on this "Baffling Earth" are fruitless and as she moves through the "Grace of Death." And there is that word "Grace," suggested in the sixth poem's "amazing sense." In this, the eighth, "In falling Timbers," the "Grace of Death," the wished-for condition of the gnat in the fifth poem is "Reward" or—in the variant—"Recompense."

"I died for Beauty—but / was scarce / Adjusted in the tomb" (J449, Fr448), ninth in the series, takes the proleptic viewpoint of the dead—not necessarily the buried-alive victim of the fallen timber but the poet capable of wearing the pain and panic of others, one who, as the fascicle's first poem says, had "Consternation compassed" (in another version, "Danger—and the Dead"). As "Falling Timbers" imitates through sound effects and broken rhythm the experience it conveys, "I died for Beauty" recreates the restored order through its absolutely even (but not monotonous) Common Meter.[6] Both, too, reflect the influence of Keats, the first ("In falling Timbers") in its high drama, the second ("I died for Beauty"), in its resolution, which is Dickinson's own "Ode on the Grecian Urn."[7]

Her rephrasing of Keats also makes the take on "Beauty" and "Truth" suited for inclusion in the fascicle in this space. First published in a form wrenched from Dickinson's own, the poem has elicited critical discussion that ignored Dickinson's own lineation and setting.[8] Returned to its place, "I died for Beauty" is more than doubly interesting and witty. On the west side of the page the victim is buried unceremoniously, the spades working furiously to extract him; on the right, the speaker is "Adjusted in the tomb." On the left, the victim and rescuer are unable to communicate ("Neither could be heard"); on the right, the two dead talk "between the Rooms" as "Brethren." They talk "until the moss had reached / our lips— / And covered up our names," which is the image she had used in the fascicle's second poem. Of Dickinson's four uses of "moss," two are in this fascicle. In "I died for Beauty," as in Shakespeare's meditations on the mutability of life, the survival of art in which the dead is perpetually alive mitigates the horror. Dickinson's speaker thus accepts the absolute fact of death with a serenity that belies Wolff's view that this and other proleptic poems present "single isolated nightmare[s]" (1986, 235). Dickinson, in fact, stops short of saying that Truth and Beauty conjoined will not live on in some form.

The fascicle's ninth poem, far from being an "isolated nightmare," in fact, has a restfulness to its dreamlike quality. Such a reading is made more obvious by noting that Dickinson follows it with "Dreams are well—but / Waking's better—" (J450, Fr449), which accommodates the movement of the fascicle mood from the panic of the frightened persona of the first poem, a speaker outside the door, to the triumph of the bold speaker of the fascicle's final poem. Largely ignored, the poem makes sense in its fascicle setting. For one thing, we hear a direct echo from Kames. Ponder notes the connection between this, "the state into which good writers put readers so that the reader will be so totally occupied with the images passing before him that he will not pause to reflect on them" (1990, 88) to Keats, to Ann Radcliffe, and to Hawthorne; whether the phrase came to Dickinson through one of them or from her own school-day reading of Kames, the words *are* those of Kames and remind us again that this fascicle implies an aesthetic statement. For another thing, this, the tenth poem, contains one particular phrase that resonates as the fascicle closes. The entire poem is a natural, not wrenching, extension of the fascicle's more famous "I died for Beauty," which ends with the soporific lines I have just quoted. Having lulled the reader to a "pleasant sleep" as Truth and Beauty, compartmentalized but communicative, talk themselves to sleep between the rooms, Dickinson wakes the reader with the tenth poem's sharply trochaic "Dreams are well—but Waking's better."

In the context of this fascicle Dickinson asserts that there are two species of dreams and two concomitant conditions of waking: the dreams of sleep that stop with the workaday world of morn and dreams linked to imagination, second sight, mystery, and insight. Such dreams contribute to what, in the next poem, Dickinson calls the "central mood" of the "inner" life. From these dreams one wakes not into the glare of morning but rather into the dark world of midnight, the world privileged, as Wendy Barker (1987) persuasively describes, by the poet, especially by the woman poet.[9] The dark provides the infinite possibilities inherent in "Dreaming—of the Dawn." It is sweeter [than that of] the robins who "gladden" the tree with musical announcements that a literal dawn approaches.

It is a "Solid Dawn . . . Leading to no Day" that the poet confronts. That Solid Dawn echoes in "Gold in Solid Bars" of the last poem. This fascicle contains two of Dickinson's only twelve uses of that adjective, defined in her dictionary (and reminding the reader of the definitions of "business" I quoted earlier) as "hard, firm, compact; not hollow; full of matter; sound not weak; real, valid, true, just, not empty or fallacious, grave, profound, not light." Better than either the invalid, hollow, weak, fallacious workaday morning (a house of prose?) and better, too, than the empty, meaningless dreams that lead to those mornings, this Dawn confronts a spacious mystery, not specious revelations of ordinary day. It draws on the Inner life to shape its Outer, as Dickinson says in the next poem.

Dreams that are formed in Solid Dawns leading to no [ordinary, prosy] day are part of the inner life that is the subject of the eleventh poem, "The Outer—from the / Inner" (J451, Fr450). This poem's speaker uses a series of five increasingly riddling metaphors, each leading to the repeated poem of self-identification. First, power is disguised (as frequently for Dickinson) in what appears to be a barefoot boy as the speaker considers the hidden identity of the "Duke or Dwarf." Second, she switches to the mobile metaphor of wheel rim and axis, the outer with its more obvious ability to transport ("and fling a dust") dependent entirely on the second, less evident, hub. Third, she speaks of the brush on canvas, regulated not by the hand only but also by something deeper than the hand that the speaker calls "the inner Brand."

With its multiple meanings, "Brand" leads the reader to the next page, for in the marketplace the word "brand" implies an immediately perceived form of identification. That common usage in Dickinson's own day does not diminish the possibilities for considering the meanings in her 1828 Webster's, which likens the brand both to lightning and to a stigma signifying infamy (Dimmesdale again). Fourth, the speaker shifts the canvas from that on a painter's easel to the human physiognomy, the "fine—Arterial Canvas" on a cheek or brow. Without completing her metaphor—she has done that on the first line—she moves to the fifth and most puzzling comparison: "The Star's whole secret— / in the Lake— / Eyes were not meant—to know."[10] Of all the comments on this "oriental" poem (Mary Cender Miller 1988), Kher's comparison of the entire poem to Thoreau's Walden Pond, in which "the whole external world is also internal" (1974, 40), is particularly helpful, especially in light of a fascicle, which, like Thoreau's meditations on the pond, surrounds the subject of aesthetic creativity.

Kher's linkage to Thoreau helps to un-riddle the last two befuddling lines, lines that Dickinson placed on the next page so that they form an inscription to the significant "At last—to be identified—." In these lines, which simultaneously summarize one poem and introduce the next, Dickinson seems to say what Thoreau says in his own compressed and complex observation on the stream he goes a-fishing in (time) with its bottom "pebbly with stars," from which one may drink deep but still not know "the first letter of the alphabet." As does Thoreau's *Walden,* Dickinson's eleventh poem touches on the limitations of knowledge, as well as on the mysterious, unfathomable riches within the lake—or the poet's creative imagination—which can at least explore the secrets of the stars.

If the Eyes of others were not meant to know any more than what is reflected in the lake or on the canvas or in the fascicle, what little of the hidden depths that are revealed leads the speaker to plead for or to claim "At last—to be identified—" (J174, Fr172). I return to this poem because this is the one that is repeated from Fascicle 8, a repetition that tests the case for contextuality. In the context of Fascicle 21 self-identity is the secret of the star in the lake. It is the brand. It is the inner life that shapes the outer. The secret, we might say, is that the speaker is or will be or was a poet. Although the word "poet" does not exist on the page, the placement of "At last" in the fascicle clarifies at least this probability.

The two burial poems and the two poems privileging dreams, darkness, and depth prepare the reader for "At last," the "repeated" poem: "At last—to be identified— / At last—the Lamps open / your side— / The rest of Life— to see" and so forth. The poem seems to cap these dialogues of the emerging poet with herself and also contains seeds of the final poems. Its opening phrase, "At last," repeated in an identical chirography in the second line, appears two poems hence in "Love—thou art high—" (J453, Fr452), and the following poems explore the value of what is only partly revealed. From awakening at midnight ("Dreams are Well"), the speaker has now moved "Past Midnight—past the / Morning Star." Although Dickinson's imagined world is full of stars (two columns of listings in Rosenbaum's *Concordance* [1964]), the reader pays particular attention to this stellar reference. At the top of this page of the fascicle, Dickinson has placed "The Star's whole secret— / in the Lake— / Eyes were not meant—to know," which is the end of the previous poem ("The Outer—from the / Inner"). Below that spillover line and below the horizontal line that is the editor's mark of separation between poems is "At last"; the words "Morning Star" are placed on their own line, echoing "the star's whole secret" of the last poem above it. Both phrases are another *Walden* echo: "The sun is but a morning star," Thoreau's last lines in that volume. Tradition pigeonholes this poem as one of Dickinson's proleptic visions. Read thus, the audience for the speaker seems to move beyond the graves in which Truth and Beauty chat, beyond even waking at midnight as in "Dreams—are well." He or she (two critics connect the speaker with an absent lover) moves into a place illuminated by lamps that obviate Sunrise.[11]

One need not discard the idea of a proleptic insight by noting that in view of the surrounding poems it seems more likely that "your side" and "our feet" are rhetorical strategies to involve the living reader in the speaker's drama of self-identification. She has just teased the reader to wonder about the star's whole secret, and then, carefully centering the poem on the page, she repeats (with fewer than the usual differences in repeated poems) the poem that fits for other reasons its placement in Fascicle 8. In the next chapter of this study, a reading of that fascicle, the difference setting makes is, I hope, confirmed. There it fits the more exuberant tone and the image clusters of wild transformations. In this, its new setting, in a fascicle concerned with the serious business of poetry, the same poem conveys not so much an explosion of gravity (as it seems to convey in Fascicle 8) as an exhausted sense of deep, well-grounded satisfaction.

Partly the impression of satisfaction results from such small chirographic differences noticeable only to the reader of the manuscripts. The longer lines and the greater frequency of exclamation points of the earlier version lighten it, lend wings to the excitement of the traveler through time and space. The version of "At last" in Fascicle 21 is more splintered, as was, increasingly,

Dickinson's mode as her hand and eyes aged so that "your side," "Morning star," and "Leagues there were" (the latter word not underscored as in the earlier version and thus without the sense of relief of a completed journey) are obviously intensified. But the greater difference is the shift in interpretation the poet's chosen placement conveys: The Morning star, for example, echoes the star's secret, and the weary sense of almost infinite leagues traveled sets up the weary narrative of the next poem, "The Malay—took the Pearl—" (J452, Fr451).

Keats, Thoreau, Sigourney, and Barrett Browning have turned up as shadows in Fascicle 21's earlier poems about poets and poetry. Now, with the fascicle's thirteenth poem, add Robert Browning. Jack Capps's (1966) identification of "Paracelsus" as one source—for all its differences—helps to unlock the mysteries of this poem. Again, Dickinson shades "The Malay" and uses the borrowed drama of deceit and treachery to heighten the contrast she has been making throughout the fascicle between the stolidity of the house of prose and the power of the poet to transcend and escape from that house. Here Dickinson's version of Browning is a story of missed opportunity, wherein a terse version of James's Strether regrets a lack of blood and impulse and courage to live. It is as Weisbuch reads it, an antiallegory leading "to a forceful moral: that nothing will come to the man who waits in selfish fear" (1972, 58). Courage is the issue of the poem as it is of the entire fascicle from the moment the quaking speaker flees from the wooden door in the first poem. If the fascicle is read as a narrative (again, a dangerous practice but tempting here), "The Malay" poses a problem: The speaker seems just to have reached a full acceptance of self and empowerment to penetrate the secret in the lake, when she or he seems to lose courage.

Even reading the fascicle as a narrative also suggests a rationale for this "Malay" poem in this place; after all, Hamlet screws up his courage several times in his drama, then falters and bemoans himself as a "Rogue and peasant slave." But the point is that the fascicle is not a single-voiced narrative so much as it is a matrix of images. Considered thus, the poem fits. On the left, or west, side of the open book the speaker imagines a secret-holding (and partly revealing) lake; on the right, or east, just opposite these lines, Dickinson's speaker says, "I feared the Sea—too / much." On the left, she iterates that line with the homonym as she hopes for "the rest of life—to *see*." These lines are directly opposite "Praying that I might be worthy—the Destiny— / the Swarthy fellow swam— / And bore my Jewel—Home." On the left (in "At last"), the speaker travels "Past Midnight—past the morning star— / Past Sunrise—Ah! What Leagues there were"; on the right, the speaker describes the "Swarthy fellow's" journey "Home to the Hut! What—lot / Had I—the Jewel—got / Borne on a Dusky Breast." The thirteenth poem continues with its own story, but the compiler of her own publication has succeeded in raising our awareness of the intertextuality of apparently disparate poems. Such artistry is reinforced by the courage, the courage lacked by the thirteenth poem's Earl.

In the fourteenth poem, "Love—thou art high—" (J453, Fr452), the Earl becomes "Ducal—at last" as the speaker rewrites Barrett Browning's "How do I love thee" in her own more richly resonating and more realistic lines. "Ducal—at last" recalls the Duke within the Dwarf of the eleventh poem as well as the opening of the repeated twelfth poem ("At last—to be identified!"). This is the first of four poems to which Dickinson gives a full page or two, isolating each from its neighbor by white space—in one case by a whole page of unoccupied paper. Although she had written some two dozen poems that she had not yet copied into a known fascicle,[12] Dickinson left space around the poems that follow her statement of artistic identity. The gaps that remain, the wider-than-usual spaces around the text, act as subliminal emphasis to the spatial imagery of all of the poems of this fascicle from the closed closets of the early poems to the wide and high distance of those final poems. As have some of the earlier poems in the fascicle, "Love—thou art high—" (J453, Fr452) has attracted much source-hunting and autobiographical commentary.[13] However, reading it in its fascicle context multiplies the poem's possibilities beyond that of a love poem.

In its context the fourteenth poem is a natural extension of the thirteenth. "The Malay—took the Pearl" is a monologue of regret; the Earl, who did not dive into the sea, failed at wooing. "Love—thou art high," which answers with another saga of failed wooing, emphasizes yet again the fathoms the wooer must cover high and low to reach the object of love. The fascicle's thirteenth poem ended with the declaration that in "the Negro's" sensibility his (the presumably white speaker's) failure or success was "alike to Him One." The speaker of the fourteenth ("Love—thou art high—") suggests that "were there two / instead of One," the couple might "reach the Sun." The speaker likens that potential union to a Rower and Yacht. He does not "fear the sea" as did the speaker of the thirteenth ("The Malay"). By the end of the first two verses of this "love" description the resonances from earlier poems in the fascicle have widened the poem's possibilities. This speaker aims not only to reach a kind of Everest peak (her Chimborazo) but also to fathom the depths—or at least to cope with them, to cross them with the power of love. Together metaphorically, the lover and speaker will form the Rower and Yacht. This speaker is at some place in the journey only imagined by the speaker of the (duplicated) twelfth poem.

The final stanza of the poem imagines Love or the object of it as "vailed." This fascicle is full of secrets: that which is beyond the wood door of the first poem; those that are revealed in the dark in the third poem; that of the little girl shut up in prose in the sixth; the man buried alive in the eighth; and—

not least—the secret in the lake in the eleventh poem. The "veil" also has to do with imagination.[14] That which is veiled seems further linked to the question of identity that recurs throughout the fascicle. Dickinson's dictionary makes a distinction between "veil" or "disguise" and "vail" (her spelling in "Love—thou art high—") or "withheld from view as the vail of the temple; concealed." This veiled/vailed love makes bliss ("joy, alacrity, exultation, the highest state of blessedness") an oddity, excluding the lover from that which the speaker (and God) calls "Eternity"—Love's other name, its "nickname" ("a name of reproach," says her Webster's, "an opprobrious appellation").

No simple love poem, "Love—thou art high" focuses on the speaker's desire for the highest, the deepest, the most inscrutable, a desire for something that is so overwhelming that its opprobrious name is Eternity and yet so problematical that it causes some who glimpse it to smile and alter—and prattle (like a child)—and die. The object so described in terms of distance, difficulty, and sometimes dubious effect remains unidentified throughout the long (for Dickinson) poem save in these gaps and spaces. In fact, Dickinson has left an entire leaf empty, the back of this completed poem. In a previous footnote appeared many possible candidates for space-fillers had Dickinson wished to fill the space. However, as if the space represents great distance, she follows that poem with a conclusion of the quest begun in Fascicle 21's fourteenth poem.

The echo is this: The voice describing Love ends the fourteenth poem with her differentiation between two states of blessedness: "Bliss—were an Oddity— / Without thee— / Nicknamed of God— / Eternity." The next voice bridges the gap of a page and a half with a "little quest romance" (Hartman 1970, 349).

> Our journey had advanced—
> Our feet were almost come
> To that odd Fork in Being's
> Road—
> Eternity—by Term (J615, Fr453)

In Dickinson's extensive exploration of "The Flood Subject" she speaks often of "Eternity." The coincidence of its recurrence, however, is heightened by the fact that in both the fourteenth and fifteenth poems ("Love—thou art high" and "Our journey had advanced") the meaning of "eternity" is hedged: In the fourteenth it is "nicknamed"; in the fifteenth the nickname is "Eternity—by Term." "Term" doubles for nickname or brand—that other word from this fascicle—with a length of time, a long terminal length, perhaps like the period of imprisonment in the closet of the little girl. More remarkable is the coincidence of "oddity" and "odd"; these are not words

Dickinson used frequently: "odd" only a dozen times, "oddity" only three. The word is subliminally underlined in the next verse with a near homophone: "Our pace took sudden awe." This in itself helps to unify the fascicle's effect; in its first poem the frightened speaker had "leaned upon the awe." Dickinson elsewhere uses "awe" as a variant for "dread," for "guile," and for "solemn." Awe is most often linked to death and to "Circumference," the "bride of awe" (J1620, Fr1636). In its longer form it is terrifying: "an awful Tempest" (J198, Fr224, F9), "the awful sea," (J506, Fr349, F17), and so forth. Dickinson's lexicon enlarges the possibilities still further by listing in addition to the expected "fear, awe, chastisement, and dread," the word "discipline." Whatever it is that requires reaching (the fourteenth poem) and that slows the pace (the fifteenth) requires and yields discipline.

In the next verse the pace slows to a stop as the speaker pauses between two branches of an "odd Fork." Unlike Frost's two roads, this fork lacks an option: "Retreat—was out of Hope," the traveler says, "Behind—a Sealed Route—." Behind the figure, in the poem's contextual web, is that latched door of the first poem and the dark partitions of the third, sixth, and eighth poems. Before the speaker are the mysterious "Cities" and, for the third time in this fascicle, "Eternity's" sign, now a "White Flag" beckoning "Before— / And God—at every Gate." The limitless vision dazzles the speaker and the reader.

To reach that "city" of consciousness, this questor (and companion: The journey is "ours" as well) must go through the "Forest of the Dead"—perhaps not the literal dead but the dead in life who in another poem inhabit the House of Prose. "The Forest of the Dead" seems a place from myth, not a Puritan graveyard but a Spenserian or Bunyanesque land of dream and enchantment. The journey through the forest iterates the weary impression of the repeated ("at last") twelfth poem. The confusion of the speaker, confronted with no easy options, recalls the "baffling" earth of the fascicle's eighth poem, even in its "odd fork." Dickinson's "fork," which may be imagined as a "jagged three-point lightning flash shape," is balanced by the next poem's "my soul grew straight." Such images as the forked road fit the spatial imagery of other poems in the fascicle in which reaches make a difference.

Such reaches and such journeys require discipline and conviction. In the fascicle's next-to-last poem, the sixteenth, the speaker has, through discipline, conviction, power, passion, and skill, attained her goal. She has risen even above the Chimborazoan heights of "Love": "I rose—because He sank—" (J616, Fr454), she says. As if the "fainting Prince" is the other, the "our" of the fifteenth poem, the speaker says she has brought him through along with herself and, as Stonum (1990) notes, has entered into a "directly reciprocal" relation with the object of love or idolatry. Secure in her self-identification and self-discipline, she has at hand the "balm." In the context of this fascicle what the speaker has that will soothe and strengthen the "fainting Prince" may be quite different from that assumed by the Jungian reading of Gelpi (1966, 119) and the more specifically phallic reading (of the poem's last line) of Wolff (1986, 455).

Read in its fascicle, the poem seems a confirmation of the repeated poem's declaration of self-identification and a preparation for the final poem's resolution of Dickinson's twenty-first book. "I rose," says the speaker, reminding the reader of the frequent burial images early in the fascicle—most notably that of the closeted naughty child. The speaker continues by positing a reason: "Because he sank." Whether the speaker intends a deity, a Rochester-like human, or her own mysterious lover is of less interest in the "plot" (always with the caveat to watch such narratizing) of the fascicle than the fact that two poems before this the poet has hyperbolized the other, the "him" to whom she sings "hymns" to the heights of Chimborazo. Now she has grown straight of soul and strong enough to support him.

Within the context of this fascicle it is of more than passing interest that the manner of support has everything to do with the art of poetry. Four times the speaker describes how she "cheered" him, "met" him, and "lifted" him: "I sang firm—even Chants," she says first. From the first fascicle's "let us chant it softly" ("All these my banners be" [J22, Fr29]) to this poem, chanting and singing are metonymies for the activity of the poet. The poet is also, as Emerson's "Poet" (in which he links the poet with "a Chimborazo under the line") put it, the teller. In "I rose" the speaker next—and then again—says, "I told him," followed by images she has literally told in poems earlier in the fascicle.

"I told him Best must pass / through this low arch of / flesh—" recalls this fascicle's second poem with its insistence that those who died ultimately "superseded" lesser later figures who are "toys" in comparison. Memory creates life and light. The "low arch of Flesh" suggests the dark of death that the light of love illuminates as in the fascicle's third poem. "No Casque so brave / It spurn the Grave," continues the teller of the poem, and the reader remembers the small boxes of the fascicle's early poems. In her own day this spelling of "cask," Dickinson's more frequent spelling, was attached to literary collections. She repeats "I told him" and offers "Worlds I know / Where Emperors [Monarchs] grow / Who recollected us / If we were true," an image that evokes the Malay and the Earl and also the meeting of Truth and Beauty in the thirteenth and ninth poems. Finally, she says,

> And so with thews of Hymn—
> And sinew from within—
> And ways I knew not that
> I knew—till then—
> I lifted Him—

The oft-noted possibilities of the Hymn/Him are accented subliminally by the rhyme "within," which reminds the fascicle reader of the careful discussion of the force within that is responsible for the magnitude and mood without in the fascicle's eleventh poem, "The Outer—from the Inner," and in which resides "the Secret in the Lake."

And then there is the language of strength—thews and sinew, both unusual for Dickinson. The meaning is obvious in the literal representation of one person supporting another. Dickinson's dictionary opens other possibilities for "thews" as well. Along with "brawn" it lists "manner, custom, habit" and "form of behavior." The habit or manner of Hymn-singing—imbedded within her from her childhood but transformed in her own poetry—is what she offers in order to "lift" the other of this poem.

Just below "thew" in her dictionary is an odd word that might have registered in Dickinson's subconsciousness in relation to this poem, to this fascicle, to the entire project: "Theurgy" is "the art of doing something which is the peculiar province of God to do; or the power or act of performing supernaturally things by invoking the names of God; magic." Perhaps it is magic that allows the little girl, Houdini-like, to rise out of the closet of prose. Certainly magic is the focus of the other fascicle in which Dickinson placed this fascicle's "At last to be identified!" That is the subject of the next chapter. For now, observe the way the first line of the final poem, "It was given to me / by the Gods" (J454, Fr455), seems to account for the miracle of power in the penultimate poem.

That opening line seems an answer to the implied question with which "I rose" ends. "Ways I knew not that—I knew—till then—" allows the poet/speaker to "lift Him" or "lift a hymn" as the preacher says. In this context the unspecified "it" of the final poem's first line is, as many have noted, obviously the gift of imagination or poetry.[15] Donna Dickenson is one of them, saying (not necessarily about this poem): "That Dickinson regarded herself as a poet among poets, even in her isolation, is clear" (1985, 112–13). Dickenson cites as evidence Emily Dickinson's "habit of jousting with established versifiers in her poem" (113). Proof is in the discipline of Dickinson's life that Dickenson lists, beginning with the fascicles themselves. These books, Dickenson believes, "she had revised and ordered into a sequence. . . . She had prepared her poems as a professional, but they were never accepted as a professional's work, and she was no longer there to defend them" (112). Further evidence of such professionalism is in her habit of sending poems, "reordering them, engaging in private competitions with established poets." Finally, concludes Dickenson, the poet "exhibited one unchallengeable sign of the professional: she kept on writing" (113).

Being Bold: Fascicle 21's Finale

So she did. Why she did is answered in the final poem of this fascicle, "It was given to me by the Gods" (J454, Fr455). The poem does not cap, it crowns a book in which a speaker—whether the same or not—opened in a timorous voice with that frightened applicant at the "Home" within which dwelt those "stolid" or "vacant" faces. The applicant, you recall, had come for "business," a word heavily freighted in Dickinson's lexicon. The speaker(s) in Fascicle 21 merge: The grieving friend attempting to hold tight to the lost one; seeing him or her "better—in the Dark," wishing to "do more"; resisting the powerlessness "to fly" or "to gad [her] little Being out—"; finding the power to escape the prison/closet of Prose; discovering that the power granted on such display is to "Distill," "Arrest," and so forth; waking to a better day; being "identified" (to this one we return later); valuing the Pearl and the Love that is "high"; advancing in a journey; and rising to newfound strength. Such a summary of the first sixteen poems of Fascicle 21 is not intended to be as reductive as a single story. Each poem has other contexts as well, but read together, they form a pattern, not a linear story or an obvious picture, but a web of metaphors for the process of making and the meaning of poems. This awareness leads the reader to appreciate Dickinson's care as a self-conscious editor, one fully aware of her own creative power.

That is the point of the final poem of Fascicle 21, "It was given to me by / the Gods—" (J454, Fr455). In this staunchly self-assertive poem the poet of the sublime announces herself. I have dropped "the speaker" from this sentence because this poem—as do the two complementary prose/poetry definitions and the repeated "At last—to be identified"—verifies Gary Stonum's observation on the Dickinsonian sublime. The speaker of this fiercely proud poem uses what Stonum calls "that volatile and elusive pronoun, the 'I' of the romantic lyric" (1990, 142). In the context of Fascicle 21 the indeterminate "it" of the first declarative line seems clear; centered as it is by the mirrored poems "They shut me up in Prose" and "This was a poet," the fascicle surrounds notions of the nature of poetry and what it takes to be a poet: For one thing, the gods give it.

This is the second appearance of plural deities. In the fascicle's fifteenth poem, "Our Journey had advanced" (J615, Fr453), the "feet" that lead to the "odd Fork in Being's / Road—Eternity by term," end at the vision of "God— at every Gate." Far from resembling the grim and tricky anthropomorphic Old Testament God, the "Burglar! Banker—Father!" of another fascicle ("I never lost as much but twice" [J49, Fr39, F3]), these gods seem to be more like muses, lately sprung up in Amherst to bestow their "gifts," when, as the speaker says, "we are new and small" (a word, recall, essential to this fascicle with its gnat, its bee, its closeted little girl).

Although the poem's first line implies that poetry's source is a kind of serendipity, a negative capability in its most positive sense that allows whatever force or surge that gives birth to those thoughts to become poems, it continues with that other necessity of the poem. The spontaneous overflow of powerful feeling must be recollected in tranquility, not only remembered but reshaped, rearranged. The lump in the throat must find its thought. And it does as Dickinson protects the gift, handling it, molding it, refusing to let it go or—in another sense of the phrase—to debunk it: "I kept it in my Hand," she says; "I never put it down—." She dares to keep it—no longer fearing the sea but touching the transforming element and herself bearing the treasure home, reversing the narrative of Fascicle 21's thirteenth poem ("The Malay—took the Pearl"). Obsessively protective of the gift, the speaker continues: "I did not dare to Eat—or sleep," recalling the deprivation implied in "It would have starved a Gnat" from the fascicle's fifth poem.

Deprivation of food, however, is unimportant in the value system of the dowered child:

> I heard such words as "Rich"—
> When hurrying to school—
> From lips at Corners of the streets—
> And wrestled with a smile.

This poet stands apart from the "they"s who furnish the House of Prose, who do not recognize that the outer magnitude is dependent on the inner, on that which is "the secret in the lake / Eyes were not meant to know." The lips on street corners gossip and prattle; they do not carry on the truth/beauty dialogue between the grave's walls. On the last page of the fascicle Dickinson explains the reason for the inner delight that causes her to "wrestle with a smile":

> Rich! 'Twas myself—was
> rich—
> To take the name of Gold—
> And Gold to own—in solid
> Bars—
> The Difference—made me
> bold.

The final stanza resonates against the poem's first. What was given to the speaker/poet by the gods has made her rich, different, and bold. We do not know whether this is the transformed speaker of the fascicle's first poem. Consider, however, the possibility that the frightened returnee to the house of stolid stares has become the bold speaker, conscious of her gifts, showing the movement in mood within the fascicle from timorousness to temerity, from terror to trust.

The adjective "solid," more than any other, links this poem with the fascicle's first ("I—Years had been"). Subliminally it calls us back to that poem in which the speaker is afraid of the "vacant" (not solid) stare; in the later version of the poem the word, in fact, became "stolid." More important, it reminds us of the first speaker's desire to pursue her "business," her "life." Just as "business" was a heavily freighted word in Dickinson's lexicon and poetry, so is "solid" and for somewhat the same reasons. The word, which appears twelve times in all throughout Dickinson's œuvre, two of those times in Fascicle 21, carries a broad range of meanings in that 1828 lexicon. Most may apply to poetry in general, but they ring particularly true for the business of bookmaking in which Dickinson is engaged: "not hollow; full of matter; real; sound, valid, true, just, not empty or fallacious." Such are the bars of gold, the poems of the speaker, who places opposite to "When we are new and small" those last lines of the fascicle: "The Difference—made me / bold."

Just so, secondary meanings of "difference" lead us backward through the fascicle to the central pair, the aesthetic statement. "Difference" is not only unlikeness but also "dispute; debate; contention; quarrel; controversy." The writer of Fascicle 21 began it by implying that the business of the poet is serious indeed, that it is something like a lover's quarrel with the world; in those central paired poems she expanded that sense that poetry de/stills, a/rests, unsettles us. Poetry, among other things, is a dialogic conversation with her forebears; not only the obvious—Keats, Carlyle, Emerson—but also the sober Kames. It is a contest between the poet's own plural inner voices, between the characters of her imagination, and between recreated literary figures. Most of all, it is a conversation with her readers. And it is potent. The potency and magic it holds is suggested throughout the fascicle in which Dickinson had already imbedded another version of "At last—to be identified—" (J174, Fr172). Why it is "another version" is the subject of chapter 3.

Poems in Their Places

Those who say that one can find patterns in any random pairing or clustering have a point. Margaret Freeman's concoction of fictitious Fascicle 41 is sobering indeed. Most of what has appeared in this fascicle by way of themes and images appear throughout much if not most of the Dickinson œuvre. Nevertheless, Dickinson's own selections bear scrutiny. She herself selected this context, and although both "They shut me up in Prose" and "This was a Poet" are among Dickinson's most interesting single lyrics, the pleasures of the text are multiplied by reading them in the proximity she herself arranged.

Contemporary readers with enough money to purchase the *Manuscript Books* (no small investment) may do what early readers could not. How, we wonder, would R. P. Blackmur modify his "Prejudice" if he had been able as we are now to remove what he called in that 1937 essay "barriers to critical labor" (1937). Listen to the discouraged opening to the essay that ends with that relegation of Dickinson to antimacassar makers: "The disarray of Emily Dickinson's poems is the great obvious fact about them as they multiply from volume to volume—I will not say from edition to edition, for they have never been edited—just as a kind of repetitious fragmentariness is the characterizing fact of her sensibility" (Blake and Wells 1964, 201). Today readers such as Cristanne Miller, Martha Nell Smith, William Doreski, and Sharon Cameron have other ways of expressing Dickinson's "sensibility." They celebrate the (probably intentional) ambiguities, the intertextuality, the multiplicities, the resistance to closure, and the modernity of Emily Dickinson's mind and prosody. Those who read her through her fascicles, looking at "the last face," as Edith Wylder (1971) calls a manuscript, see something other than what Blackmur (1937, 201) calls the "repetitious fragmentariness" of the scattered editions from 1890 to 1950 (and those that rely on early texts, some of them still, alas, used in schoolrooms). They find patterns and possibilities in interrelated details and in details of diction, of image, of etymology, of chirography, and of spatial placement of words and punctuation marks—that is to say of all that culminates in the "solid Gold," the "gold to own," of the fascicle's final poem.

As the essays in Fraistat's collection iterate, "when read sequentially, [these groupings] afford a pleasure and a significance not available to one who reads the lyrics separately" (Miner 1986, 21). Dickinson, her own and for a long time the only reader of the collections, may have assembled her books with the pleasure Michael Riffaterre, the contemporary specialist in semiotics, describes in reading a single (French) poem: "As he progresses through the text, the reader remembers what he has just read and modifies his understanding of it in light of what he is now decoding. As he works forward from start to finish, he is reviewing, revising, comparing backwards. He is in effect performing a structural decoding" (1978, 5–6). The Riffaterrean reader is engaging in the same kind of somersaulting through a text that Dickinson described, perhaps in relation to Barrett Browning: "Did you ever read one of her Poems backward because the plunge from the front overturned you? I sometimes (often have, many times) have—a something overtakes the Mind—" (1983, 30). In a sense that is what I do as I invite my reader to look backward at an earlier fascicle in which one of the crucial poems from this fascicle's focus on the nature of the poet, "At last to be identified!" rings in a different key.

CHAPTER 3

Inferring from "Duplicates": Fascicle 8's Magic

F	J	Fr	
1	165	181	A *Wounded* Deer—leaps highest—
2	152	715	The Sun kept stooping—stooping—low!
3	166	183	I met a King this afternoon!
4	167	178	To learn the Transport by the Pain—
5	168	179	If the foolish, call them "*flowers*"—
6	169	180	In Ebon Box, when years have flown
*7	170	174	Portraits are to daily faces
8	171	169	Wait till the majesty of Death
9	172	170	'Tis so much joy! 'Tis so much joy!
10	173	171	A fuzzy fellow, without feet,
**11	174	172	At last, to be identified!
12	175	165	I have never seen 'Volcanoes'—
13	153	166	Dust is the only Secret—
14	176	167	I'm the little "Heart's Ease"!
15	177	168	Ah, Necromancy Sweet!
16	154	173	Except to Heaven, she is nought
*17	170	174	Pictures are to daily faces
18	178	175	I cautious, scanned my little life—
19	179	176	If I could bribe them by a Rose
20	180	177	As if some little Arctic flower

*Poem repeated in this single fascicle
**Poems repeated in Fasicle 21

Borrowing from Dickinson's method of reading "backward" and Riffaterre's of "reviewing, revising, comparing backwards," I move to a discussion of another of Dickinson's books, Fascicle 8. The two fascicles (8 and 21) share more than a duplicate poem ("At last—to be identified"). Both encircle the complementarity between the "business" and the power of the poet. Business and power might have been strange words to use in mid-nineteenth-century America, when, as Vivian Pollak reminds us, "an antipublication cult . . . was part of a larger pattern of cultural unrest about the departure of women from their proper sphere of influence and home" (1984, 233).[1] In Fascicle 8, however, "power," specifically that connected with "magic," is key. Along with uncorking, as it were, the power contained in Fascicle 8, especially the incrementally greater power it reveals when one reads its stunning separate elements in the context of the whole fascicle, this chapter has another purpose: to explore what is revealed about reading "poems in their places" through focusing on such "repeated" poems. "Duplicate" poems—a word I use with caution, for not only are the poems rarely perfect duplicates, but more significantly they accrue new identities *because* of their settings—and provide a particularly good testing ground for the effect of reading contextually.

How conscious Dickinson was of the different possibilities inherent in the two "At last, to be identified's" may be answered in part by reflecting both on what she demonstrated in Fascicle 21 of her aesthetic principles (poets de-still, de-stabilize, surprise us; they refuse to be closeted in a house of prose occupied by those with vacant/stolid eyes who stare blankly, who do not understand the "business" of poetry) and also on the equally potent nature of the poet she reveals in Fascicle 8.

Being Identified: Two Fascicle Versions

In fact, to write poetry is almost to perform an act of magic. If Fascicle 21 traced something like a narrative of the gathering of courage and boldness by the speaker, Fascicle 8, which explores notions of the power of poetry through another network of images, has little of narrative about it. Check out the pronouns. Fascicle 21 begins, ends, and is permeated by the first-person singular; even an exception to that, a poem such as Fascicle 21's exotic Malay/Pearl tale, suggests much about that "volatile" romantic first-person "I"—especially because of the company it keeps in the fascicle. Fascicle 8, on the other hand, begins with an observation that, however highly charged with autobiographical connotations, is relentlessly observant of something else, a wounded deer, an examination of which follows. First-person poems are scattered throughout the book, and they are particularly significant as Dickinson completes the collection, but most of the lyrics she has selected for Fascicle 8—

many of them different examples of transformations, even of necromancy—are seen by an almost objective observer, one capable of connecting the sign to the meaning.

Without claiming a narrative line in the fascicle, we are nevertheless alert to the intertextuality between poems because this fascicle holds some particularly tricky examples. As we observed in the progression of stories and images in Fascicle 21, this fascicle, too, is about self-identification. In different ways but no less powerfully by the end of the twenty-poem sequence we have witnessed something like a transformation of the observed wounded victim of the first poem to the confident poet/persona of the last. By its end not only has the speaker claimed her identity in the poem that she repeats in Fascicle 21, but, in the fascicle's last poem, she actually audaciously instructs her reader how to receive her individual acts of dexterous metamorphosis.

Validating and valorizing Allen Tate's remark (now almost a truism) that "Cotton Mather would have burned [Dickinson] for a witch" (1932, 167), Fascicle 8—as Fascicle 21 does not—surrounds just that image.[2] In the sense of "Derrida's cultural commonplace," that "language's operation is to identify otherness as self, to appropriate objects and transform them into subject" (Homans 1980, 36–37), all poets use such transformational witchcraft; their enterprise depends on the condensed magic of metaphor and simile, of metonymy and synecdoche, of irony and allusion and personification. Thus, to say that Dickinson uses magic is no news. However, to note that in this fascicle magical transformations are not only method but subject *is* new.

Fascicle 8's focus on witchcraft—on acts of transformation, necromancy, transport—is literally centered by the eleventh poem's declaration:

> At last, to be identified!
> At last, the lamps opon thy side
> The rest of Life *to see*!
>
> Past midnight! Past the morning star!
> Past Sunrise!
> Ah! What Leagues there *were*
> Between our feet, and Day! (J174, Fr172)

This little poem, so rarely discussed, even by those who write specifically on the fascicles, is remarkable for the way it radiates through (or in-gathers) images from throughout the entire fascicle. For quite other reasons it does the same in Fascicle 21, where it is, as I have shown, differently lineated and punctuated and where it is placed (as it is here) halfway through that fascicle's passage from fear to boldness.

In Fascicle 8, compiled some two years before Fascicle 21, "At last" seems a gloss of the poems surrounding it. As we see in this chapter, its first words, repeated in the second line, convey the patient endurance and martyrdom of the fascicle's first (wounded deer) poem. Its second phrase—the passive infinitive "to be identified" implies supreme knowledge of self, augmented by the transforming recognition of that self by an other, perhaps the "savans" of the fascicle's fifth poem. "Lamps" shine everywhere in the fascicle, as do images of sight. "Opon thy side" (taking Franklin's lead, I am maintaining Dickinson's clear preference for this spelling) reflects the right hand of God of the fifth poem. The midnight of death, the morning star of new life, new beginnings—repeated in "Past Sunrise" and in the Leagues that *were* in a past life "Between our feet and Day"—mesh with other images of literal transport: the wagons of the "little king" in the second poem, the traveling tall-tale tellers of the twelfth, and the mysteriously conveyed alien arctic flower of the fascicle's last poem. Put another way, transaction/transport/magic occurs through pain (in the fascicle's first poem), through the effect of the sunset (the second), in death (the third), by an analogy with flowers (fourth), in relation to the ebon box (the fifth), as revealed by a caterpillar and by a volcano (tenth and twelfth)—and there are more.

Re-placing this modest poem in its fascicle context shows how it refracts from its proximate poems. Reading poems in their places is to engage in what Barbara Herrnstein Smith calls "retrospective patterning," reading backward:

> [I]n the movement from poem to poem, connections and similarities are illuminated, and the reader perceives that seemingly gratuitous or random events, details and juxtapositions have been selected in accord with certain principles (Fraistat 1986, 8, quoting Herrnstein Smith on poetic closure in relation to reading contextually).

Reading backward, retrospective patterning, and reading contextually enable what Martha Nell Smith describes as collaborative (1992, 71–75). Such reading, as Sharon Cameron points out, encourages expanding the canon (1992, 19). Overlooked poems acquire greater interest; oft-published ones take on different dimensions.

And what do we learn if the poet has placed a poem in more than one place? If, as I believe, each fascicle has its own character, its own thumbprint, its own swirl of image clusters, and its own movement and character, a poem containing (almost) the same words in one fascicle will be a different artifact by virtue of the pressure of surrounding poems when it is placed in another. Cameron touches on this probability briefly, saying that "what looks like the same poem in two different fascicles may be recognized as the same words without being recognized as the same poem" (ibid., 6). This is a bracing counter to one of the only other comments into the nature of the duplicates, that of Ralph Franklin himself. In the long preface to the *Manuscript Books,* Franklin implies that duplications may have resulted from forgetfulness or carelessness: "[P]resumably . . . she failed to destroy a worksheet" (1981, xv–xvi).

Even among the few who have written on the fascicles, few remark on what seems a significant practice. With the exception of extensive discussions of "Safe in their Alabaster Chambers" (to which I add my voice in the next chapter), commentators seem to find unremarkable the fact that from her growing body of nearly one thousand poems then available (that is, written up to the time she seems to have stopped her publication project in 1864), Dickinson *chose* to repeat between seven and eleven[3] of the poems in two different fascicles, four of which are part of this case study of the value of reading Dickinson in her own context.

Readers might possibly accept Franklin's almost exasperated conclusion (that the repetitions represented memory lapses) in the case of "I hide myself" (J903, Fr80), which appears in Fascicles 3 and 40 or "Bound—a Trouble" (J269, Fr240, Fascicles 9 and 36) because Dickinson apparently made her selections for the first pair of fascicles (3 and 40) some five or six years apart; the second pair (9 and 36) were probably separated by about three years. However, it seems less easy to believe that this woman who, as Christopher Benfy suspects, "knew all her own poetry by heart as well as huge passages of [others]" (1986, 61), forgot she had written "Ah Moon—and Star!" (J240, Fr262) into Fascicle 11 when not more than a year later she transcribed it into Fascicle 14. Just so, her use of "At last" in Fascicles 8 and 21, separated by two years, is far too canny to be the result of carelessness.

Moreover, two oddities about these repetitions argue for Dickinson's intentionality. If one accepts Johnson's numbering, emended by Franklin, as approximately correct, one discovers that most fascicles are constructed primarily from two sets of poems—that is, two (near) sequences of the Johnson numbers—often interwoven. Most have a few selections from outside the chronological order of the two sets, suggesting that the artist was choosing from her works those poems that were set off best by their placement in another group of poems from other periods. In all but one fascicle, Dickinson included one or two from a completely different numbered sequence, and of course, in one of the two appearances of a repeated poem, that poem is completely off-sequence. Thinking of the fascicles as scrapbooks, as Franklin's introduction implies, does not seem to fit this kind of construction. The patchwork-quilt metaphor more nearly does.

A second demurral to Franklin's (and Porter's and Weisbuch's and others') tendency to see these productions as repositories for poems rather than (at least instinctively) organized wholes and the repetitions as accidents is the curious feature of the placement of almost all of the nine duplications. In no case do they begin or end a fascicle, a fact that might seem to support Franklin's relegation of the poems to accidents or mistakes. However, in nine of fifteen fascicles in which duplications appear the poem is situated close to midfascicle and is almost always a gloss for those poems leading up to and away from it. "At last, to be identified," for example, is the eleventh poem in a group of twenty that compose Fascicle 8. Further, Franklin and others imply that selections (including repetitions) might have been used as fillers for empty slots below poems that ran into another page. As the chart in the appendix indicates, only two of the repeated poems were quatrains; the others were, for Emily Dickinson, the miniaturist, quite long, ranging from ten to twenty-four lines. Rather than filling blank spaces, they required more than one leaf. Moreover, Dickinson sometimes prefers leaving a page half blank, as she does in that "rest" in Fascicle 21. Remember that she had written many poems she had not gathered into her books. Clearly, as Robyn Bell says, although Dickinson "employs space thriftily, it is hardly a tyrannical concern" (1988, 5).

So I begin this discussion of the network of images in Fascicle 8 with the centered poem, one that is duplicated in Fascicle 21 with different inferences. Hold that highly charged word "inference" in mind, please, for the end of this chapter. As the repeated poem suggests, Fascicle 8 includes explorations of the past, the antiquated, the dusty—all explicit in no fewer than five poems and suggested in more. These images are linked to those descriptive of faces. All of these are clusters that intersect with and complicate the fascicle's primary design: to link the "business" of poetry making with the art and power of "necromancy." As it ends, Fascicle 8 begins with the drama of natural wonders seen in unfamiliar lights: "A *Wounded* deer—leaps highest—" (J165, Fr181).

The Transformational Power of Pain

Dickinson's wounded deer thrusts the fascicle into its transformational mode. The hunter, whom the speaker has heard "tell it" (the story) may be blending a number of stories. One is a literal hunt, something like that in a horrifying *Harper's* article: "We have known a deer to keep its position in front of a fleet pack of hounds for near a mile, running all the way. A stag was killed . . . that seemed for a while to have 'a charmed life'; for every new wound, however severe, seemed only to inspire it with renewed power to elude its pursuers" (Thorpe 1858, 619). The article, by a B. T. Thorpe, tells of one strong stag whose wound "was sufficiently large to admit a finger." Another source for this and many other Dickinson poems, note George Monteiro and Barton Levi St. Armand (1981), may be images contained in the Holmes and Barber *Book of Emblems,* which had moral stories and pictures, including one to match this poem. Both the journals and the religious tract were readily available to the Dickinson household as were hymns such as "Rock of Ages," a culturally prominent source, which, as she often did, Dickinson seems to have subverted[4]—or trimmed and tailored for her own editing purposes.

Yes, both the literal deer and the large and obvious typological allegory are there, but the language of the poem and of those that follow underscores the intersection between eschatology and the poetic consciousness. This fascicle in which "Anguish" and "Transport" are iterative words and ideas begins with the blunt announcement about the energizing power of pain. The adjective "wounded" has an important place in Dickinson's vocabulary ("We will not drop the / Dirk / Because we love the wound," says the suicidal or murderous speaker of "Rehearsal to Ourselves" [J379, Fr664, F30], and a wound is so wide in "A great Hope fell" [J1123, Fr1187] that "all my Life had entered it / And there were troughs beside"), but the adjectives in the next stanza are strange for Dickinson and highly suggestive—not only of typography:

> The *Smitten* Rock that gushes!
> The *trampled* Steel that springs!
> A Cheek is always redder
> Just where the Hectic stings!

According to Dickinson's dictionary, "Smitten" has only two meanings: "struck" or "affected with passion." It is a word she used in only two other poems, one of which would make a fine synopsis for Fascicle 8: "'Tis anguish grander than Delight / 'Tis Resurrection Pain— / The meeting Bands of smitten Face / We questioned to, again" (J984, Fr192). As for "trampled," which her lexicon defines as "to tread with contempt," this line is her only use of the word. That the pain of the wounded Deer—or whatever the deer stands for—is so particularly humiliating makes its final stanza all the more powerful. Denis Donoghue puts it mildly by saying that the speaker shows "the whirling ingenuity of the translator" of loss as gain (1965, 108) in these lines. As in the opening of another of her fascicles ("A Mien to move a Queen," J283, Fr254, F11), the real subject here is not simply a wounded character but one who must assume a defensive demeanor in the most terrible of circumstances. The speaker makes as broad a leap as did the told-about deer itself in the first stanza:

> Mirth is the Mail of Anguish—
> In which it Cautious Arm,
> Lest anybody spy the blood
> And "you're hurt" exclaim!

Later in the fascicle the speaker (or another one) exults "'Tis so much joy! 'Tis so much joy," but "mirth" is another matter. For one thing, again according to Dickinson's Webster's, "Mirth differs from joy in always implying noise." Mirth, then, is joy expressed, or perhaps it is an ersatz joy that hides the anguish. "Mail" is both what the cautious don to defend themselves from the arms of others, or, paradoxically, it is something sent—the post from Tunis delivered by the hummingbird, the song of the split lark, the letter to the world that never wrote to the poet.

By the final verse, the speaker "stands before the bitterest contingencies of chance, unabashed . . . not imperturbable or fearless" (Donoghue 1965, 109) but empowered by the "eerie transformation of anguish into energy" (Gilbert 1983, 28). Sandra Gilbert's reading of the poem is one of many, ranging from those who connect the wounding of the deer to Christian typology to those who link the wound to Dickinson's rage at her loveless father (Sewall 1980, 65, and Knapp 1989, 142–43) or to a protective stance toward her brother (Pollak 1984, 53). St. Armand links the poem to a Thoreauvian comment (1988, 232). All of these readings cast light on the poem as each scholar holds it in his or her own light, but no one has yet read the poem in Dickinson's own context, as the opening of Fascicle 8. No one has noted, for example, that the military language of "mail" and "armor" reappear in the next, the fascicle's second poem, and that three poems later we read almost another take on the wounded deer: "To learn the Transport by the Pain—" (J167, Fr178). Or that all of this leads to the pleasurable surprise of "At last, to be identified" (J174, Fr172), that poem that reappears with other connotations in Fascicle 21.

Just so, the second poem in the fascicle, "The Sun kept stooping—stooping—low!" (J152, Fr182) has been treated to a colorful reading by Camille Paglia, who sees in it a drama of rape or war and who sees Dickinson's speaker as a sadist who "avenges the feminized passivity into which God thrusts mankind" (1991, 624, 651). Indeed, this second poem *has* bloody imagery: The sunset seeps red into every corner of a kitchen in which the speaker/observer watches it. But the tone, especially when one remembers that the speaker of the previous poem was armed in "mirth," is hardly as violent as in Paglia's interpretation.[5] This sunset appears later in the fascicle in the little poem "Portraits / Pictures are to daily faces" (J170, Fr174), the poem that is situated twice within the fascicle as a kind of refrain. Sunset is to the world it touches what pain is to the deer: transformational. As the witness puts the change, it is "Transaction!" We see the scene much as we saw the wounded deer leaping, through observant, imaginative eyes. Through those eyes we see the "stain" taking over "the Hills" outside "Until the Tyrian / Was crowded dense with Armies— / So gay, so Brigadier—"[6] that, says the speaker, "*I* felt martial stirrings." The speaker, observer, perhaps a kind of

Cinderella with yearnings toward glamour, is so moved by the (not terrible) vision that she "charge[s], from [her] chimney corner" to find that "Nobody was there!"

She is the only one in the room; she must be "Nobody." Rarely negative to Dickinson (or to her Transcendentalist brothers), "Nobody" is a term of power. The word is used in only twelve poems: Two of those uses are in this fascicle. In the thirteenth poem in the series it is "Nobody" who knows the secret of death. A related word, a negative-turned-positive "Naught" also appears in the fascicle's sixteenth poem as we will see. Nobody needs to be reminded that in one of Dickinson's most anthologized poems the speaker crows, "I'm Nobody! who are you? / Are you—Nobody—Too? (J288, Fr260, F11). "Nobody" is heterodox and alive. "Nobody" is Emerson's transparent eyeball. "Nobody" is Keats's Negative Capability.[7] That Dickinson herself possessed such a gift of emptying herself in order to be capable of great observations is clear from a story her neighbor MacGregor Jenkins told of her: "She had a habit of standing in rapt attention as if she were listening to something very faint and far off," he said. "We children often saw her at sunset, standing at the kitchen window, peering through a vista in the trees to the western sky" (1984, 264). St. Armand, who quotes the Jenkins story, adds that "the daily observance of the setting sun [was] an almost holy duty" (ibid., 265). By being so open, so "Nobody," one may transform a sunset into a bustling, exciting battlefield. For that is the tone. The sun is "so gay" and "Brigadier." The cockade makes of a military insignia a cocky-sounding plume. Along with all of this, one clue to tone is that the poem shares space in a fascicle that includes the birth of a butterfly from a caterpillar and—in the next poem—of a king from a barefoot boy.

Translations, transactions, transport: quick transformations of palpable fact to meaning, of the physical body to spirit, of the individual to the universal. This action is the refrain of the fascicle. So far a deer has been wounded and thus charged with power, and the vivid panoply of sunset has become "Nobody." The fascicle's third poem, "I met a King this afternoon!" (J166, Fr183), embodies magic, too. In this one it is a barefoot boy's wagon that "transports" the speaker. But once again, the speaker is not the subject: What she saw is. This time the transforming power of the poet sees the barefoot boy, crowned with "A little Palm leaf Hat," become more and more grand. "Nobody" becomes "somebody" in the third stanza, moving through a litany of ranks (Earl, Marquis, Czar, Pope). In the fourth verse he is a "freckled Monarch" (Dickinson was freckled, too), holding the reins of a "transporting" wagon (perhaps poetry?) that can also transport royalty. In its "Barefoot Estate" (one thinks of Emerson's rousing end to "The Poet" once again, that the poet is the owner of all land tax free), the little wagon is equal to "the Royal Coach." When it was published in 1893, this poem was dubbed "My little king," a title that diminishes its grand scale of the imagination's transforming power. Just as the freckled king holds the reins to keep the vehicle in check, so the poet holds the meter at an even tetrameter until "Dare I presume to see" in the fifth verse. Daring to see, we recall, is the enterprise of the observer of the wounded deer and of the bloody sunset.

The reader may also "dare presume to see" the intricate connections between the first three poems of Fascicle 8 and the fourth one. This poem serves as a kind of pivot, reprising in the first half images of the earlier poems and then moving the fascicle in a related but more specifically literary direction in the second half. The fourth poem is "To learn the Transport by the Pain—" (J167, Fr178). Its first line harks back in meaning and mood to the fascicle's first wounded deer image; its second line ("As Blind men learn the Sun!") to the synaesthetic effect of the sunset in the second poem, and the third through sixth lines about the "homesick—homesick feet" seeking "native lands . . . And blue—beloved air!" might be the barefoot boy of the previous poem, robbed of his wagon and "Barefoot Estate."

The second half of the four-stanza poem introduces another cluster of words, images, and ideas that web with similar diction through the rest of the fascicle, diction suggesting in writerly terms those who have suffered that "Sovereign Anguish!" (of not being able to see the sunset but learning it through pain, of being deprived of home—and through such pains and deprivation of experiencing "Transport"). The lines refract off the earlier poems, helping us to understand that the power imposed by the wound to the deer, the wonder of the sunset's arrival and disappearance, and the ability of the barefoot freckled "Monarch" to Transport as he reins his cart carefully all have to do with the magic of making poetry. So does pain, as the "these," unclear referent of the "patient 'Laureates'" suggests (those in pain, those blind, those homesick for "blue—beloved air"). Here are the lines that end the fourth poem:

> These are the patient 'Laureates'
> Whose voices—trained below—
>
> Ascend in ceaseless Carol
> Inaudible indeed,
> To us—the dullest scholars
> Of the mysterious Bard!

Self-reflexively, these lines contain the language of the writer's business (signals, voices, carols, scholars, Laureates, and Bards); they point in the direction toward which the speaker wishes to be "identified" later in the fascicle. They also imply that the important hierarchy is not, for example, between all of the ranks listed in the previous barefoot-boy poem but in the huge gulf between writer (especially one who has learned "the Transport by the Pain") and reader (who hasn't), between the "patient 'Laureates'" and "us—the dullest scholars."

That hierarchy—or dichotomy—continues in the fifth poem, "If the Foolish call them *Flowers*" (J168, Fr179), in the distinction between the "foolish" and the "wiser," between those with "beclouded Eyes" (those who do not "dare" to "presume to see") and "learned angels" or "savans" (the "laureates" of the previous poem). In her even 8's and 5's, the self-consciously Belles Lettrest of this poem exhibits her own "flowers" of prosody.

The next two poems reveal even trickier linguistic play, play observable only to the fascicle reader. Dickinson, the canny editor of this book, hints at that play when she speaks of the Mysterious Bard in the previous poem. She seems mischievous, a tone borne out partly through this fifth poem's ("If the foolish") last stanza. Having berated (as she did more than once) the God who would "deny" "Old 'Moses'" his view of "Canaan," she uses heavily freighted words in the final two verses, speaking of "superfluous" sciences and "scholastic skies," and ends with the necessary comical mispronunciation of "Galaxies" at the poem's close: *Try* saying it in an orthodox manner in the grip of the poet's established rhythm as she prays:

> Low amid that glad Belles Lettres
> Grant that we may stand—
> *Stars* amid profound *Galaxies*
> At that grand "Right-hand"!

Below these lines and the heavy black line at its close is one of Dickinson's clearest statements about the possible legacy of being—or watching—such stars.

The Text: The "Promised Land"

Here's the trickiness of reading poems in their places, and here is an instance where the reader of this book will be greatly aided by looking at the manuscript books themselves; a sample of what one finds follows these pages. Exactly opposite the second stanza of "If the foolish call them flowers" (the stanza beginning "Those who read the 'Revelations'") is the opening of a proleptic poem about the legacy of the writer. The sixth poem in the fascicle begins "In Ebon Box, when years have flown" (J169, Fr180). As do the paired poetry/prose poems in Fascicle 21, Fascicle 8's paired poems resonate across the pages. On both the left ("Those who read the 'Revelations'") and the right ("In Ebon Box") pages the speaker is a reader who is using the old artifact (Revelations / an old letter) to justify her own ongoing project. "Those who read the 'Revelations'" are in the situation of those who "wip[e] away the velvet dust" on the Ebon Box. Those who stand in for Moses as he "scans" his landscape and his longing are the same who hold the "tawny" letter to the light "to con the faded syllables / That quickened us like wine."

Scanning and conning syllables: These are the actions of the attentive reader, interested in the merging of form and meaning. Reading across as well as down the page enlarges the meaning of both poems. The faded letter, held to the light, is literally parallel to a promised land. Those who deem the sciences "superfluous" are those who recognize that literal flowers ("shriveled" but surviving the "mouldering hand") are symbols of the "gallant" human soul. "In Ebon Box" continues on the next page, and so does the startling and witty evidence of care in arrangement. In addition to the musicality in the next line—the r's repeated strategically in each line, the swish of the doubled "sh" in the last line—the reader is drawn to the witty conjunction of images, for the fourth verse continues the imagined inventory of the Ebon Box:

> A curl, perhaps, from foreheads
> Our Constancy forgot—
> Perhaps an Antique trinket—
> In vanished fashions set!

Just as scanning and conning and the promised land and a letter held to the light linked the fifth and sixth poems ("If the foolish" and "In Ebon Box"), so the last portion of the sixth poem resonates against an image in the eighth (yes, there is a tiny poem in between, about which more later), "Wait till the Majesty of Death" (J171, Fr169). Opposite the lines about the curl found in the Ebon Box are these four from the eighth poem:

> Wait till the majesty of Death
> Invests so mean a brow!
> Almost a powdered Footman
> Might dare to touch it now!

These pages contain too many coincidences to discount the intentionality of the poet. On one pair of pages a "text" (the letter) is parallel to the promised land denied to Moses (remember the typology of Moses' "Smitten Rock" of the fascicle's very first poem). And on the next this little acrobatic stunt occurs. Although the concordance shows twenty-two other uses of "forehead" and seven of "brow," here they meet, brow to brow. Furthermore, the brows are joined by this little quatrain concerning physiognomy, the seventh poem in the series:

Four poems seem to unfold into each other in Fascicle 8, a fascicle dated by Franklin as compiled about 1860. The interconnected threads of the poems, fifth through eighth in the series of twenty poems, reveal themselves to the observer who reads with attention to the suggestion of images and wordplay. "If the foolish call them 'flowers'" (J168, Fr179), "In Ebon Box, when years have flown" (J169, Fr180), "Portraits are to daily faces" (J170, Fr174), and "Wait till the majesty of Death" (J171, Fr169), read in the context of each other and the rest of the poems in this fascicle, involve images of transformation and, eventually, of power. According to Franklin the paper is "wove, cream, lightly ruled, and embossed Parsons Paper Co." Fascicle 8 and Fascicle 21 (chapters 1 and 2), fascicles with quite different image clusters and concerns share one poem, "At last, to be identified!" (J174, Fr172); in addition, "Portraits are to daily faces" also appears as "Pictures are to daily faces" later in Fascicle 8. The four poems on these pages appear in the *Manuscript Books* I, 134–37. Printed by permission of the Houghton Library, Harvard University.

58   Reading the Fascicles of Emily Dickinson

Portraits are to daily faces
As an evening West,
To a fine, pedantic Sunshine—
In a Satin Vest! (J170, Fr174).

Wedged between the sixth poem ("In Ebon Box"), in which a text survives the death of its writer, and the eighth ("Wait till the Majesty of Death"), in which a "mean" or average brow is transformed by death in ways that parallel the transformation of the barefoot boy of the third poem—although, perhaps,

Inferring from "Duplicates" 59

with greater acerbity—this little poem becomes more understandable than when isolated from its context. In the face of certain death, "Portraits" seems to say, art is, as Frost later put it, the momentary stay against confusion.

If the "Portraits" quatrain were as simple as, say, an opposition of Sunset/Sunshine, Evening/Day, as it may appear to be, why did Dickinson, the tricky editor of Fascicle 8, repeat it in the same book? No one, in fact, seems to have asked why, with one alteration, these lines return in a similar placement as a bridge between two longer poems. To begin to answer the question, the fascicle reader notes that in this first appearance the question bridges poems concerning the physical appearances of the dead leftover artifacts of life. The salvaged curl—remember that Dickinson herself had at least one (in L5 she speaks of having a lock of Abiah Root's hair "as precious as gold")—lasts longer than the physical modest brow; the Portrait, the created artifact, will outlast both. Yet the dichotomy implied in the poem between the actual and the artistic appears balanced as it reprises the opening poems. Art has both its splendor—it may be as lush as "an Evening West"—and its limits: It is not the life itself, not, in other words, an actual "fine, pedantic Sunshine / in a Satin Vest." To the fascicle reader the apparent balance is skewed. That "pedantic Sunshine" and that "Satin Vest" of "Portraits" smack of the prose world, the dead shut up in Alabaster Chambers in fascicles that the next chapter treats. Sunset's colorful possibilities, on the other hand, are vividly remembered from that second poem in this fascicle.

The cluster of tricks alerts the reader for more. We are not quite halfway through this fascicle of transformations and transport. Although it is longer than most poems, the fascicle's eighth entry, "Wait till the Majesty of Death" (J171, Fr169), deserves more attention than that of the coincidence of the "brow." With its inflated language (note the heavy use of adjectives—"powdered Footman," "Obsequious Angels," "purple . . . Retinue" and "purple . . . state," and, finally and most tritely, "Modest Clay"), the poem smacks of the expected and not-quite-believed. The poet surprises our horizon of expectation by offering us the unsurprising. Nothing transforms so well as death, the poet says on the surface; death makes ordinary "Democrats" into royal personages, fit to be received "unblushingly" by "the Lord of Lords." However, the inflated (to my ears) language and the quotation marks around so many of the religious phrases tip the reader off to the possibility of parody as the poet offers other transformational images, images worthy of that particularly delicious one, the letter held to the light that, by virtue of a proximate poem, becomes something like the Promised Land.

What makes me hear parody most distinctly is another of the tricks one can observe only by reading poems in their places. Recall that in the seventh poem, the one that precedes this one, the last line—about the "pedantic Sunshine" is that it is "*In* a satin *Vest*." This eighth poem about those who "prate about 'Preferment'" and so forth begins "Wait till the Majesty of Death / *Invests* (italics mine) so mean a brow!" Serendipitous or intended, such a diction discovery must have delighted its author as it does its reader.

If the eighth poem is self-consciously parodic, the ninth, "'Tis so much joy! 'Tis so much joy!" (J172, Fr170), is also highly contrived in its prosody. Consider its relentless Common Particular Meter (88686); its mathematical ordering (three verses of six lines with three subjunctive clausal sentences); its anaphoric clauses; its perfect balance of value against value and word against word. The poem is not long, but it has true rhyme, and slant rhyme, and internal rhyme. It has alliteration and assonance. It is thus an example of the kind of art that rearranges and makes permanent the passing emotion. The word "art" or "poem" has not entered the fascicle, but all of the poems in the sequence surround just that subject.

Curiously and artfully Dickinson balances the contrivances and tricky structure of "'Tis so much joy!" against its own meaning:

> Life is but Life! And Death, but Death!
> Bliss is, but Bliss, and Breath but Breath!. . .
> Defeat means nothing *but* Defeat.
> No drearier can befall!

Having deflated—or at least leveled—the words usually inflated by nineteenth-century poets, Dickinson turns the mood with the suddenness of the Gun at Sea, the Bells of the final stanza's meditation on "gain," which ends:

> For Heaven is a different thing,
> Conjectured, and waked sudden in—
> And might extinguish me!

The heightened rhetoric of the first verse, balanced with the understatement of the middle stanza, yield to cautiously conjectural closing lines ("if I gain!" and "Heaven . . . might extinguish me!"). The effort, the "throw" ("Poor as I, / Have ventured all upon a "throw!") leads to waking sudden in a "Heaven which might be for the remains of the lovely corpse (in "the Majesty of Death" of the previous poem) or, because so many poems are about laureates, which might be the immortality of poets.

The abstractions and absences of the ninth poem are made concrete, humorous, and palpable in the tenth, "A fuzzy fellow without feet" (J173, Fr171). In this series of poems about transport, translation, and necromancy, Dickinson seems to have interposed this closely observed feature of nature between "'Tis so much joy!" and "At last," the poem that is its clear match. Perhaps she decided that between the two rather breathless expressions of transcendent experience, both of which speak of the leagues out to sea and are insistently first person, she needed this poem about "the unknowing seekers of God [who] must live without assurances, meekly, dumbly" (Keller 1979, 145). In keeping with the fascicle's focus on transformation, the homely, fuzzy lowlife has two other lives. First it takes "*Damask* Residence / And struts in sewing silk": This is the cocoon life that Jane Eberwein, who calls the poem a "seeming reversal of industrious Yankee values (1985, 169), likens to the dull everydayness Dickinson seems to be mocking. Finally it emerges "finer than a Lady" with a mission: "to tell the pretty secret of the Butterfly."

Revelations of "Identity"

Dickinson must have had great fun placing the last four lines of this poem of transformation or rather of *revelation* of a true identity on the top of a page on which she placed the poem she considered to be significant enough to enter into two fascicles. The butterfly is at last identified and can tell the pretty secret, just as in "At last, to be identified!" (J174, Fr172), the eleventh and central poem of the series, the speaker is (or will be) revealed with "the lamps upon thy side." In both poems the secret is "the rest of life *to see*!" We remember the observer of the barefoot boy/king (in the fascicle's third poem) who dared "presume to see" and of the admonition not to read "Revelations" with "beclouded Eyes" (in the fifth). Just so, we anticipate linkages in the poems in the last half of the fascicle.

The irregular rush (an interrupted common meter) of "A fuzzy fellow" and "At last" is tempered and strictly controlled in the regular trochaics of 8/5 ballad meter in "I have never seen 'Volcanoes'—" (J175, Fr165), the twelfth poem in the series and an almost perfect parallel to the first. Manner and matter merge in this compressed poem about the compressed, barely suppressed potential violence of volcanoes and, by implication, of human emotions. Outside of its fascicle placement the poem attracts much critical attention. John Pickard, for example, calls it "an abstract examination of transport and awe" (1988, 87). For Cristanne Miller it is "a pathetic cry of joy and mingled trepidation" (1987, 136); for Brita Lindberg-Seyersted it is an "ecstatic soliloquy" (1968, 45); and, most famously, for Adrienne Rich such poems are "explosive, destructive" and heterodox (1978, 177). Whether read separately or in the context of this fascicle, "I have never seen Volcanoes" is full of all of those possible readings. In Dickinson's own context, however, its power increases incrementally. "Phlegmatic" mountains bear within "appalling" violence, says this speaker, who, like the one who tells of the caterpillar becoming a butterfly or of the wounded deer leaping highest, is reciting a twice-told tale. The anthropomorphic mountain is capable of "taking Villages for breakfast" and—repeating the word but this time as a verb—of "appalling men." (She uses its root in the last stanza's "*pal*pitating Vineyard.") Having implied the comparison between volcano and human, the speaker makes the comparison overt, driving the comparison home through her double rhyme:

> If the stillness is Volcanic
> In the human face
> When upon a pain titanic
> Features keep their place—

"Faces," a subtheme of the fascicle, opened the book in "mirth is the mail of anguish"; they are brow to brow in two other poems; and they appear in the two portrait/picture poems. Just so, faces appear in at least three poems following this twelfth poem. Check Fascicle 21 for a similar gathering of such images and you will not find it. Although no poem of Dickinson may be divorced from any other poem, those within fascicles have commonalities and intertextualities that give a fascicle its particular character or thumbprint.

In this fascicle's context one need not see either the Volcano as literally "the encroaching menace of [Dickinson's] mental illness" (Cody 1971, 301) or its form as "female genitalia" (ibid., 409). It is enough, in the context of this little book, to regard the Volcano as symbolic of an "eerie transformation of agony into energy" (Gilbert 1983, 29). Controlled intensity of metrics and imagery, along with the actual content, pairs this with the fascicle's first poem. In the first, pain prompts a high leap; in this poem the speaker acknowledges a tightly lidded but felt pressure. The "Pain Titanic" of the third verse (and, in other words, of the leaping, dying deer) becomes the "smouldering Anguish" of the final verse. "The hectic cheek" of the first poem previewed the stern rigor when in this twelfth poem "Features keep their places." In the human and the mountain, however, there is trouble within. Not only are both poems twice-told ("the hunter tell[s]" and "travellers tell"), but also, in both, gunfire appears along with "Still"ness. Both end with a movement away from the hurt animal/roiling volcano to the witness of it: In the first, the deer's mail of mirth guards against the sympathetic observer's "you're hurt," and in the twelfth the focus turns to "some loving Antiquary" who, "on Resumption Morn, / will not cry with joy, Pompeii! / To the Hills return."

The Antiquary appears on the second page of the poem. He or she is an epilogue to the story that has ended with the "palpitating Vineyard" being thrown "In the dust." This ending leaves the reader with dust thrown in her eyes. The poem actually has no syntactical resolution and very little in "sense"—unless one reads it in its fascicle placement. It begins with what the traveler tells and moves to three subjunctive clauses: The first ("If the stillness is Volcanic") is of the violence contained; the second ("If at length the smouldering anguish") is of violence unleashed; and the third is of a future far beyond the eruption, not a "Resurrection" morn (Dickinson's more usual phrase), which would suggest transformation and elevation, but rather "Resumption" ("If some loving Antiquary, / On Resumption Morn, / Will not cry with joy 'Pompeii'! / To the Hills return"). Resumption implies simply placing back what has been disordered, picking up an interrupted action. These hills, says the speaker, will never, as in a film reversed, resume their stillness, beauty, fruition. They are spent, just as the deer in the first poem is dead—except in the memory and art of the "teller."

In this poem the teller merges with "the Antiquary," a word anticipated in the "antiques" of the earlier poem enumerating the contents of the Ebon Box. Used by Dickinson only in this poem, "antiquary" is a word worth playing with, as Wendy Barker does (1987, 130–32) in relation to another form of the word in another setting. One might consider, for example, antic-wary, anti-quarry, antic-query, and so forth. Dickinson's dictionary's list for the words involved in the potential pun increases the possibilities for play within the fascicle. To quarry, as a verb, may be related, her Webster's says, "to dig, to run violently, to leap"; "query" is "to seek, to inquire . . . to examine by questions, to doubt of." However many functions the antiquarian of the fascicle's twelfth poem has, what he or she discovers "On Resumption Morn" is found "in the dust." And so the poem (J153, Fr166) that follows this begins this way:

> Dust is the only Secret—
> Death, the only One
> You cannot find out all about
> In his "native town."

Whatever specific death might originally have inspired Emily Dickinson to send this poem (as many others in this fascicle) to Sue, this thirteenth poem in its own book setting begins on the same page as the stanza of the previous poem about the Antiquary. "Dust" tells the life story of the mysterious, industrious, frighteningly efficient Yankee figure, "Death" (who may or may not be the same as the Antiquary, with all of his punning possibilities, of the previous poem). The genealogy with its "Nobody knew 'his Father'" calls to mind that important absence/presence in the bloody sunset poem, the second in the series; the "native town" reminds us of the longed-for native lands of the homesick feet in the fascicle's fourth poem; and, most tellingly, the understated nature of Dust and Death in this, the thirteenth poem, calls us back to the "Life is but Life! And Death, but Death" of the ninth poem.

Understated and wry as this poem is, it nevertheless paints a grimly oxymoronic picture of death. Death is both "Industrious" and "Laconic." It is "Bold as a Brigand" (in Dickinson's lexicon, a "lawless fellow . . . robber . . . freebooter") but also "Stiller than a Fleet." How still, one wonders, is a "Fleet"? A fleet of what? Perhaps a "fleet" of birds, given that the next line is "Builds like a Bird, too!" But the Brigand/Bird has an opponent with similar traits: "Christ robs the Nest— / Robin after Robin / Smuggled to Rest!" In a poem marked by its slant rhyme (One/town, Boy/history, Sedate/Fleet), the true rhyme at its end (noted by Judy Jo Small [1990, 190]) suggests a resolution not present in other poems within the fascicle.

The poem's dry, dusty beginning shared a page with the volcano poem's dusty ending; its more affirming conclusion shares the page with the opening of an almost cloyingly sweet and almost completely ignored poem that becomes the fourteenth in this sequence, "I'm the little 'Heart's Ease'!" (J176, Fr167). It is as though "I'm the little 'Heart's Ease'!" is the speaker's description of the place to which Christ smuggles the Robins. In this poem that place is an "old fashioned" Eden. The birds become "antiquated fellows." Such intertextuality makes one increasingly resistant to notions of the accidental nature of these "repositories" of Dickinson's verse. The "lovely Antiquary" of the eleventh poem is in a line on the top of the left hand of the opened book; "Antiquated fellows" and two "old fashioneds" from "Heart's Ease" are on the bottom of the right-hand sheet. By calling attention on this one opened page to the "old," the editor reminds the reader that all through the fascicle she has been fondling old artifacts: the contents of the Ebon box, the picture/portrait, the relics of Pompeii, the dust, and the wagon of the little king. The repeated poem itself stresses long, long years with the repetition of "At last" and the italicized past tense of the last two lines:

>   Ah! What Leagues there *were*
>   Between our feet, and Day.

Historians, antiquarians, and poets use the old and transform it into the new. They perform magic.

And that is the point of the fifteenth poem in the series. To my knowledge, almost no one has commented on "Ah! Necromancy Sweet!" (J177, Fr168). Perhaps, as with several poems in this fascicle, "Ah! Necromancy" has almost entirely escaped comment because it was not published until 1929 and thus did not enter the canon but more likely, perhaps, because unless one reads it in its fascicle setting, it is bewildering, even distasteful. At first glance it appears completely weighted on what Paglia calls Dickinson's "Sadean" side (1991, 624, 651); it seems cruel:

>   Ah! Necromancy Sweet!
>   Ah! Wizard Erudite!
>   Teach me the Skill.
>   That I instil the pain
>   Surgeons assuage in vain,
>   Nor Herb of all the plain
>   Can heal!

To understand the apparent cruelty, the reader remembers that Fascicle 8 links images of transformations and pain: This poem seems to beg the "Wizard Erudite" for the power to enact tricks. Mutlu Konuk Blasing identifies the tricks as semantic, noting that Dickinson juxtaposes the traditional and the idiosyncratic, the Christian pacifist and the violent, the Latinate and the Saxon so that the reader is continually off guard (1987, 180–91).

Because the fascicle has begun with the image of the wounded deer leaping not in spite of but because of its pain, because it has spoken of the "Sovereign Anguish" that transports and because it has just explored the power of smoldering volcanoes, it is not troubling that the specific skill the speaker requests is that to "instil the pain / Surgeons assuage in vain." Pain is requisite for the skill to "instil" that pain in others. The word suggests the poet's function (as Fascicle 21 says) to "Distill amazing sense / From ordinary meanings" by destilling or destabilizing the reader, by, in other words, sharing a wound. As in the fascicle's fifth poem with its distinction between the foolish and the savan(t)s, this poem's diction connotes the subject's self-referentiality. Again, proximity is significant. The pain that is immune to the healing powers of "Herb of all the plain" shares the page with the perhaps overly sweet "Heart's Ease" and acts almost as an antidote to it. This pairing is similar to one on the previous page, also on the west side of the book. There the butterfly poem precedes the poem ("At last"), which is significant enough to be repeated in Fascicle 21. The speaker's identity now seems that of a necromancer, one who uses magic in the service of art.

Even the Wordsworthian "Except to Heaven, she is nought" (J154, Fr173) is concerned with the identity of the artist: a tiny artist, compared implicitly to a daisy, "the smallest Housewife in the grass." Like the Heart's Ease the little creature is small and others depend on it, for when it is "taken" (it does not leave voluntarily) from the Lawn, "Somebody has lost the face / that made existence—Home!" There's that face again, and it is followed as if in a refrain by a restatement of the earlier "Portrait" poem, with one essential difference: "Pictures are to daily faces" (J170, Fr174).

Portraits or pictures: Both are art. There may be a small difference to Dickinson, however. The burgeoning popularity of daguerreotypes, an art form that seemed so magical in the nineteenth century that it captured the imagination of Hawthorne (we remember that Holgrave was a daguerreotypist, for example) and seems to have impressed Dickinson as well. One imagines her staring at the representations of the revered framed faces in her own room as she wrote these lines—and as she repeated them with the change of that first word. Indeed, other than the word and two punctuation marks, the poems appear so identical that one seems almost traced from the other and is almost a picture of the other. The single word change is from the specific to the general. At least that is the implication of Dickinson's own lexicon: "[P]ortraits" are "pictures of faces drawn from life . . . the likeness consist[s] more than in the exact similitude of every feature," whereas "pictures" may be paintings or "any resemblance or representation, either to the eye or to the understanding." Both suggest a Platonic conception of reality; both are more spectacular than the "pedantic Sunshine"; both are explorations of and attempts to transform the palpable or the remembered into a new form. The editor, no mean picture maker herself (recall the sunset, the deer, and the volcano), has just mourned the loss of a little flower ("somebody has lost the face / That made Existence—Home!" in "Except to Heaven"). "Pictures" shares the page with it. There is a way to mitigate such loss, the author suggests, and that is by art. Pictures may, for example, be put in an Ebon box and uncovered many years later or perhaps hidden in a Barn, as she tells us in the next poem, which moves this fascicle toward its conclusion.

"I cautious, scanned my little life—" (J178, Fr175), the eighteenth in the series, unlike most of the past few poems in the fascicle, has attracted much intriguing critical discussion,[8] but what impresses the fascicle reader is the way "I cautious" moves the concerns of the fascicle to a new level even as it reiterates many of the themes and images from earlier in the collection. Its cynical Yankee farmer-speaker introduces a new voice. This is not an as-told-to tale such as the voice musing on volcanic power but is the voice of the poet in the guise of one who makes and stores hay. Nevertheless, the reader of the previous seventeen poems requires no more hints than the farmer/poet offers: to see that the precious hay, as those objects in the Ebon box, should be winnowed. Some would be lost, but some "would last till Heads like mine / Should be a-dreaming laid." It was these ("the latter") that the careful Yankee hid in a Barn. Here the analogy with the Ebon box contents fails, for this farmer cannot find what he has saved, and he becomes "A Cynic." In light of Dickinson's own lexicon's definition of this word, a word she uses only in this poem, we need not assume the modern meaning of the word. Her Webster's harks back to its assumed origin: "Having the qualities of a surly dog: snarling, captious, austere . . . a follower of Diogenes, a misanthrope." So the farmer is cranky; he is not necessarily a doubter or a skeptic. One proof of that is the end of the poem: "My business is, to find!" he declares, and then he tells us how: "So I begin to ransack!"

Rummaging, throwing that hay around, searching for the precious harvest is, perhaps, something the reader must do, but the speaker reflects the anxiety of the poet about what would survive and how it would survive and be found. The same editor who placed the letter, tawny now with time, opposite an image of Moses looking longingly at the Promised Land has voiced the question that would most haunt her. Recognizing, as does the speaker/farmer, that her "business" was best done "within the little Barn / Love provided [her]," she nevertheless worries. If she did not "print," how would her letters reach the world? In a sense the last two poems of the fascicle help to answer that question.

"If I could bribe them by a Rose" (J179, Fr176) is one possible answer, bribing being (in its secondary sense in Dickinson's Webster's) "that which seduces." No more than the cynical farmer (looking for his "priceless Hay"), whose "business is to find," the speaker of this penultimate poem voices a wistful urgency about her business. Repeating the word, she intensifies it (and the reader of the discussion of Fascicle 21 in the last chapter will recall the many meanings of "business"): "My business were so dear!" Two of the eight times she ever used the word in her poems, half of the times she ever used the phrase ("my business") are on the two facing pages near the end of this fascicle. Intensely self-reflexive, this fascicle is not just a declaration of the speaker's intent to become a writer (she had done so often before, especially in Fascicles 1 and 3). Rather, this fascicle explores what it is to *be* one. It involves conning and scanning, winnowing and saving, chanting and singing, and, by the end of this rather long poem, bribing and wearing down the listener until he or she finally says "Yes." In fact, the listener is primary in this poem.

"If I could bribe them" differs from the poem that preceded it ("I cautious, scanned my little life") and other stories in Fascicle 8, most of which emphasize the first person, the speaker; "I cautious" does so six times. As we near the fascicle's end, however, this poem uses the third-person plural ("they") five times, indicating an awareness of her audience, the they's who will find whatever it is she cannot find in that barn. A Rose and a Bird stand in for poetry and the poet. Both poet and poetry reappear in the last poem of the fascicle, but first, on the same page as that last poem, is the self-deprecatory notion that perhaps the world would listen patronizingly only "to drive her from the Hall!" She answers that contingency in the final poem.

The Charge to the Reader

The speaker of "As if some little Arctic flower" (Fr177, J180) is as wistful as that in the past two poems, but she seems to be saying that if the they's did try to "drive her from the Hall," she would not be deprived of her laurels. She would not be silenced. Like the Arctic Flower, she would simply

> Wander down the Latitudes
> Until it [the Arctic flower] puzzled came
> To continents of summer
> To firmaments of sun—
> To strange, bright crowds of flowers—
> And birds, of foreign tongue!

This is the whole range of "Leagues" from Amherst to Cashmere (the dichotomy is geographical and symbolic: from familiar Yankee territory to exotic, sunny, vaguely Asian climes, in which we recognize an Emersonian echo). By wandering down the "Latitudes," in fact, the poet may be covering even more than geographical territory. Her Webster's includes a sixth meaning beyond the distance from the equator: "Extent or deviation from a settled point; freedom from rules or limits; free; thinking or acting at large." Whether she intended the joke we can only deduce from the rest of those 1,775 extant poems and from the forty books into which she gathered so many of them, but she allows and even encourages such speculation in the final lines of Fascicle 8. There she gives the they's of the previous poem—and all of us whether in Amherst or Cashmere—a charge:

> What then? Why nothing—
> Only, your *inference* therefrom!

We have met the negation ("Nobody" and "naught" of previous fascicle poems reappears in the nonnegation "nothing" here), but the important new word, one of her favorites, is the one she underlined. She uses some form of the word twenty times (as a variant for estimate, as something quaint, as portentous, even, playfully, as appalling, for example).[9] As the summation of this fascicle about transport, witchcraft, necromancy, a fascicle in which faces and artifacts and dust and flowers linger as proof that the poet is at last identified, "inference" conveys how much Dickinson requires of her readers. An inference is itself an act of transport, a leap. Dickinson's Webster's definition of the word takes us toward contemporary reader response theory. It is "a truth or proposition drawn from another which is admitted or supposed to be true; a conclusion." Inferences, continues her lexicon, "result from reasoning, as when the mind perceives such a connection between ideas, as that, if certain propositions deduced from them must also be true." Although Karl Keller is right that this poem "forewarns us of [Dickinson's] difficulties" (1979, 2), the word tantalizes the reader who recognizes that the text *is* a sort of promised land. Inferring requires that the reader reach out to the possibilities imbedded in the poem or the book, but at the same time it limits the process to the text itself. As Judy Jo Small says, "While [Dickinson] accepts the instability of meaning as it [the poem] goes from world to poet to poem to reader, she invites not a wild delirium of self-indulgent personal 'readings' but a responsible attempt to get at or near what the poet had to say" (1990, 70). This "little Arctic flower," this "charming parable" (Gelpi 1966, 84) posits a heaven in which the savan(t)s, not the foolish, will recognize the flowers she ransacked and saved and ordered in these books and will understand that in them she is "At last! . . . identified" again and again as new minds draw new inferences from the letters grown tawny with time.

Drawing inferences from such evidence, evidence contained in some of the forty books she bound and left for us to ransack is the business of this study. Inferring the meaning of the altered form within the different contexts of "Safe in their Alabaster Chambers" in Fascicles 6 and 10 will be an adventure that the author and compiler of Fascicle 8 would relish.

CHAPTER 4

"Alabaster Chambers": Two Versions of Dwellings of the Dead

		Fascicle 6 c.1859				Fascicle 10 c.1860–61
F	J	Fr		F	J	Fr
1	73	136 Who never lost	1	230	244	We—Bee and I—live
2	74	137 A Lady red—amid	2	231	245	God permits industrious
3	126	138 To fight aloud, is	3	232	245	The *Sun—just touched*
4	127	139 'Houses'—so the Wise	4	233	247	The Lamp burns sure—
5	128	140 Bring me the sunset	5	163	131	Tho' my destiny be Faustian—
6	75	141 She died at play	6	207	199	Tho' I get home how late
7	129	142 Cocoon above!	7	208	200	The rose did caper
8	76	143 Exultation is the going	8	209	201	With thee, in the Desert—
9	77	144 I never hear the word	*9	185	202	Faith is a fine invention
10	130	122 These are the days	10	210	203	The thought beneath
11	131	123 Besides the Autumn poets	11	318	204	I'll tell you how
**12	216	124 Safe in their Alabaster	12	159	135	A little bread—a crust
13	78	125 A poor—torn heart	13	160	132	Just lost, when I was saved!
14	132	126 I bring an unaccustomed	14	211	205	Come slowly—Eden
15	133	127 As Children bid the guest	15	212	206	Least Rivers—docile
16	79	128 Going to Heaven!	16	270	248	*One Life* of so much consequence
17	80	129 Our lives are Swiss	17	234	249	You're right—the way
			**18	216	124	Safe in their Alabaster
			19	235	250	The Court is far away—
			20	236	251	If *He dissolve*—then—
			21	237	252	I think just how my shape
			22	224	25	I've nothing else—to bring

70

"*Has girl read Republican?*" asked Susan Dickinson across the hedge from the Dickinson homestead on March 1, 1862 (Leyda 1960, 48), referring to the appearance of "Safe in their Alabaster Chambers" (J216, Fr124). Dickinson did not need to read Bowles's journal for validation of her claims to being a poet. She had printed—at least twice—this particular poem in two different versions. Identical but for one significant verb in their first verses, the poems are syntactically nearly identical also in their second verses, but in diction and connotation they differ radically. They differ even more because of the context in which each appears. The "repetition" of this poem, so important to Dickinson scholars, affords a laboratory for the claims I have made in the first three chapters: that one proof of Dickinson's intentionality in compiling her fascicles is in reading those poems contextually. Reading contextually is particularly instructive when one discovers two different settings for a poem, whether that poem is nearly identical as in "At last," the poem that centered Fascicles 8 and 21, or significantly altered as in "Safe in their Alabaster Chambers" (J216, Fr124), a poem that Sue herself might have forwarded to editor Bowles. The revisions and variants of "Safe" are one more proof of Dickinson's diligence.

Although it may have been "given to [her] by / the Gods—" (J454, Fr455), as Dickinson claimed in Fascicle 21's final poem, poetic power needed just that: diligence, human work. Dickinson pictures herself in Fascicle 5 as "Low at my problem bending" (J69, Fr99), and she describes "Artists" who "wrestled here!" (J110, Fr111). Reflecting her Puritan heritage's work ethic, she says "Luck is not chance— / It's Toil— / Fortune's expensive smile / Is earned—" (J1350, Fr1360). Surrounding notions of diligence in metaphors, she speaks of miners, birds, and bees. The patient weaving of spiders, she says, is "Superiority to Fate." The result of such labor "Is difficult to gain / 'Tis not conferred of Any / But possible to earn / a Pittance at a time" (J1081, Fr1043). That she bent low over the problems of individual poems is clear from calligraphic designs and the inclusion of variants, which increase as the years progress, and from the many statements she made or implied on the power of the poet to escape the closed-in "still" space of prose. That she was just as deliberative in fashioning her books is equally clear.

No poem, in fact, provides more ample proof of the conscious artistry that structures Dickinson's surprises, of the pressures imposed by and the support given by her literary community, or of the value of reading poems in their fascicle contexts than "Safe in their Alabaster Chambers" (J216, Fr124). The story of its complex publishing history is well documented: that the poem was the subject of notes to Sue with the result that Dickinson changed its second stanza not once but twice,[1] that it was one of the first four poems the poet sent to Higginson, that it was one of the twelve poems published in her own lifetime, and that the poet found two of its versions suitable for inclusion in her own private printing enterprise, the fascicles.[2] However, aside from Martha Nell Smith's extensive discussion of these multiple versions as proof of "Dickinson's delight in different ways of seeing, in perspective's power over meaning and comprehension" (1985, 138), few studies have noted how the poem's changes from the 1859 fascicle, in which the poet first placed it, to the new, more intricately patterned form the poet gave it in its 1860 setting were affected by surrounding poems. Even Franklin's comment in the long entry in his variorum (159–64) is consistent with his comment in the *Manuscript Books* that Dickinson's repetitions result from memory lapses: "The nature of the variants," he says, "suggests the text to have been recalled, unreliably, from memory" (1981, 163).

Before noting the radically different tone, image clusters, and narrative thrust of those surrounding poems, listen to the wild differences between the two poems, a difference that one picks up even in Dickinson's manipulation of sound effects (all of the hard, high-pitched e's of the first, the rolling r's and hissing s's of the second.

In the two years between the binding of Fascicle 6 and that of Fascicle 10 much apparently happened to shift the look and the tone of the two versions. The first is the one that, two years after she bound it in Fascicle 6, prompted the note from Sue with which this chapter begins. That version had just appeared in the *Springfield Daily Republican,* framed by the benign title "The Sleeping" on the top and "Pelham Hill, June, 1861" on the bottom. Although the punctuation and capitalization had been "regularized" and some lines had been indented in a way they are not in the fascicle, the words and lineation of the poem are identical to that in the fascicle Franklin dates in 1859. Johnson surmises that Dickinson may have enclosed a note when she sent Bowles the poem (1960, 154), but apparently no note survives. It seems unlikely that Sue, also a good friend of Bowles, sent the note, considering the fact that this is the version Sue "evidently" (Johnson's word) challenged Emily to improve, evidence of which may be the penciled revision of the poem (the "A" version of the poem in Fascicle 10) to which Emily appended the note, "Perhaps this verse would please you better—Sue—
                                                                Emily—"

Johnson, who quotes the note that followed from Sue—tantalizing evidence of Sue's talents as editor—says that "Evidently ED, having received Sue's 'Pony Express' [a phrase Martha Nell Smith discusses at some length], again attempted a second stanza" (ibid., 152), Johnson calls the two that appear earlier in this chapter as variants B and C "variant trial substitutes." I'm not so sure they are trial substitutes. All of the versions fit in diction and tone the pitch of Fascicle 10, just as the longer lines, lighter diction, and calligraphic design fit the surrounding poems in Fascicle 6.

Fascicle 6: A Setting for Gleeful Children

Johnson's conclusion that "It is unlikely that ED ever completed this poem in a version that entirely satisfied her" (1960, 152) may not be entirely correct. For the purposes of the two collections in which she copied the two (or shall we say four?) versions, each version seems if not, for Dickinson, "entirely" satisfactory—what would have been?—certainly appropriate to her varying purposes. Consider the first version with its laughing breeze, babbling Bee (tormenting the stolid Ear), and piping birds (in ignorant cadence—little songsters who defy the rules of prosody?). In Fascicle 6 the figure who stamps the mood is clearly younger and lighter than that of many of Dickinson's fascicles, even those that have preceded this sixth. Although the fascicle begins and ends on an orphic note, between these more meditative bookends it celebrates the feistiness of a childlike persona who, as the diction of this central poem and others within the collection suggests, privileges gaiety, glee, and exultation over sobriety and somberness.

Fascicle 6's images point to a persona who prefers (or several personae who prefer) flight, risk, and freedom to gravity, safety, and rigid societal structures. Admittedly many poems and other fascicles (21, for example) reflect a similar dichotomy. Those who discount reading fascicles contextually based on the observation that one may toss up any group of poems and discover a pattern are correct to a certain extent. Nevertheless, the reader remembers that, after all, the books *are* Dickinson's, not random groupings, and that whatever she intended them to be in terms of "publications," she stamped each one with its own personality. For example, in Fascicle 6 Dickinson uses some form of "gay" or "gala" in the fifth, sixth, and seventh poems; she surrounds and defines "exultation" in the eighth; her persona assumes a "flying attitude" in the ninth; she watches birds and bees tease in the tenth and squirrels scamper in the eleventh; and she even sees the hedge as "nonchalant" in the second poem of the fascicle. The almost dizzy mood of this fascicle distinguishes it from most of the others.

One of Dickinson's habitual personae but rarely as constantly present as in this fascicle, the child, has an overt role in four of the poems (fourth, ninth, tenth, and fifteenth) and an implied presence in others. As the close of this chapter explores in greater detail, this is a female child, self-consciously female: ready for transformation, a butterfly waiting to emerge from a cocoon, interested in clothing, in playing, in striving for satisfaction. This is a child tugging at bars. Associated with the child persona are the repetitious presences of "houses" and of "home." Dickinson has woven almost all of these threads into the poems that she has placed in this book—and, for quite different reasons, also in Fascicle 10—"Safe in their Alabaster Chambers."

Fascicle 10: The Voice of the Dramatist

Compiled in 1860 or 1861, only two years after Fascicle 6, the alternate setting for "Safe," Fascicle 10, plays with quite different images: images of sight (the film on the eye, the microscope, blindness); with light (the sunrise, sun play, sunset, and the lamp that burns within); with darkness and deep places; with drunkenness and parchedness; and, as so often in Dickinson (but not in Fascicle 6), with royalty: Crowns, for example, become "diadems" from surrendering "doges" in the repeated "Alabaster Chambers" poem. Images link poem to poem, domino-like, each poem hinting of the next. Patterns such as those in Fascicles 6 and 10 (and the other books) are revealed not only as one observes the individual poems closely but also as one stands back and looks at the whole. Such scrutiny, the enterprise of this study, engages us in Barbara Herrnstein Smith's "retrospective patterning," in Martha Nell Smith's "participatory reading," and in Michael Riffaterre's discovery of "hypograms." According to Riffaterre, a hypogram is "that which appears in the shape of words imbedded in sentences whose organization reflects the presuppositions of the matrix's nuclear word" (1978, 5). A hypogram, which Riffaterre describes only in the context of French poetry but which William Doreski has applied to his study of Fascicle 27 (1986), is the unspoken center, the hub around which the text revolves. Few explanations are as helpful as Riffaterre's hypogram in describing the effect of image clustering in fascicles.

Whatever term one uses to describe reading it, what seems particularly true of the tenth fascicle, more than others in this study, is its sense of drama and discovery within which are subplots and provisional meditations. Dickinson's well-documented penchant for drama, her "habitual role taking" (1985, 183) has been considered primarily within the context of individual poems or clusters of poems outside of her own publication. This fascicle offers the drama of heightened emotion, radically conflicted thoughts and feelings, and flashes of character.

Without reducing the poems to literal autobiographical "letters to the world," one may reasonably posit that the higher pitch of this fascicle reflects the dramatic events surrounding Dickinson as she gathered the poems. The events around the annus mirabilis, detailed in biographical studies, are so extraordinary that I summarize them radically: Charles Wadsworth called; Kate Anthon came and went; Bowles published "May Wine" ("I taste a liquor never brewed" [J214, Fr207, F12])—twice. Baby Ned was born and took Sue's time, but not so much that the mistress of Evergreens could not challenge her sister-in-law to make "a peer" for the first verse of "Safe in their Alabaster Chambers." Not least, if we are to believe a twice (many)-told tale, connected, possibly with any one of these people, "Emily met her fate" (Leyda 1960, 34), and, perhaps connected with whatever that event was, the poet wrote the first of her puzzling "Master Letters."

In the public sphere events were equally dramatic. For example, the train line progressed; a balloon went up in front of the mansion house; and Edward Dickinson accepted an endorsement to be the Republican candidate for Lieutenant Governor. And on November 9, 1860, Lincoln became president, proclaiming soon thereafter his call for seventy-five thousand men. A visitor to Northampton "found the air filled with the sounds of war and the rumors of war," and by May 1861 *The Republican* noted that four students of Amherst "who reside in slave states left . . . for home, and will probably enlist in the secession army." A few months later, possibly while Dickinson completed collecting and copying the poems for Fascicle 10, Mrs. Browning died, and Dickinson began elegizing the "Foreign Lady." Any one or any combination of a few of these events might account for the difference between the childlike tone of Fascicle 6 and the high drama of Fascicle 10, although to be fair, Dickinson was by nature dramatic (reread Higginson's exhausted account of his meeting with her).

Joking to the Norcross cousins about the gift of a stagey cape, Dickinson playfully hinted at her penchant for the drama she found in such private and public events: "Do you think I am going 'Upon the boards' that I wish so smart attire? Such are my designs though. . . . May I not secure Loo for drama and Fanny for comedy?" (L225). But Dickinson needed no cousinly assistance for drama and comedy; she reveals it throughout Fascicle 10. In the spirit of retroactive reading, I want to examine this fascicle's dramatic context for "Safe in their Alabaster Chambers—" before turning back to the playful setting of the previous version in Fascicle 6.

The Dramatic Design of Fascicle 10

Strutting a transcendental exuberance, the persona of the tenth fascicle's first poem announces "We—Bee and I—live / by the quaffing—" (J230, Fr244). Every element of the slightly sarcastic poem contributes to its overtly light-heartedly dramatic mood. Lindberg-Seyersted, who particularly delights in the suggestiveness of the noun-compound (By-thyme) in the last line, says that the speaker "envisages the delirious fate of the two revelers" (1968, 111). The "delirious fate" is a phrase that binds this poem to the fascicle's last. Underlined words in this first poem ("*all Hock*," "*Ale*," and "*his*") convey excitement. The choppy lineation, quite different, by the way, in the manuscript from that in the Johnson or Franklin editions, enhances the off-balance tipsy mood of this first poem. The image of the drunkards at the "vat and vine" (an onomatopoeic bit of alliteration as in "the humming Coroner") sustains the mood as the persona answers the sober prohibitionists (preaching in Safe Alabaster Chambers?) in the second stanza's "Do we 'get drunk'? . . . Do we 'beat' our 'Wife'?"

Giddy as all this sounds, this near hedonism (and the sexual connotations of dying of nectar), the diction of "We—Bee and I" also suggests drama on a deeper level. The distinction in the poem's second and third lines—"'Tis'nt *all* Hock—with us— / Life has its *Ale*"— suggests two grades of intoxicants known to Dickinson from literature,[3] if not served up from the sideboard on Main Street. That which is rare and valued as distinguished from that which is common (hock/ale) fail in equal measure. In the face of that failure, "We chant—for cheer." The fascicle ends with the notion that when one has "nothing else—to bring," one just "keep[s] bringing These," a pronoun with no referent unless one steeped in Dickinson fills in "poems" or "chants." Such is the symmetry the fascicle reader comes to expect.

The word "chant," associated elsewhere in Dickinson's work with nature's sounds,[4] has liturgical uses as well, of course, enhanced in this fascicle's first poem's "Latest at the Vine— / Noon—our last Cup." Origin of the wine, the vine is a metaphor for Christ ("I am the vine"); noon is associated by Dickinson (as Cynthia Griffin Wolff has discussed at length [1986]) with an hour of transcendence; and the cup, as Dickinson implies in "Cup of Anguish brewed for the Nazarene" ("Proud of my broken heart" [J1736, Fr1760]), holds the sacred wine memorializing that death. In Dickinson's lexicon the "cup's" meaning is spelled out:

> 3. in a *scriptural sense* sufferings and afflictions: that which is to be received or endured. 'Oh my father, if it be possible, let this *cup* pass from me.' Matt 26.4; blessings 'Good received' . . . my *cup* runneth over.' Take the cup of salvation.'"

This tipsy poem thus also connotes a drama that reaches its pitch by the eighteenth poem, in which the Alabaster Chamber divides sharply the worlds of the spiritually living and the conforming dead-in-life. Even the "humming Coroner" plays on these two levels. Dickinson's lexicon tells us that the coroner is so named because his office "is concerned principally with the crown."

The "crown"—this word placed on the bottom of the page and on the same plane as the word "Coroner"—is what the speaker "plays" with in "God permits industrious Angels—" (J231, Fr245). In fact, appearing in the fascicle's twelfth and nineteenth poems ("A little Bread" [J159, Fr135] and "The Court is far away" [J235, Fr250]), the crown is a central image in Fascicle 10, especially in the diadems of the repeated poem. If the first poem's second stanza had been a rebuke of sorts to the "Alabaster Chambers'" stolid dead, untouched by the noon that is the moment of death in the first poem, this second poem continues that rebuke. Even angels may play, says the persona (continuing the balance in her tone, the poet's own play and industry), as she tells the story of her drama with an angel. This angel is no wrestler but rather a charmer who entices the speaker to forget the dreary schoolroom routine and, in her private drama, play a queen. "How *dreary— / Marbles /* after playing *Crown!*" exclaims the speaker. Dickinson's opposition of "Play" with this select angel on the one hand and "*Marbles*" on the other suggests the opposition of the Alabaster setting of those safely dead in life, on the one hand, with the implied active life of those willing to risk, to subvert, to be powerful and alive.

Dickinson appears to have arranged other parallel pairings between the second ("Angel") poem and that repeated eighteenth ("Alabaster") poem. In both she not only dichotomizes between a stupefying "marble" existence and the light play with something like angels, but she does so in a similar narrative structure. The narrator begins from the stance of one who lives among the dead, entombed in a schoolroom ("Angel") or grave ("Alabaster"), senses the giddy action of another world "above them," but returns to the reality of the silence and stolidity of death.

On a more literal level about a sunset, "God permits" is followed by "The *Sun—just touched* the / Morning" (J232, Fr246), a sunrise poem that continues to play with the dichotomy between the alive "Happy thing" and the "*unannointed*" thing (sunset/poet) deprived of her "*Crown.*" In the opened book the line "After playing *Crown*" in the second ("Angel") poem is almost exactly opposite to "The Morning . . . / Felt feebly for Her Crown—" just as the lines about the "industrious Angels" who are allowed to play are opposite to the description of Morning as a "*supremer—" / A Raised—Etherial* thing" on "*Holiday.*" Reading across as well as down the pages of these books is part of the fun of "participatory reading."

Fascicle 6, as I discuss at the close of this chapter, features childlike joy set against sunset, death, and Swiss lives, along with the coolness of autumn and the chill of Alabaster Chambers; Fascicle 10, on the other hand, privileges images of warmth, fire, wicks, and sunlight, against which the dark icy stolidity of this version of the Alabaster Chambers is all the more stark. "The *Sun—just touched* the / Morning," in fact, tells just that story. The departure of sunset "leave[s] a *new necessity*! The *want of Diadems!*" Whether the "new necessity" is to desire the crown, the diadem, or whether it is *not* to have it (that there is a necessity to want—the economy of desire), the story is one of staggering loss. The speaker feels "feebly for her crown" but instead finds only "her *unannointed forehead.*" That is the end of the poem on that page, where "crown" meets "crown" in the opened book. But the poem has another line. Perhaps it was the simple expedient of running out of room that led Dickinson to place "Henceforth—Her only One!" on the next page. The "only one" is the unseen crown on the unanointed forehead (something to keep in mind for the "unshriven" heart on the fascicle's last page).

Before that, there is a more immediate bit of intertextuality: Visually and contextually the line that spills over from the previous poem becomes a title for the fascicle's fourth poem, "The Lamp burns sure—within—" (J233,

Fr247), in which the poet eschews the need for outside inspiration. Because the unanointed head, perhaps unsanctified (and subversive), is independent and self-isolated, "the busy / Wick / At her phosphoric toil" does not need the "serfs—[to] supply the oil." Throughout her work, using imagery of fire, heat, light, and oils, Dickinson constructs this web of metaphors for the process and effect of writing poetry; consider, for example, "The Poets light but / Lamps— / Themselves—go out—" (J883, Fr930, set 5). Poets, says the speaker of this later poem, are the source of light; they are their own suns, lighting others as "Each Age [becomes] a Lens / Disseminating their Circumference." They do not need either the sun (third poem) or the serfs (fourth). That the Slave in this poem, as the Sun King in the third, is faithless is nothing to the poet: "The Lamp burns golden—on— / Unconscious that the oil / is out— / And that the Slave is gone." The poet does not need but makes and supplies oil (as in "Essential oils—are wrung—" [J675, Fr772, F34] and elsewhere). Slave and serf, minor characters in this little drama, may seem exotically out of place in Amherst, but in this fascicle's depiction of crowned heads and doges, perhaps they are not. Moreover, they may serve as only somewhat hyperbolic representatives of women, even privileged nineteenth-century women in lawyers' homes. They may also represent those who must remain in Alabaster Chambers as "Tribes—of Eclipse—in Tents— / of Marble."

The stance of the independent, self-fueling, light-and-warmth-producing poet, free of serf and slave, is repeated in the poem that faces it, Fascicle 10's fifth poem, "Tho' my destiny be Fustian—" (J163, Fr131). As does the repeated "Alabaster Chambers," which was part of a conversation with Sue, this poem has a specific context other than the fascicle. Ruth Miller reads it as a possible riposte to Bowles for having published an overly sentimental poem, "The Portrait" (1968, 120–22). The line to the Hollands suggests still other meanings (Keller 1979, 200). Within Fascicle 10's context, however, the line contrasts the ordinary or fustian to "damask fine" and "a silver apron." The speaker, whose "destiny be Fustian" and who appears as a "little Gipsy being" (along with the addressee) will not be victim to the "Frosts" that lay "their punctual fingers" on the finer damask Rose. The fascicle is inching closer to the dichotomy between those who, in variant B of "Safe in their Alabaster Chambers," are the victim of the "Frosts unhook[ed]—in the Northern Zones," those unlike the sturdy, conformity-resistant poet with her unanointed forehead who will live as "Roses of a steadfast summer / In a steadfast land."

The first five poems of the fascicle have their own low-key drama; the cast includes the drunken bee, the playing angel, the disappointing sun, the scorned faithless serf and slave, and the proud if fustian poet, living her superior life from within. They are followed by two poems reflecting dramas verging on the melodramatic. In fact, they seem parodic of the "damask" story of popular taste so scorned by the speaker of the fifth poem.

"Tho' I get home how late— / how late" (J207, Fr199) posits a dramatic situation Dickinson readers readily recognize, a situation fraught with what Vivian Pollak calls "the psychodynamics of desire in which pleasure is enhanced by a prior context of frustration . . . by a previous experience of pain" (1984, 124). Specifically, it recreates the imagined notions of a person, one who sounds to me like a romantic egoist or a self-dramatic child, out too late and too far. The character thinks (with some pleasure?) of the surprise and relief of those who have stayed up without hope, waiting and waiting for "Decades of Agony" and "Centuries of Way," phrases that may make the fascicle reader think of "Grand go the Years" and the "Staples—of Ages" that "have / buckled there" in the "Alabaster" poem, touchstone for the book. Two phrases that Dickinson has isolated on their own lines—"How late" and "and dark" convey the speaker's dread as she wistfully thinks of those gathered with "long-cheated eyes" around the fireside. She imagines those eyes meeting hers, but she leaves the drama a cliffhanger.[5]

If the sixth poem is an imagined melodrama, the seventh, "The Rose did caper on her cheek—" (J208, Fr200), is a sweetly quaint and slightly comic tale. The speaker is, as William Shurr notes, a "voyeur" (1983, 66), peeking in on a courting ritual that ends with the blushing, nervous man and woman moving toward a relationship in which their "troubled little Clocks / Ticked softly into one." However self-contained this rather saccharine courtship tale might be (its clock imagery is similar to the wedding message Dickinson included in at least two letters—L805 and L902—which also appears as J1569, Fr1598), it also has contextual relationships within the fascicle. Not only does it face the other melodrama in the opened book, but it also sets up two of the poems on the next page (the back of this one). That next page, left on the open book, holds three separate poems: "With thee, in the Desert—" (J209, Fr201), "Faith is a fine invention" (J185, Fr202), and "The thought beneath so slight / a film—" (J210, Fr203), each of which may be discussed in relation to the melodrama of "The Rose did caper" of the preceding page. To take the last one first, that on the bottom of the page: It requires little imagination to link the rising and falling "boddice" of the woman, so nervous that "Her fingers fumbled at her work—" of the seventh poem's courtship poem, with the thin image of the "slight film" that barely hides the "surge" of "the Appenine" in the fascicle's tenth poem, a poem that, in Dickinson's manner of overlapping images, connects with later poems in the fascicle as well. Move up to the top of the page to the poem that immediately follows the little melodrama. The quatrain of the eighth poem, almost a sequel to "The Rose," might script one of the demure lovers from that sweet "caper" poem. If one of the lovers gained courage and speech, he or she might say,

With thee in the Desert—
With thee in the thirst—

> With thee in the Tamarind wood—
> Leopard breathes—at last! (J209, Fr201).

Whether a passionate declaration from lover to lover or a cry from a Ruth figure to a Naomi ("whither thou goest, I will go"), "With thee" builds the drama to a pitch that is checked by the skepticism of the next poem. It has a third function as well. One word encourages the reader to read the quatrain and the fascicle in which it is the eighth poem as the development of a self-directed, inwardly supported poet who claims the right to "tell" us how the sun rose—to control, in other words, the figure she depicted as a male teasing force in the third poem. Dickinson alludes to the power by which that happens in the strangeness of "Tamarind," a word she had chosen only once before, in the first poem of the sixth fascicle (the one containing the earlier version of "Alabaster Chambers").

Linked with the poetic principle through its use in Poe's "Sonnet to Science,"[6] "tamarind" suggests the opposite of the safe, stolid, sleeping meek. Poe rails at "Science! true daughter of Old Time," possessed of "peering eyes" and "prey[ing] . . . upon the poet's heart." Equating "Science" with a "Vulture whose wings are dull realities," Poe ends his sonnet:

> Hast thou not torn the Naiad from her flood.
> The Elfin from the green grass, and from me
> The summer dream beneath the tamarind tree?

Dickinson's dreamy, potent quatrain seems to speak for the rich imaginative possibilities of poetry as opposed to science. But look at the ninth poem, which follows it on the page:

> Faith is a fine invention
> For Gentlemen who *see*—
> But *Microscopes* are prudent
> In an Emergency. (J185, Fr202)

From the woman whose letters often reflect doubt, the statement, which Robert Weisbuch calls "an all out attack on fatuous faith" (1972, 113), has a personal ring. It also has a context; "Faith is a fine invention" seems an answer to the passionate, imaginative quatrain that precedes it, and it anticipates "Safe in their Alabaster Chambers," another assault on "fatuous faith" waiting four pages ahead. Dickinson includes this poem also in Fascicle 12, where it shares the page with "A transport one cannot contain" (J184, Fr203). There Dickinson intensifies the quatrain by enclosing "Faith" in quotation marks, and there (Fascicle 12) the quatrain seems one voice—not necessarily the dominant voice—in an ongoing interior conversation. Here, in Fascicle 10, however, it has an amused, reflective tone continued in "The thought beneath so slight / a film" (J210, Fr203) on the bottom of the page. Along with that "boddice," which harks back three poems, the word "film" interests the attentive reader. Associated more with sight (that which Gentlemen can improve with microscopes), the subject of the previous poem, "film" is an odd covering for "thought," but the next poem, the eleventh in the series, "I'll tell you how the Sun rose" (J318, Fr204), makes even more use of synesthesia.

As the page on the left enacts a drama in three parts (holding "With thee," "Faith is," and "The thought beneath"), "I'll tell you" encloses its own dialogue, a dialogue Dickinson makes more obvious by doing something strange for her, placing a horizontal line between the two main sections of the poem. "I'll tell you" contrasts "tell[ing]," based on what one sees, against not "knowing" what one cannot see. "I'll tell you how the Sun rose," says the speaker, using fanciful bright images; then, after that odd slash-line mark, she continues, "But how he *set,* I know not." The speaker may not know, but she surmises in subdued tones: "There seemed," she says, "a purple stile," over which a submissive "flock" was led away by a "Dominie in Gray."

Even though almost every commentator on this often anthologized "I'll tell you" has put the poem in the context of its inclusion as one of the four poems enclosed in the first letter to Higginson (with this fascicle's version of "Safe in their Alabaster Chambers"), and even though it was praised by its first readers of the 1890 edition as "a dainty caprice" with "rhythmic delicacy" (Buckingham 1989, 113, 20), no one has yet noticed its neat fit in the context of this fascicle. The division between the two parts reenacts the kind of dialogue we can hear among the three poems (those three stunning quatrains) that precede and face it and also that in those "Alabaster Chambers," where by the end, "Midnight in Marble— / Refutes—the Suns—."

Having plunged "the flock" into darkness in the eleventh poem, Dickinson continues the drama, envisioning the speaker now like "Old Napoleon— / the night before the crown" and also as a character plunged not only into darkness but into some kind of debtor's prison, begging for "A little Bread— a / Crust—a / Crumb" (J159, Fr132). As elsewhere, Dickinson provides alternative readings of the poem in lineating it so that combinations of the words placed on separate lines, "Crumb / warm— / and sweet / more, / life!" form an imagistic cluster within the larger poem. Whether read thus or in its usual form, the poem adds to those meditations on the economics of desire that provide some of the drama of Fascicle 10. Dickinson's diction also suggests motifs from earlier in the fascicle, especially from the first "Bee and I" poem in the "demijohn" (a wicker-enclosed bottle holding from one to ten gallons) and even in "not *portly,* mind." But it is the puzzlingly terse reference to "old Napoleon" who is "Conscious . . . the night before the Crown," who illustrates the value of reading contextually. Until a better explanation of the source of Dickinson's historical image comes along, let us suppose that she is referring to the little dictator's decision not to be crowned by the pope but to crown himself.[7] Self-coronation is the work of the poet-persona in the fascicle's second poem, in which she is "playing crown," and by implication in the nineteenth, when she intercedes for a Sovereign.

She also uses the poem to introduce a new motif that meshes with that of the economics of desire. The first of four poems in the fascicle's second half use the image of the sea and/or sailor: "A little bread—a crust—a / Crumb" ends with "A *Sailor's* business is *the shore!* / A *Soldier's—balls!* Who asketh / more, / must seek the neighboring / life!" In the next, the fascicle's fifteenth poem, which faces "A little Bread," the persona is "Just lost, when I was saved!" (J160, Fr132)—perhaps from a sea disaster, a metaphor, like passing across the stile or crossing the shore, for death.

"Just lost" enacts the drama of the second chance, the near-death experience that only whets the appetite, evoked in the previous poem, "A little Bread," for the experience of ecstasy or of death. "Called Back," as this was titled when it appeared in the *Independent* (Johnson, *Poems* 117), offers an option to being enclosed in "Alabaster Chambers," as in the poem toward which this fascicle is moving. The synesthesia of seeing things "by Ear unheard, / Unscrutinized by Eye" takes the fascicle reader back to "The thought beneath so slight / a film"; the second stanza with its image of "the awful doors / Before the seal" takes us ahead to the duplicated "Alabaster Chambers," and the final stanza of this thirteenth poem with its "Slow tramp [of] Centuries, [while] the Cycles wheel" parallels those "years—in the Crescent above them—" around which "Worlds scoop their Arcs— / And Firmaments row."

That last stanza, however, spills to the verso of the sheet, where it serves as a kind of introduction to and hence a recontextualizing of one of Dickinson's most discussed, especially in erotic terms, poems of passion, "Come slowly—Eden!" (J211, Fr 205). Mabel Todd, who had access, after all, to these books, titled the poem "Apotheosis" in the 1890 edition. Perhaps she, too, read it as an extension to the thirteenth poem; perhaps "Come Slowly" in *this* context is neither a death wish nor a "liebestod,"[8] but an extension of the drama of escape from "Alabaster Chambers." Certainly it is physically an extension of the same idea in "Just Lost," when the speaker tells the harrowing tale of a close escape from entering the "awful doors." In fact, that page contains three linked poems. Linked subliminally through iterative long e's that line the right margin (tarry/wheel/Steel/Centuries/Eden/Thee/Bee/sea/thee), they are also ordered in sense: the first (the last verse of "Just lost"), expressing a yearning to trespass mortal bounds as in "Alabaster Chambers," not literally physical death but the spiritual death in life of the timorous world of social expectations; the second, "Come slowly," imagining a metaphysical union with a different kind of "chamber," one that provides nectar and balms experienced only by those who suspend fear and inhibitions and caution—however slowly and bashfully; and the third, "Least Rivers," a two-liner at the bottom of the page, indicating elliptically complete subsumption in a force larger and more powerful than the speaker. All three poems, often read in erotic terms, may be seen as part of another drama, that of the artist who loses self in the creative life. All three, in a sense, could be titled "apotheosis," Todd's title for "Come slowly," not so much as we think of the word today as an exalted ideal but rather as an exaltation to divine rank or stature.

Facing the three poems that build to the two-line conclusion of the fifteenth poem is the much longer "*One life* of so much / Consequence!" (J270, Fr248). That this is less a poem of sexual attraction and obsession, as Weisbuch, for example, sees it (1972, 24–25), than of the quiet drama of choosing a vocation that is borne out by poems that succeed it. Among those who read the poem as a drama of self-discovery are Greg Johnson, who says that it is not a romantic lover but Dickinson *herself* that is of so much consequence that her clarity of vision "burns" (1985, 129), and Wendy Barker, whose comments on this poem might be made as well about the fascicle's fourth poem, "The Lamp burns sure—within," suggesting once again the intertextuality of the fascicle. Barker says that in this poem "Dickinson affirms the durability of her imaginative vision. For this small, glowing circle of interiority, for this pearl of great price, the poet is willing to 'spend' her life" (1987, 116). Each significant phrase of "*One* life" points toward such a reading. Consider the way the diction of this sixteenth poem in the fascicle links to the language in the poems that surround it. The first two stanzas' willingness to spend all, to dive into a "full" sea for a priceless, special pearl, though the speaker knows it will "*cost* me—*just a life!*" takes us back to the "Least Rivers—docile to some sea. / My Caspian—thee" of the previous small poem. In the third stanza we learn that the gem for which the speaker would dive is "*Intact—in Diadem!*" That diadem, we remember, appeared at almost the same position on the page earlier in the fascicle when the departing "Sun [that]—*just touched* / the morning" disappeared, leaving "The *want* of *Diadem!*" As in this sixteenth poem, that third poem and the twelfth, the little Napoleon poem, "A little Bread" concerns self-coronation. And here we have a poem that ends: "But *Monarchs*—are *perceptible* [through an inward lamp or through the microscope?]— / Far down the dustiest Road!"

As so often the last line ("Far down . . . ") spills onto the verso side of the paper, where, as also so often, it almost becomes the title for the fascicle's next poem, the seventeenth in the series, "You're right—'the way *is* / Narrow'— (J234, Fr249). For four poems the persona has been moving toward this eschewal of the world of Safe Alabaster Chambers by moving *toward* the greater life, the sea life, the Monarch life, the pearl and crown, the acceptance of the role of poet or at least of powerfully self-sufficient woman. With the seventeenth poem the persona demonstrates the choice she has made to reject with barely concealed scorn the polarized, mercantilistically tainted vocabulary of the Patriarchy. Those quotation marks around the biblical borrowings from Matthew 7:13–14 and the underlined words at the end underscore the disdain for what Albert Gelpi calls "the legalistic categories of the federal theology" (1965, 46). In fact, the persona speaks with such force in "broken rhythms" that Sewall likens the dramatic sense to Browning's monologues (1980, 716), reminding the fascicle reader of the other dramatic monologues within this fascicle (the first "Bee" poem; the sixth, "Tho' I get home how late"; the seventh's blushing couple; and those three short poems that followed). As are some of Browning's speakers, this speaker of Dickinson challenges accepted doctrine throughout the poem: Heaven is "'The *Good* man's—*Dividend*'— / And *Bad* men—'go to Jail' / I guess." She shows how far removed from that kind of narrowness and dusty thinking she wishes to be, how far away from the stolid who stay "Safe in their Alabaster / Chambers—" she is.

Placing the two poems opposite each other seems as pointed an editorial pairing as the prose/poetry dichotomy she presents in Fascicle 21 ("They shut me up in Prose—" [J613, Fr445] posed against "This was a Poet—" [J448, Fr446]) except that in this case the paired poems are not so much contrasts as comparisons. So we see the "narrow" road of the poem on the left poised against the sterile "Alabaster Chambers" of the darkly dead; we see the gate that is difficult to "Enter in—thereat—" poised against the Rafter and Roof of the Alabaster Chambers; we see that "*purples*," the "price of *Breath*," and the "*Brokers*" who dole out discounts and wages of sin and virtue are poised against the whirling world with its royal doges, even they, who must "surrender— / soundless as dots—on a / Disc of snow." At the bottom of the page, we find the "*Bad* men [who] 'go to Jail'— / I guess—" poised against Variant A: "Spring—shakes the sills— / But—the Echoes—stiffen," a horrifying version of a permanent jail, one at least as bad as those traditional hellfires against which Dickinson's Puritan forefathers warned. Such contextualizing is what makes this reader brazen enough to question the comment of Johnson that Dickinson never "completed this poem in a version that completely satisfied her." The changes made in "Safe" from the Fascicle 6 version to this one tighten the effect of implied skepticism, something Higginson, once a minister, seemed not to mind when he included this version of the duplicate poem in the thirteen poems he sent to *Century*, although he also spoke of its "too daring condensations."[9]

By the time she wrote to Higginson, Dickinson already knew for herself that this poem was alive—in both its versions. She knew, too, when she wrote Sue, that this version was "frostier." Look back at the changes: Whereas the version in Fascicle 6 imitates in its neat calligraphy and its imagery of breezes, birds, and bees more traditional poets (in a moment I show how perfectly this fits what precedes it), this one has a more jagged, fierce look. The poet chops the first line short so that "Chambers" and later "The Resurrection" and "surrender" and "Disc of Snow" occupy their own lines, emphasizing doubt or—possibly—anger. The most obvious and telling of the other changes in the first stanza is that the "meek members" no longer "sleep"; now they "Lie." While "sleep," that which knits up the raveled sleeve of care, connotes resignation, rest, renewal, and comfort, "Lie" has more insidious possibilities. Not only does "lie" imply something stiff and inflexible (a patient lies on an operating table, an inert object, for example), but its punning possibility "weights the whole poem towards irony and skepticism" (Orsini 1981).[10]

Such unalloyed disbelief as the poem in this fascicle reveals belies the readings of those who use the version published in the 1890s' editions, combining the second stanzas of the two fascicles and omitting either of the two variants. This version with its silence and ice and mysterious discs of snow has an eerie existential emptiness and loneliness; its white nothingness reflects Melville's whiteness chapter and previews Frost's "Snow falling fast, oh fast" with its "blanker whiteness of benighted snow / With no expression—nothing to express." There seems a gulf of teleological acceptance between the lines of the poem in this fascicle and the poet's letter to Judge Lord near the end of her life that "On subjects of which we know nothing . . . we both believe and disbelieve a hundred times an Hour, which keeps Believing nimble" (L750).[11] With such adamant disbelief as this version of "Safe" projects "the court [of Heaven]" must have seemed very "far away," which is how she begins the nineteenth poem in Fascicle 10.

Virtually every line of "Safe," in fact, is witness to Dickinson's weaving skill. This repeated but radically altered poem, read as it almost never is in its fascicle setting, suggests, as well as concatenates against, other poems within the book. Check the list: The morning that cannot touch the meek members recalls the fascicle's eleventh poem, in which Dickinson likens sunrise to the busy actions of children; meek members are those who are so imprudent as not to use a microscope. "Grand go the years" recalls the "Centuries of Way" of the sixth poem, and the Firmaments that "row" and the worlds that scoop their arcs appeared in the rotations of sunrise and sunset of the tenth poem, which in turn picked up the image of the teasing Sun touching and leaving Morning in the third; in turn, that image returns in the twenty-second ("I've nothing else—to bring" [J224, Fr253]), the fascicle's last poem. Diadems and Doges, too, appeared in the preference for the crown over marbles in the second, and so forth. Both "Midnight" and "Eclipse" appear in the fascicle's twentieth poem ("If *He dissolve* [J236, Fr251]). Finally, the last lines of the first variant, "Staples of Ages—have / buckled—there" holds, as the *OED* reveals, a possible link in imagery with the preceding poem. "You're right—the way *is* / narrow." Cynthia Griffin Wolff reminds us that "staples" might be the nails that fixed Christ to the cross (1986, 319), but Dickinson's own dictionary provides several other possible meanings for "staples" and hence for the line and the entire poem: The Saxon root of the word, says Webster, is to set or fix. The line may mean, then, that those notions fixed in orthodoxy have buckled. The dictionary continues with the familiar meaning of principal commodities so that the line may also refer to economic certainties that have perished. It may, yes, even in 1828, the date of one of her Webster's, be that metal loop that holds manuscripts together; thus, the line may imply that meaning itself has buckled. The *OED* provides one more secondary meaning. A staple is a mineshaft smaller than the principal one. If that buckles, the collapsed dark interiority is like polar darkness.

There is no resurrection here. Spring, a metonymy for resurrection, unavailingly shakes the "seals." The "Song of Solomon" (8:6) admonishes believers to set God like "seals" on their hearts. A seal is an "act of confirmation": It is a "royal mark . . . [and] a mark of property." A seal may indicate a promise or contract, but here, in "Safe" in "Alabaster Chambers," the word in its stiff context implies the brokenness of that contract. In the end, all that has stapled the ages, all of the seals that promised meaning rather than silence, disappear: "Staples—of Ages—have buckled—there—" or, as she puts it in the next variant, "Midnight in Marble— / Refutes—the Suns—."

Having pushed the stiff, cold, distant, meek members as far down and narrow as possible, Dickinson returns to a conversational tone with "The court is far away— / No Umpire—have I—" (J235, Fr250). "*That*—Empire—is of Czars— /As small—they say—as I," she continues. The Empire, the court from which the speaker is excluded, is "Umpire-less," lacking an intercessor, but the notion that the Czar and she are equal shifts the tone from pathos to assertiveness. By the end of the poem with all of its royal imagery, the speaker meditating on the vagaries of Grace (Christ being the sought-after "Umpire," the one who might "intercede" for her—or *not*) has declared the outrageous (to those "meek members"): She has dared to suggest that she, the poet, and the Savior could share or even swap roles. When she asks for the power to intercede, she is asking for what a poet has: the power "to mediate; to interpose." After all, Emerson had implied as much in his catalogue of roles the poet holds: "Sayer, Priest, Announcer." Dickinson's delight in wordplay might have led her also to consider the germinal activity of the poet's process and effect, the poet as inter-seed-er.[12] If the court is so distant that she disbelieves she will enter, the poet has one recourse: through her art to take control of power otherwise denied her. Her texts make permeable the borders of faith and doubt, acceptance and rejection, light and dark; they are her way of wresting control from patriarchal systems, of worsting God.

The fascicle is closing. On the next pages, the compiler arranges two poems, twenty and twenty-one in the series, which seem opposing voices in this fascicle's drama of the speaker's continuing religious quest. Consider the many ways the first of the two, "If *He dissolve*—then—there / is *nothing—more*" (J236, Fr251) is echoed by the next poem, "I think just how my shape / will rise—" (J237, Fr252). Indeed, if the echo isn't exact, the fascicle reader again sees the way images answer each other, concatenate against each other. The poem on the left, "If *He dissolve*," is marked by negation, darkness, and blindness, all familiar from previous poems in the fascicle. It is full of absences: the possible dissolution of faith (deistic or mortal); the blank "*nothing—more*"; the totality of "Eclipse" (a reprise from "Alabaster's" "Tribes of Eclipse"). It reverses expected hope: not Easter sunrise but "sunset," not the bright hope of Christmas but "*Faint* Star of Bethlehem— / *Gone Down!*" Such is the first half of "If *He dissolve*" on the left. On the right are the first two stanzas of "I think just how my shape / will rise—," in which the speaker meditates on the very elements of faith she has just negated. Characteristically she hyperbolizes them, picturing what it would be like to be "forgiven," the word that appears twice in the poem—both times in the quotation marks that usually signal irony, an irony sharpened by its rhyme with the last word, "unshriven."

Answering—or continuing—the eclipse and darkness of a faith that fails, there would be, the speaker suggests, an equal disappearance act should she be granted grace and gathered "*Out of Sight*—in Heaven." That is, after all, where the meek members go. On the other hand, if the Star of Bethlehem, faint at that, go down (in the poem on the left), there seems some tiny hope (in that on the right) as the speaker quotes the Christ who was born by that star. Paraphrasing Luke 12:6, the speaker thinks of the weight of the Gospel's words: "that you—*do* [so?]—*late*—'*Consider*' *me* / The 'sparrow' of your care."

Suffering (near death) is the focus of the third and fourth verses of both poems as they face each other. Again, the poem on the left is darker, more urgent, as the speaker implores intercession—a reverse intercession from the biblical idea that the *person* of Christ informs God on behalf of man: "*Would not some God inform* / Him—" that the speaker is dying, perhaps as a later poet put it, "piecemeal of emotional anaemia" (Ezra Pound's "The Garden")? Dickinson's words are not that different: "Say—that a *little life*—for / *His*— / is *leaking—red*." The reader may be horrified at the next line, as the speaker calls herself "*His little Spaniel*"—and many have discussed it,[13] but the next line "*Will he heed?*" need not be submissive and plaintive; it might be the way the fawning dog demands dominion over the master.

The question ("Will he heed?") might also be a bridge in the dramatic construction of the fascicle, a bridge between the statement of dark despair in "If *He dissolve*," on the left, and "I think just how my shape will rise," on the right. There's a conversation, too, in another set of answering lines. Opposite the image on the left of a mortal, bloody wound of the deserted speaker ("A *little life*—for / *His* / Is *leaking*—red") is the third verse of "I think just how," offering specious solace. As with the quotation-marked sparrow in the previous stanza, this pious hope rings hollow. The persona is not comforted by the biblical promise. The hollow ring of quotations in the second of the paired poems ("Consider" me / the "Sparrow" and "forgiven" in "I think just how") seems to signal the tenuous beliefs of those "meek members of the Resurrection."

The last lines on the back page further shatter any platitudinous comfort the speaker has suggested: "Until—delirious—borne— / By *trust*— / I drop my Heart—*unshriven!*" Recalling that the fascicle began with the poem that, when the book is opened, is opposite to these lines, "We—Bee and I." In that opening poem the Bee seems delirious in another sense so that the fascicle reader is struck by the movement in this book from relatively carefree images of drunken bees, industrious angels, and sunrises to this last page on which all of that bright hope and trust that has made the speaker delirious and that all of those "meek members" probably believed ends: The speaker says, "I *drop* my Heart—*unshriven.*" The words recall the eighteenth poem, in which diadems dropped, but in this poem it is faith itself that drops. Conning that verb "drop" (as the speaker does with "Forgiven") may make one think of the expulsion from Eden of the first couple; it may connote the clumsiness of one delirious in some way, or—radically different from such suggestions—it may suggest assumed power. This drop may not be accidental; it is willed. All options have dissolved, based as they were on empty promises. "Unshriven"—separated from its referent (I), isolated by the dash, and punctuated with a heavy exclamation point—challenges orthodoxy.

If the speaker fails to achieve, fails, in fact, to ask for forgiveness of the master or lord, whether mortal or theistic, the speaker in the twenty-first poem seems on the way to becoming the woman whose power is in her art. That is what she says in the last powerful (but largely ignored) poem:

> I've nothing else—to bring,
> You know—
> So I keep bringing These—
> Just as the Night keeps
> fetching stars
> To our familiar Eyes—
> Maybe, we should'nt mind them
> Unless they did'nt come—
> Then—maybe it would puzzle us
> To find our way Home— (J224, Fr253)

Dickinson sent an only slightly different copy of this poem to Bowles, Johnson guesses, with some flowers (1958, I:161). From the tone and context in this fascicle, however, the pronoun referent might not be flowers but poems. For the poet, triumphant over a disappearing sun and a disappointing God, the poems so carefully woven together ward off bewilderment about the "way Home." That Home may be the one on Main Street, inhabited by the stern father; perhaps it is the silent, waiting home, site of the sixth poem of this fascicle, the dramatic "Tho' I get home how late— / how late." Read another way, the home may be the one that will substitute for the Court that is so far away, a more hospitable home than the one believed in by the "meek members of the resurrection" who now lie, cold, cheated, marbleized, in their "Safe" Alabaster Chambers. The "home" with which she ends Fascicle 10 involves risk; it involves the making of poetry.

"I keep bringing these— / Just as the Night keeps / fetching stars," she has declared. Fascicle reading reveals how carefully contrived, how variable in mood, how complex in structure are her collections of "these." Such a study shows that the same poem ("Safe in their Alabaster Chambers"), keynote of both fascicles, radiates out also within Fascicle 6 in a radically different way. Whereas we have seen it in Fascicle 10 as part of a grim investigation of options that threaten to cut the speaker from her authentic voice, much more briefly let us see how "Safe" (or an early version of it) acts in Fascicle 6 as a grave but also playful jibe at those incapable of flight and fun.

Laughing Light: Alabaster Chambers in Fascicle 6

No less heterodox in its context in Fascicle 6 than in Fascicle 10, the early version of the poem, the one that Sue challenged Emily to improve, "Safe in their Alabaster Chambers" looks and means something different in this earlier context. In the first place, it shares the page with another verse from another poem, one that prepares for its particular thrust. In the second place, it looks much neater—and is. As Sharon Cameron points out, Dickinson's early "publications" appear much more finished than the later ones (1992, 8). Not until Fascicle 5 do those cross marks show up, offering us multiple possibility words. Fascicle 10's version of "Safe" with its two whole verses as options or additions is a fascinating oddity. Fascicle 6's poem seems more benign, tidily positioned between two almost horizontal lines. And its diction more nearly fits the lighter tone of this book. If Fascicle 10 seems bitter, Fascicle 6 is more ironic, sarcastic—and lighter. Its first poem, "Who never lost are unprepared" (J73, Fr136), begins the fascicle with a traditional idea (and with three words important in Fascicle 10 as well: a Coronet, an Emperor, and the "cooling Tamarind"). The idea is one of Dickinson's most often explored: that loss and pain, particularly that achieved in battle, sweetens the prize. The notion that at death an Angel might "Write 'Promoted' / On this Soldier's brow!" anticipates breezes that might laugh at the dead interred in Alabaster Chambers below. Written before the Civil War, this poem embodies idealized battle, not the literal "Scarlet Maryland" of "When I was small, a / Woman died" (J596, Fr518, F24). "Who never lost" envisages another kind of life, death, and scarring. As Barton Levi St. Armand notes, Dickinson "knew two kinds of death" (1984, 100). With less fierceness than in the Fascicle 10 version, "Safe" suggests those two kinds: the complete nonlife of the "meek members of the Resurrection"—in both senses. These members may be literally dead, but the poet's focus is on their spiritual, intellectual deadness: on the "stolid ear" that cannot perceive the light laughing breeze or the babbling bee, representatives of another kind of life.

Much less exhaustively than with the three fascicles I've already discussed, I want to show how "Safe in their Alabaster Chambers" is as appropriate to the tone and collection of image clusters in Fascicle 6 as the later version with its variants is for Fascicle 10. Reading the fascicles attentively allows us to see that what Curran said of Wordsworth's collection, *Poems in Two Volumes,* is as true for Dickinson as it was for Wordsworth: Both are "in ceaseless motion among contraries; but in their composite unity, there is the undoubted equipoise of a great artistic vision" (Curran 1986, 238). By tracing my reading of these four fascicles and offering some further observations in the next two chapters I do not mean to foist one interpretation over another. Rather, I hope to interest others to focus their Dickinson reading on doing so in the context she provided, to join what Rosenthal and Gall called the "revolution."

"Revolution": That is the crux of the little poem about two flowers (ladies), second in the series, "A Lady red—amid the Hill" (J74, Fr137), a poem that ends by implying the benefits of revolution, change, risk. The flowers bloom, they change when the "tidy Breezes" come, perhaps the same breeze we feel in the to-be-repeated "Safe." The kind of Revolution experienced by the "ladies" is, as the last line of the second poem, says—slantwise—"strange." There is an archness in that nonchalant Hedge that doesn't recognize the Springtime Revolution, and there is an archness, too, in the lines that face those, the end of "To fight aloud, is very brave—" (J126, Fr138). There the "Angels go / Rank after Rank, with even feet— / And Uniforms of Snow." Those uniforms are what interests me in the context of the tone of this fascicle. Used by Dickinson only in this one poem, the word used as a synonym for an outfit or costume turns those "angels" into visions of cloudiness. However, as a synonym for that which carries the insignia of rank and that which deindividualizes its wearers, it conveys Dickinson's disdain for those who dwell in the "Safe . . . Alabaster Chambers" of the twelfth poem. Under "uniform," in fact, in Dickinson's dictionary, appears this sentence: "It is the duty of a Christian to observe a uniform course of piety and religion."

Indeed, one turns the page and finds the speaker refuting that duty in "'Houses'—so the Wise Men tell me—" (J127, Fr139), the fourth in the series. The apparent plaintive tone belies the acerbity one hears reading the poem in its context—though even without the acerbic "Safe" and other contextual clues the poem itself seems sarcastic: Again there are those telltale quotation marks around the biblical passages; there is the arch tone of "so the Wise Men tell me"; and there are those slantwise subjunctive lines. Mansions must (we think: "should") be warm, must exclude the storm, must be snugly built. These mansions (players with language will think: man/scions—the patriarchal constructions) are built by "his Father," whom—with devastating parenthetical understatement—the speaker claims not to know. Finally, "Could the Children find the way there— / Some, would even trudge tonight," implying, of course, that they cannot find that mansion/bastion of the traditional story and they will not trudge. Of course, they may be better off: They might not end up in "Safe Alabaster Chambers" to be laughed at by the breeze and babbled at by the bee. As if freed from such constraint, the next, much longer, more fanciful poem, "Bring me the sunset in a cup" (J128, Fr140), shouts with a kind of children's glee in a series of demands and questions, all leading to the desire "to fly away, / Passing Pomposity." Not to want "Uniforms of Snow," not to want entombment, wanting, rather, to be free from Pomposity: This is the thrust of the repeated "Alabaster Chambers" poem—in this fascicle.

As the fascicle moves on toward that focus poem, the next four poems all feature images of escape, specifically the escape of a female figure who feels trapped or entombed. After a whimsical "She died at play" (J75, Fr141), a meditation, presumably, about day but easily analogous to the concerns of someone *not* wanting to be stifled and kept from playing, the editor of this small volume places a triumphant poem of perfect freedom. Listen to Wendy Barker on the seventh poem, "Cocoon above! Cocoon below!" (J129, Fr142): "The poet's primary business is paradoxically the result of constriction and isolation within the smallest and most universal of all dark interiors, that of the embryo. The poet, like the embryonic butterfly or bird, must relish silent nourishment from the dark circle of interiority" (1987, 123). And Barbara Mossberg extends the image. The poet daughter, says Mossberg, "is the cocoon, bursting with words, yet confined and shut up; she has a 'secret' creation no one can see; her dutiful daughter contains, protects, and hides her present and future greatness as a poet" (1982, 172). Although neither Barker nor Mossberg is speaking of the poem in its fascicle context, the descriptions of both explain the way the imagery of this seventh poem prepares for "Safe" and the way it meshes with the poems surrounding it. This cocoon will be transformed to something so free that it competes with the laughing breeze and babbling bees above the "Alabaster Chambers." In her Butterfly form she will take "A moment to interrogate, / Then wiser than a 'Surrogate', / The

Universe to know!" Lawyer Dickinson's daughter would know that "surrogate's" secondary meaning is "Judge of probate / wills and testaments." Whether she is challenging our own "surrogate" (Christ?) or her own father and his peers, she is claiming grand power. That power leads to the next poem, in which she defines and gives a giddy edge to the poet's definition of "Exultation."

According to the editor of Fascicle 6, "Exultation is the going / Of an inland soul to sea" (J76, Fr143). In going "Past the houses— / past the headlands— / Into deep Eternity," the speaker escapes the fate of those entombed in "Alabaster Chambers," heedless of breezes, bees, and laughter. This expansive, joyous poem shares space on the page with "I never hear the word 'Escape'" (J77, Fr144), an eight-liner that continues the theme, opposing "A flying attitude!" to imprisonment, specifically to being a child "at my bars," struggling and failing to escape. This image returns in another poem about children (flowers) in their cribs near the end of the fascicle. Meanwhile, Dickinson has chosen what would become one of her most discussed and quoted poems to face the "Exultation" and "Escape" poems, both of which express a wistfulness for freedom.

"These are the days when Birds come back—" (J130, Fr122) is, of course, more than one of the most heartbreaking poems ever written about "Indian Summer," its rather reductive title in the 1890 edition. That the author realized her success seems clear; the poem exists in at least three versions, the other two differing little from this one, where, positioned between the wistful children and an acerbic poem about traditional (male/old) writers on Autumn, its meaning unfolds incrementally. Here the poet, cannier than those "Wise Men" (from the "Mansion" poem several pages earlier) who would offer unconvincing solace, spurns the "sophistries of June":

> Oh fraud that cannot cheat the Bee
> Almost thy plausibility
> Induces my belief.

"Fraud" leaps out, especially in relation to the reference in the "Mansion" poem to the children who "don't know" the Father and who "could [not] find the way there." In such a context, this reads as a poem of spiritual longing and loss.

The tone (but not the import) changes to exasperation and self-determination in the poem that follows the final stanza, a stanza in which the outcast child asks to share the "sacred Emblems." "Besides the Autumn poets—sing" (J131, Fr123), says the sharp-tongued speaker as though it's not enough to be denied belief in sacred scripture; besides that, one cannot count on the secular scripture of romantic poetry. The skepticism and sadness of "These are the Days when

"Alabaster Chambers"

[Manuscript facsimile in Emily Dickinson's handwriting:]

> Perhaps a squirrel may remain
> My sentiments to share.
> Grant me, Oh Lord, a sunny mind
> Thy windy will to bear!
>
> ———
>
> Safe in their Alabaster Chambers,
> Untouched by morning
> And untouched by noon.
> Sleep the meek members of the Resurrection
> Rafter of satin,
> And roof of stone.
>
> Light laughs the breeze
> In her Castle above them.
> Babbles the Bee in a stolid Ear,
> Pipe the Sweet Birds in ignorant cadence
> Ah, what sagacity perished here!
>
> ———

Perhaps no "duplicate" poem shows so dramatically how reading "Poems in their Places" yield more possibilities for interpretation than those read out of the context supplied by Dickinson. In Fascicle 6 (about 1859 and written on the same stock of paper as Fascicle 8, the first version in the smaller handwriting of the earlier years follows the last verse of "Besides the Autumn Poets—sing" (J216, Fr123). In this fascicle the context is far less dark than that in Fascicle 10 (about 1860), in which Dickinson suggests an eerie existential emptiness of "dots—on a Disc of snow—" Much has been written about these changing versions, including the six pages in Franklin's *Variorum* (I, 159–64), but little has been made of the context provided by the fascicle settings. Printed by permission of the Houghton Library, Harvard University.

Birds come back" merges into the outright scorn for the "Autumn poets" in the poem Sandra Gilbert calls "an elliptical expression of literary scorn" (1986, 132). The "child" cannot trust—cannot participate in—either sacred or secular scriptures: not the invitation of the Last Supper nor the poems of those such as Bryant and Thompson, whom, Capps says, Dickinson "loved" (1966, 111). It is tempting to think that the "blue and gold mistake" in the previous poem might be a pun on the most famous Autumn poem, which begins "Seasons of *mists* and mellow fruitfulness," turning the idealizations of Keats into an *ache* in the woman who also recognizes the hazards in the haze. Dickinson linked the two poems ("These are the days" and "Besides the Autumn poets sing") in sending them together to Bowles, about whose tin ear Sewall berates with the kind of scorn Dickinson showed for her Autumn poets: "Both of these are so superior to the verses the *Republican* habitually honored as to defy comparison" (1974/1980, 476).

Midway through the poem, "autumn" blends into a frozen stillness. The eyes of elves, says the speaker, are touched by "mesmeric fingers," as if somehow the poets, as the season, have the power to hypnotize one to sleep, a sleep that is the subject of the next poem. She ends her poem about the "prosaic," "incisive," and "ascetic" season—and poets—with a kind of shrug of her shoulders, one that leads directly—in the space it occupies and the sense it conveys—to the poem she repeats in Fascicle 10 in such a different form. These lines lead to the Alabaster Chambers, which follow on the same page:

> Perhaps a squirrel may remain—
> My sentiments to share—
> Grant me, oh Lord, a sunny mind—
> Thy windy will to bear!

Below these lines there's the neat horizontal line and then the poem around which this chapter revolves and toward which this fascicle has been surging.

"Still" and "Sealed" in the "Autumn Poets" poem prepare the reader for the sealed Alabaster Chamber, and this stanza, which spills into the space of the Alabaster Chamber, seems an inscription for it. The playful squirrel prayer appears to be to God, whose will may blow haphazardly and not always pleasantly in those cold Puritan New England churches. "Will," that loaded word in those churches, appears significantly in the inscription in the book that Benjamin Lease tells us influenced "These are the days" (1990, 54–55). Here is what is written on the inscription page of Dickinson's own copy of the *Imitation of Christ,* which makes doubly poignant the disappointment of the speaker in some of this fascicle's poems:

> His will entire be God's will resign'd,
> And what pleas'd God, pleas'd his devoted mind
> Thrice happy saint, remote from haunts of ill,
> Employed in hymn, and dispossess'd of will.

The *Imitation* continues, "O Jesu, teach me like thyself to fly / This poisonous world, and all its charms defy." The Amherst poet begs with less sincerity. In the first place, the speaker does want her own will; that of the deity is windy, with all of the connotations that word carries of pomposity as well as of shiftiness. One squints at the manuscript, too, wondering whether "will" could be confused with "wile," partly because of the poem's placement in the fascicle. Dickinson is about to address the frigid rigidity of those who are unthinkingly attentive and faithful to the windy will of this God.

Before exploring the poem, now in its fascicle place, I offer this observation (yet again) on the symmetry of the pages. On the left, the western side, of the open book and opposite them on the right, the eastern side, are the little prayers that are the last lines of two poems and simultaneously the prefaces of those that follow ("Thy sacred emblems to partake . . . " on the left; "Grant me, oh Lord, a sunny mind . . ." on the right). Almost exactly opposite each other, below the little prayers are the characteristic Dickinson dark lines separating one poem from another and also calling attention to the way one may read the pages horizontally as well as vertically: Opposite the stanza on the snow, haze, and prosaic days of "Autumn Poets" is the stanza on the stolid stillness of the meek members of the Resurrection; opposite the stanza on the stillness of winter is the stanza on the movement of life above the casket of the dead.

Those may be the physically dead, of course, but given the context of this fascicle and the nature of the exchange with Sue about the poem, they may be—more likely are—the dead in life. Before exploring that pivotal poem, I tender another word about this stanza that forms a bridge between the two poems, an epigraph of sorts to those "Safe in their Alabaster Chambers." Braving the still, sealed winter world of the "Autumn Poets," the squirrel is the creature with which Dickinson identifies. In other poems the squirrel is almost always in motion, like the child who appears in other poems of the fascicle. It is "rampant," "giddy," "running," and "playing."[14] As in Emerson's "Fable," the squirrel is the tiny principle that is the equal of the gigantic Himmeleh (in J862, Fr506, "light" is equally accessible to both). When the squirrel/poet/speaker begs for "a sunny mind" to bear "the windy will of God," she suggests that the Calvinist deity is literally in harmony with winter. Judged by its juxtaposition on the page with "Safe in their Alabaster Chambers," it appears that what is hardest for the speaker to bear of the windy will at odds with her own Power is not necessarily physical death but a torpid state of life suggested in the richly textured two stanzas of this version of J216, Fr124.

The first line of "Safe in their Alabaster Chambers" conveys the saccharine niceness of funeral parlors. It is fussy and feminine as in "Sweet—safe—Houses" (J457, Fr684, F32), where the chambers are lined with satin. The Alabaster Chambers are hardly the "Chambers of the Cedars" in "I dwell in Possibility" (J657, Fr466, F22). Rather, this hard white gypsum belongs to the House of Prose. Dickinson's lexicon notes that Alabaster is also a measurement for wine or oil, reminding us of the child who wanted to join the feast of bread and wine. In these hard, unyielding, overly ornate compartments or chambers sleep the meek members of the Resurrection. A less-loaded verb than the "lie" in the Fascicle 10 version, "sleep" is nevertheless intensified by its near rhyme. These are the "meek" who should be inheriting the earth. These are the opposite of the squirrel/child/poet of the fascicle's earlier poems who claim a kind of power. As in the squirrel image of the previous poem (and so many others), this one owes much to Emerson. In "Brahma" he declares with the kind of scorn we see in this series of Dickinson poems, "Thou meek lover of the good / Find me [Brahma] and turn your back on heaven." Dickinson's speaker seems to have heeded Emerson's strong, heterodox words. It would be better, she suggests, to do just that, turn away from the meek members assembled and find a life free of dichotomies such as good/evil, devils/angels, comfort/pain. It would be better to be "ignorant" of expected drawing room codes, undependable bible stories, and autumn poets. It would be better to be one with the laughing breeze and the babbling bee, both of which, of course, are loaded with metaphoric possibilities to the Dickinson reader.

The fascicle reader turns the page to find one of Dickinson's most trenchant parodies, "A poor—torn heart" (J78, Fr125). Such a tone is suggested by more than one context of the "torn heart"; along with the poems that precede it and at least one of the four poems that follow and complete the book, it has another context, a note to Sue accompanied by a representation of Dickens's lugubrious Little Nell's mourning grandfather (Capps, 97; Martha Nell Smith has also discussed this at length). In this thirteenth poem, angels pick up the sorrowful heart "Intent upon the vision / Of latitudes unknown" (we smile at the echo of "flying attitudes" in the ninth poem, "I never hear the word 'escape'") and carry it to God in the "blue havens" (the laughing breeze blowing over the Alabaster Chambers). The figure in the poem seems to be a child, as is the figure pleading to be allowed to the sacrament in the tenth poem.

On the other hand, between this poem and one that continues the lighter tone of this fascicle (lighter than the later Fascicle 10 anyway), is the utterly serious, stunningly heterodox "I bring an unaccustomed wine" (J132, Fr126), the fourteenth in the series. It was "thine immortal wine" for which the speaker of the tenth poem longed and from which she felt excluded and cheated; here the speaker is no longer begging but giving. She has the power to save others with the draught she once lacked. Not another version of death, this poem posits a way to live in the face of death akin to that of the Christian existentialist. The wine may not save the thirsty, but the speaker continues to "bear the cup" to slake the thirst of one who may be able to drink it. Put another way, as poetry itself is an "unaccustomed wine," she offers her poetry that it may satisfy another. Before the poem ends, its quoted line "Unto the little unto me" (Matt. 25:40) recalls the New Testament's central message and also recalls the continuing presence of the child in this fascicle. The last line jolts with its apparently nonsequitous follow-up: "When I at last awake." Reading the poem in this its fascicle place clarifies its mystery. "When I at last awake" from that metaphoric alabaster chamber of a death in life, then I will be able to bring the sunset in a cup or join the laughing breeze, babbling brook, and busy bees.

"When I at last awake" is opposed in the next poem, situated just below it on the page, "As Children bid the Guest 'Good Night'" (J133, Fr127). The slaked lips of the fourteenth poem become the "pretty lips" of flowers in this fifteenth poem. In the first stanza the children (flowers), "reluctant turn," rather like those in Longfellow's sonnet "Nature" in which the about-to-die are compared to children who don't know how much they need to sleep and how wonderful "the unknown" beyond will be. Harking back to the fascicle's sixth poem, "She died at play," the alliterative second stanza likens heaven to a garden or a playground:

> As children caper when they wake
> Merry that it is morn
> My flowers from a hundred cribs
> Will peep and prance again.

These capering, prancing children, risen freshly awake from their cribs, seem reenactments of the fascicle's most celebrated poem, the soon-to-be-rewritten "Safe in their Alabaster Chambers." Here, too, the children have been well behaved in their safe (perhaps satin-lined) homes, well trained in manners by some careful mommy. But they break the bonds of convention, refusing to be interred in the safe chambers. As they rise from their cribs, they suggest the bars tugged at by the speaker of the fascicle's ninth poem. These children have come uncribbed in the fullest meaning of the word. Dickinson's dictionary lists not only a manger and a small cottage under "crib" but also the verb: "to shut or confine in a narrow habitation; to cage." These children are so uncribbed, in fact, that they break some basic societal taboos: They "peep" and "prance." Although the poet is speaking overtly of flowers peeping over the rims of their boxes, she has placed the poem in this context in which it is legitimate to see the metaphoric children as naughty enough to "peep," not only violating discretion and privacy but also peeping into the sacred, seeing through façades, investigating the forbidden. This is the business of the poet who says "My business is, to Find!" ("I cautious, scanned my little life—" [J178, Fr175, F8]). The children may not be waking up in another life, not, certainly, in the conventional heaven of "meek" members of churches. They may be waking up to the heaven that is on earth if one is uncribbed.

Such is the powerful implication of the penultimate poem in the sequence. As a musician friend pointed out about an Aaron Copland setting of this poem, the first five notes of "Going to Heaven!" (J79, Fr128) are sung in exactly the upwardly rising inflection of the stationmaster's call. Not only that, says Maryann Sewell, a student of Dickinson in music and a performer of many of the settings, but the closing words, "the ground," come down hard; they seem to be Copland's parody of "amen." Sewell's observation and the wit of her own performance perhaps influences my reading of this poem, which might otherwise—like "A poor torn heart"—seem pious, albeit puzzling. But Sewell's interpretation of Copland's interpretation is perfectly consistent with the context of the spunky poem. The voice seems that of the child, an "astonished" one who doesn't like the "dim" sound of the place (those Alabaster Chambers, after all) and tries to convince herself of the value of the destination by reminding herself of Sunday school teachings: "And yet it will be done / As sure as flocks go home at night / Unto the Shepherds' arm." The child of an earlier poem kissing or hugging the guest with the Good Night becomes the sheep heading into the Shepherd's arm.

In the second stanza, too, the speaker is a child, perhaps whispering conspiratorially to another child, asking him or her to "Save just a little place for me / Close to the two I lost!" Remember the opening poem of this fascicle: "Who never lost are unprepared / A Coronet to find!" The parallel is intensified in the next line; the speaker specifies the garb appropriate for heaven: "the smallest 'Robe' . . . and just a bit of Crown." Further, "Going home," the phrase the child speaker uses at the end of the second stanza as a euphemism for heaven, calls us back to the "Houses" and "Mansions" of the fascicle's fourth poem, the claustrophobic "Alban House" of the fifth poem, and "Alabaster Chambers" of the twelfth. The indeterminate pronouns of the final stanza ("I'm glad I don't believe *it* / . . . I'm glad they did believe *it*") seems pretty clear by this time in the fascicle. Although the first "it" may refer to the line just before (that the friend will go ahead and save a place), more probably it harks back to the poem's opening: that the speaker is going to Heaven to be gathered in like a lamb to the fold. Such orthodox assurances from the meek members of the resurrection are not for this feisty speaker, who nevertheless is glad that her departed friends had the faith that made their dying easier. A third "it" in the poem: "For it would stop my breath—" seems less indeterminate; what would kill the poet would be an easy belief.

As the poem that she repeats in Fascicle 10 implies, being shut up in "Alabaster Chambers"—Jane Eberwein likens them to bank vaults (1985, 32)—is no fun. This speaker is greedy for a full, fancy-filled, frolicking life: "I'd like to look a little more / At such a curious earth." Many things are "curious" to the poet: trinkets/flowers, a cloud, the memory of the past, God, and "His memorial institution," communion.[15] The "curious Earth" of this poem contains such poet's human activities as "health, and laughter, curious things" in "I cried at Pity—not at Pain—" (J588, Fr394, F19). All that comprises the active, probing life on a solid earth, then, is privileged over the safe sleep of death as Dickinson's "Alabaster Chambers" poem in all of its versions insists. The specious solace of "Autumn poets," reprised in the last line of "Going to Heaven" in "the mighty Autumn afternoon / I left them in the ground," and the "sophistries" of Indian Summer have failed to comfort this speaker/child/lover of earth.

Sharing the page with this declaration—that life fully and even dangerously lived is preferable to the death in life of unquestioning acceptance of social conventions in Alabaster Chambers or the religious dogma of the windy preachers about the windy will of God—is this final poem:

> Our lives are Swiss—
> So still—so Cool—
> Till some odd afternoon
> The Alps neglect their Curtains
> And we look—farther on!
>
> *Italy* stands the other side!
> While like a guard between
> The solemn Alps!
> The siren Alps
> Forever intervene! (J80, Fr129)

The afternoon of the burial service with its amen thud of finality has become in this last poem of the fascicle a day of revelation, of unveiling of mystery. Implicating us ("we") in her discovery, Dickinson works with three geographical metaphors parallel to image clusters from throughout the fascicle, but particularly in the Alabaster Chambers.

In the first, those meek members immured in Alabaster are Swiss: "so still—so Cool" and so Calvinist. Geneva (Dickinson's closest other reference to Switzerland is in "Geneva's farthest skill" in "A Clock stopped" [J287, Fr259, F11]), the birthplace of John Calvin, resonates in opposite ways from *Italy*, a country that obviously intrigued and attracted Dickinson. Even had the Brownings not lived there, Dickinson (the Dickinson whose persona rejects safe Alabaster Chambers) might have been intrigued with the country noted in one of her textbooks for its "low delights" as opposed to Switzerland with its "nobler race" (Capps, 107–8). But the Brownings did live there. Italy was the location of poetic power. Between the Swiss serenity and stolidity and the Italian vividness the cloud-curtained Alps stand guard. Between the imaginative play of breeze and bee, of the scampering squirrel and the adventurer who assumes a feisty, risking "flying attitude" on the one hand and the obedient children kissing guests, the autumn poets who revere what the poet sees as specious sophistries and false promises on the other, the curtains are usually drawn. In the words of a *Harper's* journal Dickinson may well have read, the Alps' Mount Blanc "seems so near the sky that the blue firmament kisses its brow. It is so far off, yet so near, so bright and pure, that angels might be sporting on its summit and be safe from the intrusion of men. It is a *solemn* mountain" (from *Harper's* 14 [1856–1857]: 740). The unnamed author of this passage (721–40) describes Mont Blanc as Dickinson does in this fascicle's final poem: "[A] cloud is gathered like a halo on its head; but it rises and vanishes." Just so, in Dickinson's poem "The Alps neglect their Curtains / And we look farther on."[16]

In this context, as the culmination of a gathering of poems about two ways to live, the "daring figure" posits, as Greg Johnson puts it, the "sheltered" and inviolate geographical positions of Switzerland against the "celestial city," reached only through the "siren Alps," through which the quester must pass (1985, 146). The quester, however, cannot pass, as this poem implies, because the "solemn, siren" Alps "Forever intervene." "Our lives are Swiss" would then seem a wistful if not mournful end for a book that includes so much play. Perhaps it is, but before one closes the book, one is rewarded by a close look at the back of the opened book. Following Dickinson's advice to read backward (prose fragment 30), the reader notes that with the book opened, the last poem, now on the west side, becomes a preface for the first, now on the east side. As elsewhere—in Fascicles 1, 3, 14, and 40, for example—the circularity provided by reading the poems "backwards" in this way provides new interpretive possibilities. In Fascicle 6 the stanzas on our Swiss lives so far from the richer shores of *Italy,* so unattainable, are opposite the second stanza of "Who never lost," the first in the sequence:

> Who never climbed the weary league—
> Can such a foot explore
> The purple territories
> On Pizarro's shore?

Italy's dark mysteries and Pizarro's exotic Shores[17] were withheld to all but those who brave the siren Alps or the dangerous seas, those who travel weary leagues away from the safety of Alabaster Chambers toward the locus of the poetic imagination.

That Dickinson intended such linkages is suggested by a detail outside this fascicle: some three years after she laced together the seventeen poems of Fascicle 6, this book's version of "Safe in their Alabaster Chambers" was printed by Bowles. For this version, identical (but for punctuation and lineation) to that in Fascicle 6, Dickinson had appended a line of reference: "Pelham Hill, June 1861." In his variorum Thomas Johnson remarks that she had done so because she may have remembered a visit to an old burying ground there. No doubt that is true, but reading the poem in this fascicle suggests another reason for the mountain image. Of course, we cannot know what she intended and what happened serendipitously. Intentionality, that contested and unanswerable ground, is slippery. How can we measure the distance between what the artist put there and what we find there? Does it matter, just so long as we stick with what actually exists on the pages, always watchful for inferences? By reading what she selected to be seen and read in a particular order and grouping in the (I hope not too painfully) detailed method through the first four chapters, we become participatory readers of texts full of surprises.

Rereading Dickinson in this manner may reify her poems, or it may revolutionize our interpretation of individual poems. In the next chapter I wrestle with what these books may have been to her, and in the next, the penultimate one, I suggest some similar pleasures from other fascicles and face those hard questions of intentionality, hoping that Dickinson would say again, "The poets light but— / Lamps— / Themselves go out" (J883, F930 Set 5), as she encourages us to *see* the refractions of the lamps she lit.

CHAPTER 5

"Whatever it is—she has tried it": Exploring the How and Why of the Fascicle Project

>Whatever it is—she has tried it—
>Awful Father of Love—
>Is not Our's the chastising—
>Do not chastise the Dove—
>
>Not for Ourselves, petition—
>Nothing is left to pray—
>*When a subject is finished—
>**Words are handed away—
>
>Only lest she be lonely
>In thy beautiful House
>Give her for her Transgression
>License to think of us—
>
>Variants:
>*When the subject is taken
>**The words are withered away
>
>J1204, Fr1200[1]

To attempt to unravel across a century the "intentionality" of a poet who prized the slant route of truth (J1129, Fr1263) is to court mistakes and frustration. Certainly I cannot solve mysteries about which there is no proof; nevertheless, having shared some of the delights of discovering *what* Dickinson left in those fascicles, I turn briefly to considering *possibilities* for the how and why. However "backwards" it may seem to do so here, I move toward the end of this argument through the beginning; before discussing origins, I wanted to show results, the products.

Studying the Fascicles

Analyzing Dickinson's individual lyrics has become almost an industry. Split this lark and you'll find diverse music, bulb after bulb reserved for feminist, historicist, deconstructionist, or old-fashioned "new" critics. Another way of grouping the history of Dickinson scholarship, a history of criticism that is readily available in many of the books listed in this bibliography, is that suggested by Jerome McGann: three groupings of critical stances, leading from Wordsworthian to Kierkegaardian.[2]

Reading poems in their places (Fraistat's term for contextuality again) suggests that although each fascicle has variety, each also has its own voice so that each grouping elicits readings roughly in keeping with one or the other of these schools. Fascicle 40, for example, subject of the Oberhaus study, indeed lends itself to the first kind of reading in McGann's scheme, that "clearly drawn from a Wordsworthian and, more generally a Christian (Protestant) model" (1983, 22–26); Fascicle 40 is a startlingly devout book, startling in light of so many poems in other fascicles that are not. The flowery Fascicle 1 might invite the same school (Christian) of criticism, but Fascicle 14, in which Dickinson placed a poem almost identical to one in Fascicle 1 ("The feet of people walking home" [J7, Fr16]) lends itself more easily to the second of McGann's school (the Mellor School of skepticism). And we have already seen how Fascicle 10 invites the third and darkest (Kierkegaard/Praz) school. With this in mind, here is a brief chronology of those few who have taken seriously the challenge of reading the poems contextually, those who, in the words of Ruth Miller, let Emily Dickinson's choice guide them.

Although at the 1986 Folger Conference Miller, the first to take seriously the possibilities of reading Dickinson in her own collections (fascicles), claimed to have changed her mind about some of her conclusions, and although her pre-Franklin book was based on an ordering Franklin has corrected, her approach to the gatherings helped to define both what Dickinson's purpose was and what it was not. Warning readers not to find a chronology, not to find meaning in possible recipients, and not to find any single event or subject reflected by any one fascicle, Miller concluded that each fascicle has a range of feelings and subjects and that single fascicles have "polar feelings" (248). Her description of the books as "long link poems" (249) previews that of Rosenthal and Gall's as "Modern Poetic Sequences" (1983).

From the 1970s on, at least four dissertations[3] focused on the fascicles, and in 1983 the first major book, that by William Shurr, which chapter 1 outlines, attempted to interpret the fascicles as revelatory of the personal romantic crisis of the poet. That book, along with the private publication of Martha O'Keefe, began a discussion that failed to convince Franklin. Although Franklin made the last three of the dissertations and the two absolutely different books (one rather notorious, the other privately printed and known to only a cluster of people) possible, he has not joined the (slim) ranks of those who consider the fascicles as intentional compositions rather than repositories of her verse. Just so, as chapter 1 also reviews, few of the major scholars became interested in the value of letting Dickinson's voice guide them through her groupings in the fascicles, and several voiced outright scorn at those who did so. Franklin's disavowal of such attempts, courteous as it was, is perhaps the most daunting. Two years after completing his work, he maintained that "Emily Dickinson probably felt the need for an audience outside her domestic scene, but she did not prepare the fascicles for such an audience, nor for publication" (1983, 16). Knowing the raw material best, he is convincing when he tells us that the evidence for such intentional publications is not borne out by the apparent manner of their assemblage. To be sure, his words are cautionary, but he ends his *Studies in Bibliography* article with this somewhat ambiguous sentence, "Constrained by time, the fascicles may present the poems, recurrent in their concerns and strategies, in gatherings that appear to have design" (20).[4]

One need not claim what Franklin (and those who heed him) warns against: finding a tight "thematic, narrative, or dramatic structure" (ibid., 17) for the fascicles. Indeed it is too bad that some of the earliest work seems to do just that. On the other hand, that bad start does not obviate the need for a new approach, one that respects the books as evidence of Dickinson's mind at play at particular moments in her artistic life. Such serious public beginnings at doing so have been demonstrated by Sharon Cameron, Dorothy Oberhaus, and members of a panel at the 1997 MLA in Toronto under the moderatorship of Martha Nell Smith: Robert Bray, Paul Crumbley, Marget Sands, and this writer. Responses to all of these have been debated with spirit within the various Dickinson chatlines and journals for over a decade with little bridging of the chasm that separates those who privilege working with the Dickinson manuscripts and those who consider such studies fanciful, obsessive, and misguided.[5]

Why and How: Dwelling in Possibilities

In all of this contentious discussion whirling around reading Dickinson through her own manuscript books, no one, it seems to me, has satisfactorily tried to explain *why* Dickinson might have attempted her editing project or how she went about it.

One cannot look long at the little volumes—any of the forty—without *seeing* Dickinson's self-determination as an organizing poet, a crafter of books as well as of stunning and complex lyrics. Obviously, the fascicles are products that reveal their producer's experiences, education, and preoccupations. They are not necessarily, however, personal narratives or essays. Thus, although we might situate the production of the fascicles against the general background of what is (tentatively) known of her life as she compiled each—as I did in the preceding chapter—I do not mean to imply a one-to-one relationship between those events and her poems. Because that first study, Shurr's "Marriage," did so, it seems appropriate to address the complex subject of the reciprocity between the autobiography and the lyric statement.

I neither believe nor am comfortable in my disbelief that all or even most of the poems are "autobiographical," except as the "supposed person" of whom Dickinson spoke to Higginson. With that proviso, I agree that the poems as a whole may be read as what Weisbuch calls "archetypal autobiographies" (1972, 39) or even archeological autobiographies: layered and compressed and distorted levels of memory, desire, and consciousness. The lyric, in the words of Celeste Schenck, is a "serial effort at sketching a self in time and over time" (1988, 290). How consciously autobiographical—or not—that "serial effort" may be, it is complicated by what Alicia Ostriker has pointed out is particularly true of the woman poet, who simultaneously "resists discovery" and "yearns for discovery" (1986, 65). What Ostriker says about Margaret Atwood is incrementally greater for Dickinson: She "insists on our knowing that she is difficult to discover ["I hide myself—within my flower"], submerged—and possibly hostile—yet discoverable" (ibid.). In that an autobiography is, in Shari Bentstock's words, "an effort to recapture the self" (1988, 11), Dickinson's poetry is more often than not autobiographical. Nevertheless, I am suspicious of efforts to tell too literal a story from the traces Dickinson has left in the fascicles, especially when the telling of that story is based on a collection of poems from disparate contexts known and unknown. Poems in the fascicles almost certainly have been removed from their initial impetus still further by a conscious artist.

For the purposes of my study—and this is an extraordinary challenge in itself—I am interested in the way the voice of the poet moves from the dead to the mourner, for example (in Fascicle 3), from the host to the guest (in Fascicle 40), and from the believer to the skeptic within a single fascicle as the editor/author arranged the poems (obviously written earlier, sometimes many years earlier) in a new setting. That they are, to some extent, predicated on autobiographical experience is undeniable. That they are also carefully crafted artifacts and that the new entity they form, the twenty-second poem of a twenty-one-poem sequence, let us say, has its own validity is equally undeniable. Reading this new entity requires that we look closely beyond the individual words and poems to the intersection of words and poems. The *gnome* revealed in the physio*gnomy* of the web itself[6] created not a single strand, not even, necessarily, a collection of dialectically opposed images and ideas within each fascicle, but rather a web of interconnections. It is among those interconnections that we begin "to ransack!" (J178, Fr175 F8).⁷ As long as the fascicle reader understands that Franklin has regularized what are diverse sizes and thicknesses of paper, he or she will come as close to the original source (Dickinson's worktable) as it is possible to be to any poet.

Difficult as it is to meet Dickinson with the kind of attention I have paid her through the fascicles, it may be easier to discover *what* she was doing than *why* she was doing it. Thus far, this study has focused on the texts themselves, and they seem the best evidence of a seriousness toward the editing project, but this chapter also looks at evidence outside those texts that might give us clues: first at the gentle pressure of family example and culture; second at what she said and inferred about writing and work itself; finally this chapter considers what others who practice her art today have to say about their editing goals and methods. None of these can solve the mystery of creativity, but they help to surround it with a network of possibilities. A hint at answers to those overlapping questions may be the opening of a letter to Susan Dickinson when she was twenty-three: *"Write! Comrade, Write!"* (L105).

Five years after she wrote this note at the top of the letter that was entirely a poem, she selected that poem—minus the admonition at the top of the page—for her first "book." One senses that she is not only rallying Sue but also herself to diligence at her life's work. Although most Dickinsonians date the debut of Emily Dickinson as a self-conscious, serious poet from the first letter to Higginson in 1862, her evolution in her vocation was lifelong and almost inevitable. That, beginning in 1858, she went beyond the creation of individual Acts of Light to the self-publication of some forty books was only somewhat less inevitable.

In the first place, as Higginson's preface to the 1890 edition points out, Dickinson worked within a tradition well established, particularly in New England, that of the Portfolio Poet. Although Emerson's description of the private poet makes such a label for Dickinson pejorative, the "portfolio" tradition of private, unedited poetry provided Dickinson with a niche among contemporaries steeped in the romantic tradition.⁸ Emerson's description of earlier writers does not match Dickinson's method: "[B]eing not written for publication, they lack . . . finish [and] rhythmical polish," he had said, and even worse, "These are proper Manuscript inspirations, honest, great, but crude. . . . The writer was not afraid to write ill" (1912, 147).

However demeaning to our ears Emerson's words may seem (in the context of the romantic tradition in mid-nineteenth-century America they would not have seemed so), perhaps Higginson's use of the term tended to influence Dickinson's earliest carping critics. And if she wrote "portfolio poetry" in any sense of Emerson's description, she was in good company. Far from crude but certainly private (for a while) were the earlier lyrics of Anne Bradstreet, whose poems were also "robbed" of her and published widely. Two hundred years after Bradstreet declared herself "obnoxious to each carping tongue,"[9] women writers outside the portfolio tradition, from the widely read Lydia Sigourney to Dickinson's friend and neighbor Helen Hunt Jackson, produced individual collections, often small and flower-bordered, and filled the pages of the proliferating gilded anthologies. Such American women and their British sisters, Jean Ingelow and Barrett Browning, anticipated an answer to Romney's challenge in Barrett Browning's influential *Aurora Leigh* (1856):

> Women as you are,
> Mere women, personal and passionate,
> You give us doating mothers and perfect wives,
> Sublime Madonnas and enduring saints!
> We get no Christ from you—and verily
> We shall not get a poet in my mind (II:44).

Unless Barrett Browning's Romney meant a "genuine" poet in the Marianne Moore ("Poetry") sense, he was wrong. It was an age, as Hawthorne put it, of "Scribbling Women." Their work filled the voluminous literary journals and those gilded anthologies covered and dotted with pictures of curly-headed soulful women, but none to my knowledge was as original, startling, culturally resistant, and funny as Dickinson, who famously resisted such a context as those volumes provided. As St. Armand says, Dickinson "was of her age as well as beyond it" (1984, 12).

Second, she came from a writing family. Tireless and careful correspondents, Dickinson's parents courted through letters and, although the results, edited by Vivian Pollak, lack anything approaching the range, charm, and surprises of those of their daughter, they reveal respect for daily writing. Dickinson's own practice of writing letters to some ninety-three known correspondents in her life (Tingley 1987, 15) was bound so tightly to the writing of poetry that the two enterprises are sometimes difficult to differentiate. Family members wrote everything from doggerel to serious essays. Alfred Habegger goes so far as to say of rather sappy verses of the young Emily's mother (also Emily) that "These lines [the rather pathetic quatrain he quotes] from just before [the young poet's birth] could not be mistaken" for Dickinson's, but they do reflect the "consolatory purpose" of some of Dickinson's work (2001, 67).

From childhood Dickinson was encouraged to write vividly. As a schoolgirl she wrote "strikingly original" compositions and probably contributed to a school publication called "Forest Leaves" (Sewall 1974/1980, 342, 350). By the time she was twenty, she had seen her work ("Valentine Eve") in print; even though it was far from her later quality, the unsigned poem in *The Indicator*, which begins with the traditional invocation, "Awake ye muses nine," announced that another Dickinson had joined the ranks of writers.

Third, as even the rather labored and artificial valentine shows, Dickinson had a gift. For all the discipline and craft she brought to refining, containing, and continuing her enterprise, Dickinson reminds us at the close of Fascicle 21 that the initial impulse for poetry—as with Frost's "lump in the throat, a homesickness, a heartsickness"—was "Given to [her] by / the Gods" (J454, Fr455, F21). It often came to Dickinson unsought: "A Thought went up my Mind" (J701, Fr731, F35), she says, or "It struck me—every Day / . . . And let the Fire through— / . . . It Blistered to my dream—" (J362, Fr636, F31). As easily as the gift of poetry could come, she acknowledged in these poems, it could drift away, as these poems continue. Another might seem to play into Franklin's conclusion that the fascicle project was an effort of safekeeping and retrieval:

> Heavenly moments . . . [are like]
> A Grant of the Divine—
> That Certain as it Comes—
> Withdraws—and leaves the
> dazzled Soul
> In her unfurnished Rooms (J393, Fr560, F27)

No doubt the books did help her to save and order the fruits of those heavenly moments, but, along with the tricky evidence within the fascicles, there's this: Dickinson "decided to be Distinguished," as she told her cousin Louise Norcross (L199). Child of Puritan overachievers, whose influence was strong, she had at age fifteen crowed that her one composition of the term "was exceedingly edifying to myself as well as everybody else. Don't you want to see it?" (L6 to Abiah Root). She teased her "Brother Pegasus" over his verses (L110), and she made no secret of her desire to make Sue and Austin "proud of me—sometime—a great way off" (L238 in that remarkable correspondence with Sue about "Alabaster Chambers"). Problematic as her relationship to print may have become, letters and poems attest to the personal ambition of Emily Dickinson from a young age. Natural gifts, a fine education, parental encouragement, hard work, and ambition, however, do not necessarily lead to great poetry; as Vivian Pollak says, "great art has a human history" (1988, introduction). The personal and spiritual dramas, along with the reading that took life in her mind and poems, have been the subject of most other Dickinson studies. Precisely what led Dickinson to accept the directions of lines in her library—Emerson's to "insist on [her]self" and of Thomas à Kempis to "Fly the tumultuousness of the world as much as thou canst" and work daily (or nightly)—is unrecoverable.

Unrecoverable, too, is the precise impetus for gathering her poems into booklets. Well documented, although not in the fascicle context, is the influence of

Barrett Browning's *Aurora Leigh,* written two years before Dickinson gathered her first book. Itself a full novel in verse, it might provide a source in that its eponymous writing heroine says, "Behold at last, a book. . . . If life-blood's fertilizing, I wrung mine / On every leaf of this" (Part V, 168). Another of her favorite writers, Emily Brontë, made prepublication books, first copying them into one notebook, from which she rearranged them for another. Margaret Homans says of Brontë's practice that "the apparent care with which the poems were chosen and arranged indicates . . . [that] she is consciously developing a myth of the imagination" (108–9). Whether Dickinson knew this fact or not, she must have known that such a practice was common for professional writers. Chances are she *was* following traditions of those she so admired and about whom she did read as much as she could. Barrett Browning, "that Foreign Lady" ("I think I was enchanted" [J593, Fr627, F29]), whose picture hung on Dickinson's bedroom wall, appeared in many letters, especially those to Bowles and Higginson in 1862. As for Brontë, who died in 1848 when Dickinson was an impressionable eighteen, probably devouring obituary stories, she was a "favorite" of Dickinson's. So said Higginson, who read from Brontë at Dickinson's funeral.

Martha Nell Smith has uncovered an inspiration much closer to home than these, however. She discovered in "a commonplace book of Sue's" that "tucked inside of it was a fascicle of poems in Sue's early handwriting (1850s). They were not her poems but were poems from Prescott, Poe, and others." Smith concludes that "fascicle-making was part of the manuscript culture in which Dickinson was deeply embedded." Along with the fascicle of Sue's, Smith found one made by Sue's sister Martha (not her daughter Martha). As Smith has been telling the rest of us for a long time, "we, in the twentieth century, have been seeing Emily's [works] through the machine of the printed book." Dickinson, on the other hand, saw her works as part of a culture that was all around her, that of the handmade book.[10]

Thus, the inspiration for the fascicle project may not be entirely irrecoverable. What is certainly recoverable—thanks to Lavinia, whose determination to bring her sister's work to print took her to Sue and then to Mabel Loomis Todd and Higginson—is the result. As I outlined briefly in the first chapter, thanks to the Harvard and Amherst libraries, whose troves both Johnson and Franklin used, and, of course, thanks to Franklin one may read Dickinson in an almost unmediated form. Recovering the intentional and serendipitous surprises Dickinson left there is both simplified and compounded by the self-publications.

It is simplified because one discards the usual complications of arriving at authorial intentionality that McGann explored in *A Critique of Modern Textual Criticism* (1983). Because Dickinson had no editor, unless she collaborated with Sue—and this possibility is tantalizing, especially to scholars such as Martha Nell Smith—there is no mediating editor or printer. The authorial construct is free of the "history of transmission and . . . history of production" (121–23). Reading the fascicles eliminates the problems of authorial intention that McGann posed: Gone is the difficulty of "choosing less-than-final intentions" because a reading of a particular edition "will capture . . . someone else's intentions" (34); gone is the peril of problematical readings that result from using a text produced by "a struggle between the pen of the author, the pencil of the editor, and the mechanized tools of the printer" (48).

One need not, as McGann puts it, "try to reconstruct a lost original document" (66). Franklin has completed that heroic task. Both his own account of his process and the internal evidence of the results, the reconstituted fascicles, indicate the extent of his accuracy. We need not "distinguish . . . between a history of transmission and a history of production" (123) because the fascicles were not publicly transmitted. With Dickinson's fascicles, alone in the canon of major writers, except perhaps for Blake's illuminated privately printed books and Whitman's visions and revisions in *Leaves of Grass*, editorial changes (in the form of Dickinson's variants) "spring from a single *fons et origo*" (49). McGann's reminder that "the very term 'authority' suggests the author is taken to be—for critical purposes—the ultimate locus of a text's authority" is particularly true of the fascicles. Leaving aside important questions such as the existence of more than the known forty fascicles and the whereabouts of some of the missing leaves Franklin lists in his appendix, what remains is Dickinson's own work.

On the other hand, recovering Dickinson's intentions is complicated by the contradictory statements Dickinson wrote about "print" and "publication" and the lack of any known comments about the forty books she was binding, except possible hints such as "I've nothing else—to bring, / You know— / So I keep bringing These—" (J224, Fr253, F10). Any conclusion about whether Dickinson yearned to have her "letter to the World" (J441, Fr519, F24) read or she sincerely disdained publication, that being "foreign to my thought, as Firmament to Fin" (L265 to Higginson), must be highly provisional. Both of these last comments were recorded in 1862, her *annus mirabilis*. All we know is that she apparently did not choose to publish in print, except in a small way, as Karen Danderand discovered, in support of the war effort.

The concomitant difficulty, however, is in judging whether Dickinson intended the books (or the poems within them) to be read as finished. This is not a problem imposed by those almost private productions of Blake and Whitman. We do not know to what extent her books, the fascicles, are those she might have left had she decided on or been offered encouragement and a trusted collaborative editor. I am not alone in being grateful that she did not have such help, although some contemporary poets, such as Marilyn Nelson, whose help I elicited for this chapter, praise such collaborations. Dickinson's habit of altering lineation, punctuation, and diction in versions of poems she sent to differing recipients and in the poems she repeats in a second fascicle is witness to her resistance to closure. That openness is what encourages the reader who must insist on this as Dickinson's own form of self-publication to play with her, a play validated by the closest possible reading.

Play—deeply serious play—is what those who have read and written about Dickinson and who are practicing poets themselves report as an attitude in their editing. Fifteen American poets weighed in on my questions to them about the challenge of selecting and placing poems in their places. Although they *do* write for print, most of them in differing ways agreed that Dickinson, who did *not*, was probably self-conscious as an editor and probably faced the same kinds of decisions as they did. Their helpful comments are recorded in greater detail in Gudrun Grabher and Martina Antretter's collection, *Emily Dickinson at Home;* I excerpt from the sometimes long letters they wrote in response to my questions, not to *prove* that Dickinson worked in the same way but to show the common habits and attitudes and to suggest that Dickinson may well have shared their agony in decision making and their joy in the finished products.

"Low at [Their] problem bending": Dickinson's Fellow Editors

To be sure the poets do not speak in one voice, but there are enough similarities to make it possible to imagine Dickinson in her own workshop. Among the fifteen are Richard Wilbur, whose "Sumptuous Destitution" essay is basic to Dickinson scholarship; Alicia Ostriker, who devotes much of her *Stealing the Language* (1986) to the woman she calls "America's first radically experimental poet, and . . . the first woman poet whose poetic language and structures systematically register and resist the dominance of masculinity and rationality in culture" (43); and Sandra Gilbert, whose groundbreaking *Madwoman in the Attic,* with Susan Gubar ([1979] 1984), helped to shape subsequent thought on Dickinson.

Wilbur, Ostriker, Gilbert, and other practicing poets—most of them with more than two or three volumes of published work—talked about their practices in weaving poems into new volumes and offered educated guesses about Dickinson's. Charles Wright and Richard Wilbur were the only poets among the fifteen who said that chronology is the largest factor in their editorial arrangements of poems. Wilbur, for example, sounds much like Franklin about Dickinson:

> A collection of mine generally contains all the satisfactory poems which have been written since the last collection. Each poem of mine exhausts my present

sense of the subject, so that I don't write suites or clusters of poems on a single theme, and don't aim at unity. When the poems of a book of mine cohere, it is simply because I wrote them and have certain persistent concerns.[11]

Nevertheless, Wilbur, who elsewhere in his letter acknowledged that, for example, the openings of his collection are carefully considered, is somewhat guardedly open to the notion that Dickinson may have made use of more complex arrangements: "I think it quite possible that she, like Yeats or Stevens, was conscious of creating thematically clustered poems, and bound some of her related pieces together."

Unlike Wilbur, who makes the process sound almost effortless (his books seem to me to belie that), most respondents (see Appendix A) spoke of the labor and thought, almost the agony, they invest in putting poems in their places and voiced strong suspicions that Dickinson worked with similar intentionality. So many spoke of the process as happening "on the floor" that we turn with new interest (perhaps even amusement) to Dickinson's comments on her familiarity with the floor: "[T]he Dust behind I strove to join / Unto the Disk before— / But Sequence ravelled out of Sound / Like balls opon a Floor" (J992, Fr867). Dust balls bouncing around, frustrating order, suggest a metaphor for the difficulties of ordering the piles of poems. Elsewhere she says, "The Pile of years is not so high / As when you came before / But it is rising every Day / From recollection's Floor" (J1507, Fr1337). Such metaphoric "floors" in Dickinson's vocabulary are palpable to Betty Adcock, who says, "For me a book arrangement usually means sitting on the floor with all my new poems, spreading them out around me and grouping them. . . . This can take days, and no one can walk on that floor! I group and regroup, sometimes toward variety and sometimes toward relationships between poems." Linda Pastan offers the same picture, saying that when she has "fifty or sixty poems finished, I spread them around me and try to discover which deserve to be in a book and how these relate to each other." Alicia Ostriker speaks of the "horribly hard, confusing work of selecting and rejecting and then . . . *arranging*" poems. "The floor," she says, "gets covered with poems, grouped into various categories, regrouped, sequenced, exchanged with each other; the order shifts and re-shifts, the sections of the book form and change places." Annie Finch tells a similar story, saying that she works until her poems follow "each other with the kind of tension and inevitability I required." These poets and more remind of us of Dickinson:

> Low at my problem bending,
> Another problem comes—
> Larger than mine—Serener—
> Involving statelier sums.

> I check my busy pencil,
> My figures file away.
> Wherefore, my baffled fingers
> Thy perplexity? (J69, Fr75, F5)

These practicing poets speak of the balance of work and intuition, Wilbur saying that the process of arranging a book "is an intuitive process; some of my decisions are nothing I can explain," and Alicia Ostriker likens the work to that of a painter:

> You've seen a painter working at a canvas, stepping back to look at what's just been done in the upper right-hand corner, and going back to the painting to fiddle with something in the middle left . . . the process of creating a composition in which every part coheres is more complicated than the painter could *describe* to you—but that is what artistry is all about.

Sometimes, according to the poets, the process is beyond even what we might call "intuition." Sandra Gilbert wrote of a complete suspension of logic in relation to the birth of *Ghost Volcano*. She was working, she explained, on a different collection when in the wake of the shock of her husband's sudden death, "One night I actually dreamed a solution" to the problem of fitting one poem into the collection on which she was working. That poem, "Widow's Walk," became crucial to *Volcano,* the new book she would soon be completing.

For the most part, though, indescribable as the process seems to be to poets, they indicated the great care they invest in editing. Every single correspondent spoke of the importance of first and last poems in a sequence. Even Wilbur, whose earlier comments seemed to understate the difficulties, says, "I incline to feel that the first poem of one of my books should not stump the reader." Allowing the obvious response that *all* of Dickinson's poems "stump the reader" to some extent, we recall that the first of each sequence studied so far indicates the direction in which the remainder of the poems will go. Julie Fay, Sandra Gilbert, and Natasha Saje particularly emphasize the importance of entrances and exits from sequences in books. Do they write poems specifically for sequences? Excluding those who write intentional sequences almost as narratives (Charles Wright, for example, and Julie Fay in her first book), most poets say that they do not often write "to fill a gap."

Saje speaks of the "trajectory" of the poems within a collection, "a trajectory from fixity to play, disorder, openness . . . from constraint to possibility"; Linda Pastan speaks of the "shape of a book (its opening and closing, the way poems face each other on the page)." These, says Pastan, "are all important to me, [but] I never think about them while I am actually writing." The poets' attempts to describe their process and their products find varying metaphors, all of them helpful in describing the fascicles of Emily Dickinson. Debra Kang Dean speaks of the poems in a collection as "cluster[ing] together like iron filings"; John Solensten speaks of "multiple unitary devices" that cluster like "prism shards." Turning the figure, he speaks of them as akin to "musical structures—ragtime and jazz and the fugue with theme and voices and the dying away of voices." Almost all speak of the poems in "dialogue" with each other, a pattern that we have already seen, particularly in the two poems (Prose/Poetry; Still/De-stilled; and so forth) in Fascicle 21, with which this study began. The next chapter offers many more examples.

These practices and patterns are as old as Petrarch, who, says Neil Fraistat, "rearranged *Canzoniere* nine times." Fraistat points out that Petrarch "visualized *Canzoniere* as an elastic form: one allowing him to shape and reshape all of the shorter poems he wished to acknowledge publicly within an overarching if continually refocused vision" (1986, 6). Each essay in Fraistat's collection, as each of the letters poets wrote in response to my questions, tries a different metaphor, but all of them acknowledge an impulse toward shape.

Such is what I have attempted in the previous four chapters, using as a sort of test case the effect of a duplicate in each of the four fascicles (8 and 21, each with its own version of "The feet of people walking home," and 6 and 10, each with a rather radically revised "Safe in their Alabaster Chambers"). To round out the enticement for others to do their own readings, I offer one more chapter in which I show that from her first to last fascicle Dickinson's words *live* (as Higginson resisted telling her they did) in extraordinary contextural relationships. The Amy Lowell–type play has yielded discoveries that I don't think evolved from my own ear (as Franklin warns). The discoveries— these doublings, mirrorings, and other patterns of themes, images, syllables, and sounds *are,* in fact, Dickinson's—the only ones we have outside of the contexts she provides in letters. Dickinson may or may not have been conscious of all the contextuality of relationships within the fascicles any more than she might have been of the intertextuality observed in virtually every thematic study of her work. That is not to say such findings as those in the next chapter are not valid. She encouraged them in "A word is dead / When it is said, / Some say." Her answer to what "some say" is "I say it just / Begins to live / That day" (J1212, Fr278).

CHAPTER 6

Asking/Giving Uncommon Alms: From Fascicle 1 to 40

Fascicle 1 c. 1858

F	J	Fr	
1	18	21	The Gentian weaves her fringes—
2	6	24	Frequently the woods are pink—
3	19	25	A sepal, petal, and a thorn
4	20	26	Distrustful of the Gentian—
5	21	28	We lose—because we win—
6	22	29	All these my banners be.
7	23	23	I had a guinea golden
8	24	13	There is a morn by men unseen—
9	323	14	As if I asked a common alms—
10	25	15	She slept beneath a tree—
**11	7	16	The feet of people walking home
12	26	17	It's all I have to bring today—
13	27	18	Morns like these—we parted—
14	28	28	So has a Daisy vanished
15	29	29	If those I loved were lost
16	30	6	Adrift! A little boat adrift!
17	31	xx	Summer for thee, grant I may be
18	32	32	When Roses cease to bloom, Sir,
19	33	33	Oh if remembering were forgetting—
20	4	4	On this wondrous sea—sailing silently—
21	24	10	Garlands for Queens, may be—
22	35	35	Nobody knows this little Rose—

***"The feet of people walking home" is the poem, which is repeated, with subtle variations, in Fascicle 14. Although almost identical in words and form, the poem's two differing contexts (the two fascicle groupings) offer possibilities for revisions in interpretation; this is consistent with the contextual aesthetics discussed in chapter 2 in which "At last, to be identified" becomes part of a complex of poems related to powerful transformation, whereas in Fascicle 21 the same poem is part of a reflection on aesthetics—the nature of poetry and of the poet. Just so, as chapter 4 argues, two quite different versions of "Safe in their Alabaster Chambers" reflect the different contexts of Fascicle 6, full of play, children, and small animals and Fascicle 10, in which the world depicted is more often insidiously suggestive of existential emptiness.

Fascicle 14 c.1861–1862

F	J	Fr	
1	319	304	The maddest dream—recedes— / unrealized
2	277	305	What if I say I shall / not wait!
3	240	262	Ah, Moon—and Star!
4	278	306	A shady friend—for Torrid days—
5	271	307	A solemn thing—it was— / I said—
6	272	308	I breathed enough to take / the Trick—
7	238	309	Kill your Balm—and it's / Odors bless you—
8	239	310	"Heaven"—is what I cannot / reach!
**9	7	79	The feet of people walking home
10	582	414	Inconceivably solemn!
11	422	415	More Life—went out—when / He went
12	423	416	The Months have ends—the Years—a knot—
13	424	417	Removed from Accident of Loss
14	299	249	Your Riches—taught me—Poverty.
15	583	419	A Toad, can die of Light—
16	332	420	There are two Ripenings—
17	584	421	It ceased to hurt me, though / so slow
18	310	422	Give little Anguish,

(Missing? Poems unknown)

Of all the fascicles in this study, this is the most problematic because of the inclusion of the separate sheet of paper for "The feet of people walking home." Obviously, others may differ on this conclusion, but it seems to this reader to fit so well where Franklin has surmised that it belongs that it is further evidence of Dickinson's intentionality. As in each of the pairings, this setting suggests that the poem, more innocent and almost merry in its flower-filled context of Fascicle 1, may be reflective of the frustration of a speaker (or speakers) struggling with frustration and loss. The first and eighth poems of this fascicle may imply that one cause for the frustration is a failure to receive the kind of approbation for or at least recognition of the poetic power of the poems such as those the poet sent to Higginson.

Fascicle 3 c.1858–1859

F	J	Fr	
1	58	67	Delayed till she had ceased to know—
2	89	68	Some things that fly there be—
3	90	69	Within my reach!
4	91	70	So bashful when I spied her!
5	92	71	My friend must be a Bird—
6	93	72	Went up a year this evening!
7	94	73	Angels, in the early morning
8	95	74	My nosegays are for Captives—
9	96	75	Sexton! My Master's sleeping here.
10	97	76	The rainbow never tells me
11	98	77	One dignity delays for all—
12	88	78	As by the dead we love to sit,
13	99	79	New feet within my garden go—
**14	903	80	I hide myself within my flower
15	11	38	I never told the buried gold
16	49	39	I never lost as much but twice,
17	50	118	I hav'nt told my garden yet—
18	51	41	I often passed the village
19	12	32	The morns are meeker than they were—
20	52	33	Whether my bark went down at sea—
21	53	34	Taken from men—this morning—
22	13	35	Sleep is supposed to be
23	54	36	If I should die,
24	55	37	By Chivalries as tiny,

** Here again, hidden midway in the fascicle is the poem that will appear again in another fascicle, Fascicle 40. In both cases the editor (Emily Dickinson herself, of course as we have every reason to believe) placed the poem on the bottom of a sheet on the "west" side of the opened book. That is almost all that is similar about the two versions. Separated by six years, the two settings provide radically different interpretive possibilities. Here in Fascicle 3 the impression produced by the voice–largely because of the surrounding poems–is that of a speaker fiercely skeptical. In Fascicle 10 the same poem takes on a devotional tone, far from the mood of this earlier setting.

Fascicle 40 c.1864

F	J	Fr	
1	827	820	The Only News I know
2	961	821	Wert Thou but ill—that / I might show thee
3	962	822	Midsummer, was it, when / They died—
4	902	823	The first Day that / I was a Life
5	963	824	A nearness to Tremendousness—
6	964	825	"Unto Me"? I do not / know you—
7	965	826	Denial—is the only fact
8	966	827	All forgot for recollecting
**9	903	80	I hide myself—within / my flower.
10	904	828	Had I not this, or / This, I said,
11	905	829	Between My Country— / and the Others—
12	906	830	The Admirations—and Contempts—of time—
13	907	831	Till Death—is narrow / Loving—
14	908	832	'Tis Sunrise—Little Maid— / Hast thou
15	967	833	Pain—expands the Time—
16	968	834	Fitter to see Him, I / may be
17	969	835	He who in Himself believes—
18	970	836	Color—Caste—Denomination—
19	909	837	I make His Crescent fill / or lack—
20	971	838	Robbed by Death—but that was easy—
21	972	839	Unfulfilled to Observation—

** Hidden also in Fascicle 40, the little poem which had appeared midway in Fascicle 3, takes on a different tone. In this fascicle, the speaker looks with "compound vision," backward and forward on moments of reverse and advance, claiming the power over her material ("I make his Crescent fill or lack"), even as she moves beyond her own "Color—Caste—Denomination," beyond "locality." In this last fascicle there is a stillness, even in what may well be an elegy for the war dead (these poems were compiled in 1864), "Midsummer was it, when / They died—." Whether or not Dickinson intended this to be her final edition, it ends with "a Revolution / In Locality—" and a "Night" that may be better than the "Suns." While the reader wishes for more and while the writer wrote over 100 other powerful poems after those she gathered for this collection, these poems seem to provide a "perfect" ending (a word repeated three times, more frequently than in any other fascicle), almost a benediction.

Having delved rather deeply into four fascicles, two pairs, in that each contains another version of a repeated poem, this chapter glides more quickly through four other fascicles, two other pairs, to show that jolts of astonishment such as those noted are found everywhere. The canny editor (Dickinson) seemed to delight in such surprises from the very first fascicle, collected in 1858 to the very last, some six years later.

Fascicle 1 begins—and ends—with a mock funeral and a benediction in which bee, butterfly, and breeze substitute for the orthodox trinity. Throughout the remaining poems in the twenty-two-poem sequence, other trios act as shadows of that playful threesome. The fascicle bustles, suggests a lark, a romp. Everything is in motion. The earth turns on its axis ("Frequently the woods are pink—" [J6, Fr24]); the stars swing ("There is a morn by men unseen—" [J24, Fr13]); the linnet flies free ("Morns like these—we parted" [J27, Fr18]); and the dead "dance," "game," and "gambol" on a mystic green (also "There is a morn").

All of this happens in a woodsy garden, beginning with the autumn of the gentian and moving to the summer of the rose. There are nooks for daisies, some columbine, orchis, crocus, and anemone sprinkled throughout as the persona poses as gardener, her "little spade" ("All these my banners be—" [J22, Fr29]) in hand. Indeed, in the sixth poem of the series the speaker "sows" (sews) her pageantry. Morning is privileged over night in this garden; at least four poems of the poet, who later claims "the dark" that she "adores," focus on the coming morning.[1] This garden is out of reach of the Burglar and the cheater ("All these" [J22, Fr29]). It is a space to re/collect ("*Oh* if remembering were forgetting" [J33, Fr9]) what the "teller" doles out. Each image, each word used in this impressionistic introduction to the fascicle project exists in its own relationship, figurative and literal, within its poem. Like the flower image itself, Dickinson's little force explodes, blossoms, and multiplies, each part seeding new images in its fascicle setting.

As she does three years later in Fascicle 14, in which she repeats the poem in a radically different context, Dickinson centers the fascicle with "The feet of people walking home" (J7, Fr16). Isolated from its setting in these two fascicles, "The feet" has invited a discussion that reveals the value of reading poems in their places. Ted-Larry Pebworth and Jay Claude Summers in a 1969 *Explicator* call the poem "an unusual example of orthodox Christianity" (item 76). Just so, Jane Eberwein notes the "happy mood" even as Dickinson confronted issues of immortality (1985, 232). However, Greg Johnson has a darker view, finding in it an "overt expression of a death wish" (1985, 145), and Cynthia Wolff finds "bitter irony" (1986, 148). By comparing the settings for the poem in the two fascicles (1 and 14), the reader sees the validity of each reading—but each is more relevant to the context of one or another of the two fascicle settings.

The first fascicle first: These poems gather a jaunty momentum by the repetition of tripartite construction in the two poems that follow the initial benediction. The visual flourish of "Frequently the woods are pink—" (J6, Fr24), the fascicle's second poem, apparent only to the fascicle reader, underscores that tripartness. Note the way the "f's" of its first three lines wave like flags down the poem. Below those three flying "f's" are two sets of threes in the third poem: the "Sepal," "petal," and "thorn"; the "flask of Dew— / a Bee or two— / A breeze a caper in the trees." And across from the waving "f's" of the second poem, in the fourth, also a flower poem, "Distrustful of the Gentian" (J20, Fr26), is another evidence of Dickinson's delight in editing. In this case the ear picks up the echo of the visual "f's": the "*f*luttering of her [the gentian's] *f*ringes," along with the "per*f*idy," and the *ph*antom meadows."

Four poems into the fascicle, the gentian of the first poem has evoked doubt, and the tone of the fascicle modulates. These are not simple flower poems; many, among them Margaret Homans (1980), have discussed the seriousness of Dickinson's play with flowers, her reversals of "ordinary meaning" in the feminine symbolism and the power of the small. Dickinson begins her fascicle productions, grounding her work in beds of flowers and calling attention to them throughout the book through such appeals to eye and ear.

United by such imagery, the first fascicle is far from uniform or univocal, moving from the brisk playfulness of its beginnings to explorations of the economy of loss. Throughout it is full of surprises for the attentive reader. The fourth poem ("Distrustful" [J20, Fr26]) ends with a hand reaching toward a distant heaven, for example, and is followed on the page by a poem that, when it is noticed, is usually wrenched apart from it: "We lose—because we win—" (J21, Fr28), in which the hand becomes that of a gambler who tosses the dice again. Turning the page, one finds a longer meditation on loss and gain in "All these my banners be" (J22, Fr29), and so forth.

If the fascicle's seventh poem, "I had a guinea golden—" (J23, Fr12), enacts a drama of loss of inspiration, the eighth, "There is a morn by men unseen—" (J24, Fr13), declares that the poet, as Joanne Feit Diehl puts it, is finding "the ground of poetry" in "an alternative territory" (1983, 159). Situated on the leaf before the central poem, which is repeated in another fascicle ("The feet of people walking home" [J7, Fr16]), this eighth poem anticipates it: Alike in structure (each is twenty-four lines with six of those lines spilling into the next page), each is a resurrection poem, the celebratory dancing feet of "There is a morn" yielding to "the feet of people walking home." Each suggests a Heaven reminiscent of the Swiss Alps (Sue was in Geneva in 1858, don't forget—albeit the one in New York—at about the time these poems may have been gathered).

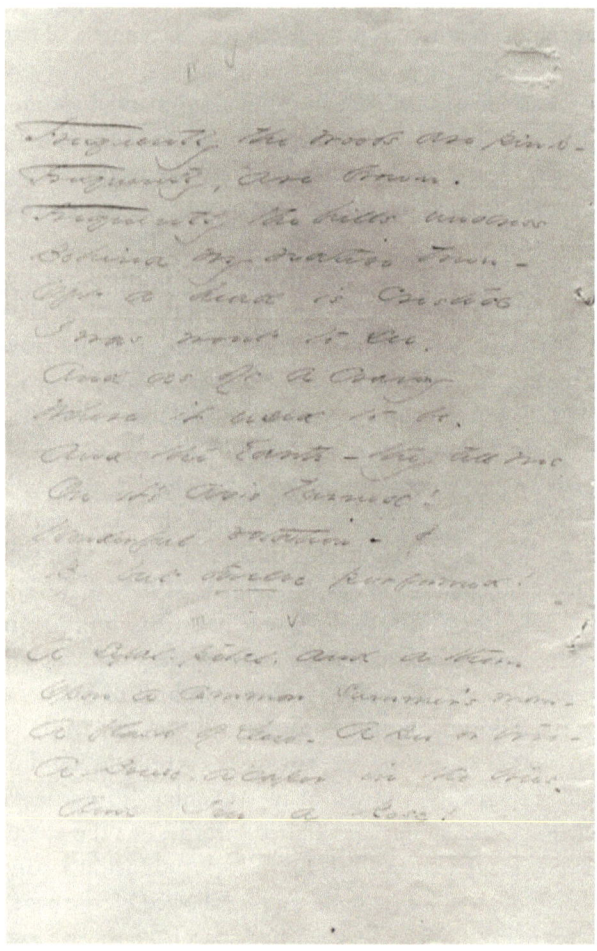

"Frequently the woods are pink" (J6, Fr24). Source: Archives and Special Collections, Robert Frost Library, Amherst College.

Between the two longer and similar poems is the quick thrust of the ambiguously worded "As if I asked a common alms" (J323, Fr14). Syntactically two fragments of sentences, "As if I asked a common alms . . . / As if I asked the Orient," initially puzzles, even frustrates the reader. On its own this shorter poem seems an enclosure of that mysterious empty space, the gap, which interests those who find in Dickinson an existential soulmate.[2] The unnamed something the speaker asks for is not kingdoms, not the Orient, not a Morn, though it is akin to each. One clue to the identity of those alms is another context Dickinson provided: She included "As if I asked" four years after the approximated date of this gathering in a letter to Higginson, where it follows, without a break, this introduction: "The 'hand

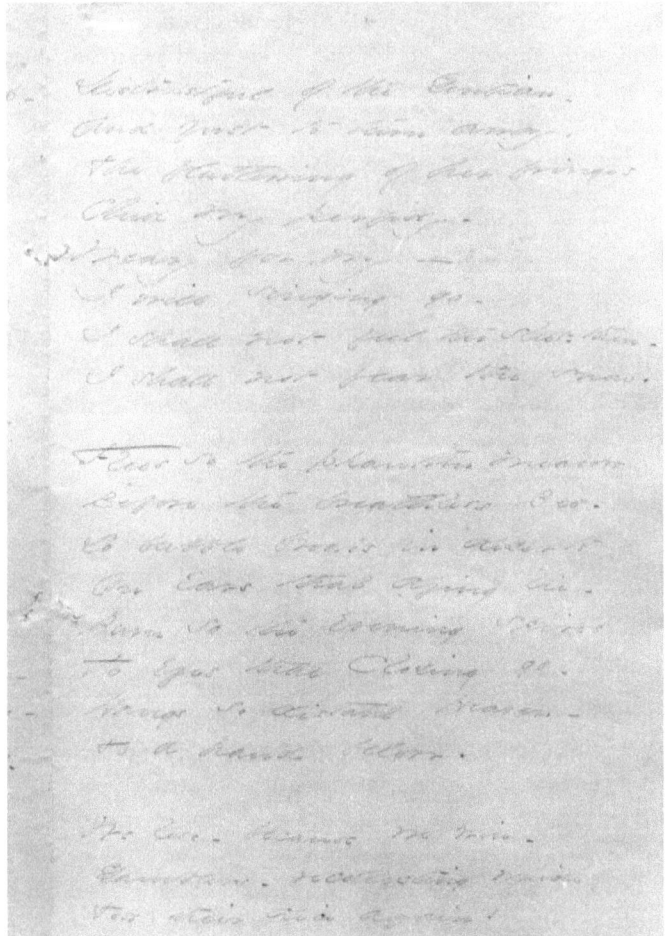

you stretch me in the Dark,' I put mine in, and turn away—I have no Saxon now" (L265). Significantly, this is the letter in which Dickinson asks Higginson to be her "preceptor," a linkage that suggests that the wished-for "common Alms" relates to recognition of her poetic gifts and skills.[3]

Such a reading reifies Dickinson's placing the "common Alms" in this fascicle," and the intertextuality between contexts reifies the studies of scholars, such as Martha Nell Smith, who correctly insist on reading between various venues. This is a fascicle, remember, in which flowers and gardens are metonymies for poems and poet. When she wrote the same poem to Higginson, in which it appears in an almost identical form, the "a's" of its first words drift down the page on the right to remind us subliminally of that "alms" on the right, whether those alms are the grace to write or the grace of a kindly reading.

The context supplied by the letter to Higginson fits the context in this fascicle. This little common meter bridge ("As if I asked") between longer poems follows logically and directly the preceding poem ("There is a morn" [J24, Fr13]), which ends with almost the same words: "And flood me with the Dawn!" The twice-expressed yearning for some kind of rebirth is repeated in the even tinier poem nestled at the bottom of the page: "She slept beneath a tree" (J25, Fr15), the tenth in the series. Rarely discussed, except as "simple,"[4] it takes on greater complexity and interest when read in its fascicle setting. The speaker's "foot," recognized by the not-born flower, merges into "The feet of people walking home," the poem that centers this fascicle and that is repeated in Fascicle 14. In more ways than I can detail here,[5] the central, repeated poem picks up or anticipates every other poem in the fascicle. One can almost imagine the poet sifting through patterns as a quilter does for designs that are neither linear nor pictorial but pleasurable and suggestive.

Answering the plea for alms in the fascicle's ninth poem, for example, the speaker of the twelfth offers alms, saying, "It's all I have to bring today—" (J26, Fr17). The alms, the gift, the grace may be in the form of a literal flower (one imagines another context: a note with a gift) but more probably in the form of a poem, maybe even a book of poetry. This gift "could tell," says the speaker, who accompanies it with her "heart, and all the Bees / Which in the Clover dwell," taking us back to the fascicle's opening.

Between this twelfth poem with its three-part gift and the end of the fascicle, in which the flowers and the tripartite construction return, the editor inserts a series of meditations on silence—or death, particularly that on the sea. They seem an interruption—and are—until we consider that the little ship in the sixteenth poem, "Adrift! A little boat adrift!" (J30, Fr6) "shot—exultant on" and that the twentieth, "On this wondrous sea—sailing silently" (J4, Fr3) is the one that precedes Dickinson's instructions to Sue, "Write! Comrade, Write!" in the letter sent to Geneva. The ship sails into eternity, and the poet, as the fascicle ends, offers a rose to the reader rather than "Garlands for Queens" (J34, Fr10). The rose, symbol of "Chivalry, Chastity, and Equity" (that tripartite construction again) is the stuff of which the attar comes, attar that in "This was a Poet" (J448, Fr446 F21) is distilled; in other words it is poetry. Another rose poem shares that last page of the first fascicle. If one opens the fascicle and looks at its cover pages, the last poem (now on the left) leads to the first (now on the right of the opened book), suggesting the cycles, rebirth, a kind of eternal use, adding (the Bird/poet) to the characters of the initial blessing (Bee, Butterfly, Breeze):

> Nobody knows this little Rose—
> It might a pilgrim be
> Did I not take it from the ways

And lift it up to thee.
Only a Bee will miss it—
Only a Butterfly,
Hastening from far journey—
On it's breast to lie—
Only a Bird will wonder—
Only a Breeze will sigh—
Ah little Rose—how easy
For such as thee to die! (J35, Fr1)

It might be easy for the rose to die, except that it is lifted up to us, readers who continue to discover its multifoliate suggestions as we read the fascicles, of which this is the first.

The "Feet of People" and Issues of Power and Print

By the time Dickinson copied that central poem of Fascicle 1, "The feet of people walking home" (J7, Fr16), into a similarly central position in what we now call Fascicle 14, her world had changed. Compiled against the backdrop of the opening of a war, the feet have changed from those strolling through a garden to those gathered in troops or on graveyards. In this period, too, she initiated "the most important correspondence" of her life, that with Higginson (*Letters,* 388). The poems selected for this book provide a striking contrast to those in Fascicle 1, and the repeated poem demonstrates the value of reading contextually.

If the first fascicle announced an effort to give shape to an already clearly articulated ambition "to be distinguished," Fascicle 14 interrogates the problematical extension of that ambition. Blessings in bees and breezes and gifts of flowers and poems give Fascicle 1 a kind of gentleness. This almost totally different setting (Fascicle 14) for an almost identical poem ("The feet" [J7, Fr16]) is most of all different in the attitude it reflects toward "Power." Power desired, thwarted, robbed, and won is an overt concern in four of the sixteen existing poems and seems a hypogrammatic shadow in virtually every one of its poems. By this time Dickinson, who lied to Higginson ("I made no verse—but one or two—until this winter—Sir—" [L261]), had become a poet aware of "authority and potency," as Gary Stonum points out (1990, 128). By this time Dickinson had, in fact, self-published at least fourteen books (these fascicles), selecting from at least three hundred poems to do so.

How much—if at all—were the poems in this fascicle and the letters to Higginson an appeal for the kind of attention that might lead to publication? Martha Nell Smith argues persuasively—and many scholars agree with her on this—that Dickinson eschewed the marketplace and that the fascicles are evidence of a strategy to subvert and triumph over the tyranny of "print." This fascicle suggests that Dickinson was rather inconsistent on the subject. The poems of Fascicle 14 might be as one stage in an ongoing dialogue the poet conducted with herself. On the one hand, she claimed in that letter to Higginson to be a neophyte; on the other hand, she indicated that she was already considered at least a member of the local literati:

> Two Editors of Journals came to my Father's House, this winter—and asked me for my Mind—and when I asked them 'Why,' they said I was penurious—and they, would use it for the World—
> I could not weigh myself—Myself—. (L261)

This is her second (known) letter to Higginson, written after he apparently responded with faint praise to the poems she enclosed in that first famously timorous letter ("Are you too deeply occupied . . ." [L260]). She responds to his apparently tepid assessment ("Thank you for the surgery") and answers in playful hyperbole his apparent questions (about her companions, her reading, specifically, Whitman) and ends with praising his work and appealing to his judgment again. This was ten days after her first letter to him. Two months after that first flurry of correspondence she answered both his praise ("Your letter gave no Drunkenness, because I tasted Rum before—") and his criticism ("You think my gait 'spasmodic' . . . You think me 'uncontrolled'") and makes her most famous statement about publishing:

> I smile when you suggest that I delay 'to publish'—that being foreign to my thought, as Firmament to Fin—
> If fame belonged to me, I could not escape her—if she did not, the longest day would pass me on the chase—and the approbation of my Dog, would forsake me—then—My Barefoot-Rank is better—. (L 265)

Coupled with the evidence of her overture to Higginson and her continuing correspondence with him, Fascicle 14 suggests frustrated ambition.

Listen to the echo (or anticipation?) of the letter to Higginson in Fascicle 14's first poem (J319, Fr304): There's a chase, a barefoot boy, and something (fame? publication? approbation?) that tantalizes and slips away:

> The maddest dream—recedes—
> unrealized—
> The Heaven we Chase—
> Like the June Bee—before
> the Schoolboy—
> Invites the Race—

Stoops to an Easy Clover—
Dips—Evades—
Teazes—Deploys

and so forth.

The Bee that promises but does not provide "steadfast Honey" is far from the one invoked as blessing in the first fascicle's first poem. Just so, the second poem, "What if I say I shall / not wait!" (J277, Fr305), reflects impatience, if not frustration. In an *Explicator* article I more fully explore the almost suicidal desperation of this Hamlet-echo. There is none of that in Fascicle 1, just as there is no flower imagery (other than that crocus in the repeated poem and a jessamine/jasmine in another) in Fascicle 14, most of it straining against the conventional belief in "lips of Hallelujah / [which] Long years of practice bore."

However, into this fascicle (Fascicle 14), so radically different in tone, Dickinson appears to have placed in a similarly central position "The feet of people." Admittedly, knowing with certainty its position is complicated by the two problems confronting Franklin in its restoration: The first is that the fascicle's final poems may be missing; the second, that rather than being written—as almost all of the other poems were—on previously folded sheets, sharing the space there with other poems, "The feet of people" seems to have been inserted after it was sent to someone or to have been removed and then replaced (see Franklin's explanation in the *Manuscript Books* (1981) and in *PBSA* (1979, 353–54). Dickinson's use of the poem again shows that she could think of it in a new way, privileging it for different reasons each time. This is what other readers do, of course. Thus we read, on the one hand, David Porter's take on "The feet of people walking home" (aligned more or less with those of Pebworth and Summers and Jane Eberwein) as "a simple affirmation of a private faith in immortality" (1961, 145), and, on the other, Cynthia Griffin Wolff's as "bitter irony" (1986, 148). Reading the poem in its two settings, as neither Porter nor Wolff did, reifies even polar readings such as the one by Porter, fitting well the way the poem works in Fascicle 1, the one by Wolff, appropriate to the context in Fascicle 14.

Although we may not know for sure *why* or even *whether* Dickinson placed this once-used (folded in two places) single sheet between the more customary folded and piled stationery pages, we can *see* evidence of clever self-publication. As in the poems "They shut me up in Prose" and "This was a poet," there are poems answering others in Fascicle 14. "What if I say I shall / not wait" (J277, Fr305), for example, faces "Ah Moon—and Star / You are very far" (J240, Fr262), a poem that ends by declaring sadly, "I cannot go!" On the next two pages are two poems that appear to be about women (those who are too limited by feminine contingencies, perhaps, to leap the moon), about friendships, and again, about disappointment: "A Shady friend—for Torrid days—" (J278, Fr306), on the left, and, facing the "Shady friend" and syntactically reflecting it, "A solemn thing—it was / I said— /A Woman—white—to be—" (J271, Fr307).

"Solemn": Of the twenty-four times Dickinson uses the word (in nearly eighteen hundred poems), four of them are in this fascicle. Fascicle 1 was *not* "solemn": The bees did not cruelly tease, nor did dreams. The moon was almost reachable. The speakers of the first fascicle's poems pose as coy, flirtatious, and playful, even as they speak seriously of gains earned from loss. In Fascicle 14, however, the speakers strive—often for death itself—in a landscape of pain. War rumbles in the background. A teasing God/universe is up to conjuring trickiness. That is a solemn thing in itself, but the first overt use of the word in this fascicle is the declaration in the fifth poem in the sequence that it is a "solemn" thing to be a "Woman—white," to be what the "Sages call . . . small": in other words, perhaps, to be the poet constructing the work, the poet who answers those sages by swelling at her sense of the power of the so-called "small." Although in the early, faulty, 1896 edition Higginson and Todd, who amputated the strong last two stanzas of the poem, titled the remaining stanzas "Wedded," white was not necessarily bridal in the nineteenth century, but it *was* the costume of the woman poet ("The Wayward Nun" in Juhasz [1983a, 32]), in this case one who dared to take on the majority opinion that would label her "small."

In the same fascicle all of the panoply of war—Parades . . . Pomp . . . A pleading Pageantry . . . Flags . . . Music . . . [and] Drums too near—is "Inconceivably solemn!" (J582, Fr414), the tenth in the series. There is "solemn News," too, in the eleventh poem, "More Life—went out—when / He went" (J422, Fr415), the story of the death of someone uncommonly fine. Between the two poems that begin with the overt use of "solemn" are four that in import are just that. Below the end of the fascicle's fifth poem's assertion that the poet is strong enough to "sneer" at those who do not see the force in the "small," the fascicle's editor writes "I breathed enough to take / the trick" (J272, Fr308). How can one live when one is nearly smothered? One "simulate's" a life. Something has been so nearly lethal to the speaker of this poem (faint praise, perhaps, or—not forgetting the larger world—war drums in the distance) that the only strategy is to "descend / Among the Cunning Cells / and touch the Pantomime / Himself / [and feel] How numb ("cool" is the variant) the Bellows feels!"

The implied gasping violence of this common metered poem continues in the poem that faces it: In one the poet "sneers" back at those who diminish the force of her "small"ness. Then, in the next she "simulates" a life "among the cunning Cells": "Kill your Balm—and it's / Odors bless you—" (J238, Fr309, the sixth poem). The aggressive thrust of the phrases that follow:

"Bare your Jessamine to the storm . . . Stab the bird" taunts the reader or God or the system of the universe. Keller is right in speaking of "the wolf in all of Dickinson's sweetness": "The poet is assertive. Poetry is daring. Audacity is an aesthetic. . . . There are rewards to the risk" (1979, 292). Keller's words are more descriptive, however, of the poet or her speaker(s) in Fascicle 14 than the one we met in Fascicle 1.

It is by now a truism that the flower (balm and Jessamine—Dickinson grew jasmine in her hothouse) and the bird are metaphors for the poet. The "maddest perfume" that lingers both echoes the fascicle's first poem and, because it is so much like that first one, leads to the next poem, the fascicle's eighth, in which " 'Heaven'—is what I cannot / reach!" (J239, Fr310). Heaven hides "Behind the Hill." Although the speaker says that "Paradise—is found" there, she follows it with the discouraging news that "Her teazing Purples" are "decoys" for the "credulous." Certainly the notion of a conniving, frustrating, tricksterish universe or deity is not orthodox Protestantism. Following poems that suggest such heterodoxy, "The feet of people walking home" (J7, Fr16), lineated—but, significantly, not punctuated—exactly as it was in Fascicle 1, seems puzzling. Although its imagery was indeed a focus for much of the first fascicle, "The feet of people" also contains images that echo poems in this fourteenth book so opposite in tone. First, because of the apparent bitterness of the surrounding poems, one guesses that here the feet of people walking home may be battle-weary feet; they may be those dead honored by the "Inconceivably Solemn" parade of the poem that follows, or they may be the Hamlet-like figure of the second poem meditating on "fil[ing] this mortal— / off." And the needed patience—the "Long years of practice"—will be the point of "There are two Ripenings" (J332, Fr420), the fascicle's sixteenth poem. There's more: The pearl imagery, for example, anticipates the fascicle's thirteenth poem, "Removed from Accident of Loss" (J424, Fr417), in which "the Brown Malay" is "unconscious" that of "Pearls in Easter Waters / Marked His." The line, one that seems almost spit out by the frustrated speaker, "Larceny [is] legacy," stings as do those poems that prepare the way for it; if we inherit a kingdom, this fascicle implies, we do so in a system that is not wholly honest, open, or fair.

Contextual pressures also shape a new take on the poem's final stanza. In Fascicle 1 the village, the angels, the abbey, and the triumphant last line, "Such resurrection pours," were linked with other poems. Here the serial images of blankness, distance, and darkness suggest reasons for Dickinson's situating the poem in this new setting. The figures that "fail to tell me" and the classics that "vail their faces," not to mention the punning verb in "How far the village lies," convey the skepticism of the very last image of the extant fascicle: the soundless, expressionless stoic vision of "Death— / who only shows his Granite face / Sublimer thing [way] than speech" (J310, Fr422). Just so, the repeated poem's key line, "My faith that Dark adores," sets up the startling opening of one of this fascicle's oddest poems: "A Toad, can die of Light" (J583, Fr419), the fifteenth in the series. That strange ode to death as "the Common Right / Of toads and Men" fits this fascicle as it would not fit, say, Fascicle 1 or Fascicle 40.

It is as dangerous to ascribe biographical motives to one of the fascicles as to any of the poems; nevertheless, the despair of so many of these poems and the focus on death, certainly more than in Fascicle 1, might reflect several kinds of pain associated with the date Franklin assigns to this fascicle (about 1862). Not only is this the year she began her tentative association with Higginson, whose responses must not have elated the hopeful poet, but it is also the year she wrote the sad letters to her cousins and to Samuel Bowles recounting the death of "brave Frazer—'killed at Newbern' . . . by a 'minnie ball.'" (L255, L256).

Fascicle 14, chosen for this study because its centered poem provides a test case for the way context affects interpretation, it having been centered also in Fascicle 1, ends mysteriously. Franklin explains that it may be missing a leaf, one part of the folded paper having been ripped away. I am tempted to think, however, that the poem that is the last surviving one in the fascicle, is Dickinson's own way of ending this meditation on disappointment and death. She had followed her toad poem with "There are two Ripenings—" (J332, Fr420), a fairly long poem in which the speaker seems to be exhorting herself to patience, and, facing that, a poem that seems to reflect sheer weariness, "It ceased to hurt me, though / so slow" (J584, Fr421). The ambiguous "it" and the equally ambiguous "something" that "had obscured the track" (one thinks of those "feet of people walking home") to something like resurrection have taken their toll. "The Grief—that nestled close / As needles—ladies softly press / To Cushions Cheeks— / To keep their place—" has almost been assuaged. And "almost" is the operative word. The speaker cannot explain the learned consolation, the movement from the frantic tone of the fascicle's first poem, only its effect:

> Nor what consoled it, I could
> Trace—
> Except whereas 'twas Wilderness—
> It's better—almost Peace—

Below these four lines is a Hamlet-like ending ("the rest is silence"):

> Give little anguish
> Lives will fret—
> Give Avalanches,
> And they'll slant.

Straighten—look cautious for
Their breath—
But make no syllable, like
Death—
Who only shows his Granite face
Sublimer thing [way]—than Speech—. (J310, Fr422)

Without noting the fascicle context for this poem (her book appeared the same year the *Manuscript Books* were published), Joanne Feit Diehl speaks of Dickinson's "stoicism of silence, the relinquishment of her art" that follows "overwhelming experience": Diehl also speaks of the "awe" in this the fascicle's last poem, saying that "the result and reaction to Dickinson's private loss becomes a precondition for her fragmentary form of art" (1981, 24). Reading Dickinson in her fascicles expands that assessment. Emily Dickinson could not know in 1862 "if fame belonged to [her]," as she told Higginson. That was not in her power to arrange or to know, but what was in her power was to shape her growing body of work, the speech hurled in the "Granite face" of death that was all around her. For some two years, perhaps with some form of publication in mind, she had chosen these books as one way to shape that speech. Whether consciously or serendipitously, she provided each little book with its own design. Each design, in turn, shapes the effect of its components so that, for example, "The feet of people walking home" has a darker, sharper effect in this wartime fascicle than it had four years earlier in the flowery first.

That difference is signified by the difference in punctuation, something that is observable only in the manuscripts. The two versions of "The feet" appear to be almost identical; they even break at the same line, spilling on to the next in both cases with "Whose peasants are the angels." In fact, when one holds the two side by side, the second seems almost a carbon copy of the first. The one change, however, shows the power of what Paul Crumbley—who believes the fascicles to be "finished works" (1996, 11)—calls "inflections of the pen." Crumbley takes the title of his intriguing study of the Dickinson dash from Dickinson's L470: "[A] Pen has so many inflections and a Voice but one." Although Crumbley does not discuss specifically either the use of the end mark (the period) or this particular poem, the example of the different versions of the same poem in Fascicles 1 and 14 reifies Crumbley's call for "readers to take seriously the uniquely Dickinsonian grammar, orthography, and punctuation" (ibid., 28). I would add to Crumbley's advice that readers need to take seriously as well the different uses to which she puts those details in two versions of the same passage. When it appears midway in Fascicle 1, "The Feet of People" is punctuated at the end with an exclamation point; in Fascicle 14, the exuberance implied by such a mark is not just muted; it seems stamped out by the round, large, final period. By such small marks she "hid herself" in Fascicles 3 and 40, both of which focus on—and reveal—the "Granite face" of Death.

"I Hide Myself" in Fascicles 3 and 40

When Dickinson selected "The Only News I know / Is Bulletins all Day / From Immortality" (J827, Fr820) as the opening of what appears to be her last fascicle, she alluded to both the timeliness and the timelessness of her poems and announced the general concern of both fascicles in which she "hid herself." The news that was not news was that of death. That Dickinson constantly tweaked the meaning and margin of death, of course, is no news, but in Fascicles 3 and 40 she explores the subject in such radically different settings that they form an appropriate conclusion to this study of the way context shapes meaning.

Readers of this book know well the numbers of young and old family members and friends whom Dickinson had lost by 1858, when she compiled Fascicle 3. By 1864, when she compiled Fascicle 40, she also had, of course, as a constant reader of her father's journals and a member of Amherst's first family, become familiar with national carnage. Yet Fascicle 3's vignettes of the grieving watcher at bedsides reveals a Dickinson closer to that described by Cynthia Griffin Wolff: "[P]erhaps this God of absolute cold has concocted a cosmos that functions primarily as an experiment in human anguish" (1986, 321); Fascicle 40, on the other hand, in which Dickinson placed a poem almost identical to one in Fascicle 3, places her closer to the mystical Dickinson of Inder Nath Kher: "In the midsummer of mind," he says, "death is like 'The Summer closed upon itself / in Consummated Bloom'" (1974, 209).

Two years before Dorothy Oberhaus published her extensive study of Fascicle 40, I had engaged in a similar study. Frankly, I was amazed at the orthodox devotion reflected in this fascicle, so that I was not surprised at part of the Oberhaus theory. Although it may be a stretch to see all of the forty fascicles as forming "a single œuvre," in which Fascicle 40 is the climax of a "conversion narrative" (1995, 87), as Oberhaus does, her conclusions that this fascicle is "a meditation" (ibid., 9) is inescapable. So thoroughly and elaborately has Oberhaus analyzed the fascicle we believe to be the final one (the proviso inherent in this sentence might be one challenge to complete acceptance of Oberhaus's theory) that this discussion focuses primarily on the different voice I hear in Fascicle 3, which contains a duplicate poem.

Both fascicles 3 and 40, separated by six years, almost hide the repeated poem in an identical position on the bottom of a sheet on the west side of the booklet. Unassuming as it seems in isolation, however, the little "I hide myself" in this context seems a coded assertion of poetic identity, or rather, identities. As with "The feet of people" in Fascicles 1 and 14, this poem becomes a different artifact within its altered setting. In Fascicle 3 the impression produced by the voices is fiercely skeptical, the stance existentialist; in Fascicle 40, as Oberhaus shows so thoroughly, the voice is so meditative that Oberhaus claims the speaker to be Christ. Fascicle 3 conveys impatience; Fascicle 40, a serene anticipation of the end of finite time.

Speaking usually from the point of view of a small observer to death's puzzling manifestations, poems in Fascicle 3 speak of "Mystery," "riddle," and "enigma," each a synonym for the state that is beyond telling. Built into that structure are at least two of Dickinson's most idiosyncratic and potentially heterodox statements on death: "Some things there fly that be—" (J89, Fr68), the second in the fascicle, and "Sleep is supposed to be" (J13, Fr35), the third from the end (note the near symmetry). The loose narrative seems to reach a crisis in the sixteenth poem, the angriest poem in the fascicle, in which the bereaved mourner rails at her "Burglar! Banker—Father!" This "loose narrative" should not be confused with the kind of plotted narrative Shurr tells—or even with the kind of religious devotional Oberhaus finds; it is closer to a train of linked vignettes. Each succeeding poem picks up and turns to a new light an angle or image from the previous poem. Poem leads on to poem through associative clusters of words and images.

Fascicle 3 poses a barrage of questions about death. Is it ceasing to know? Is it knowledge that cannot be put down? Is it the view of the eye of the humble tourist? Is it captivity or victory? Flight or rest? The hidden or the revealed? Each poem poses a new question. Equally the fascicle queries the hortatory act: the tension between the telling and the keeping of silence. In seven of the poems this is a specific refrain, and it is implied in the other poems as well. Both concerns emerge in the first poem, "Delayed till she had ceased to know" (J58, Fr67).

Although Higginson later selected this three-verse, common, particular poem as one of the fifteen he chose for his *Christian Century* article and although several have posited interpretations of this poem,[6] most readers are baffled by the characteristic gaps and inconsistencies of "Delayed." For one thing, the gender of the subject is slippery; three times the one who has "ceased to know" is female, but by the end that subject (masculinized, then neutered) is "a king / Doubtful if it be crowned." For another, there's that missing direct object: "[T]o know" *what?* asks the reader. "It would be" *what,* and *what* is the "it" in the second stanza? Why the heavy beat of iterated Delayed/Delay/lay in the first stanza and the conditional mode of the "Had not" and "if there may be" of the next two stanzas? So much is missing in this poem that the reader thinks again of the Riffaterrean hypogram, that shadow inherent in but unstated and hovering just outside the formal elements of the poem. Cristanne Miller's study of Emily Dickinson's grammar, particularly of Dickinson's "nonrecoverable deletions" that "allow a freedom of association and narrative movement" (1987, 30) is helpful, but perhaps the most helpful way to approach the riddles is to replace this poem in its fascicle context, where the jarring tone of "Delayed" continues in the second poem's riddle.

In "Delayed," the speaker hovers around the friend who has "ceased to know," attributing her own doubt to her subject, but she herself delays until the poem's last line—the overt statement of doubt. She could not "have guessed" what lies beyond. The unfulfilled yearning "to know," the inability to "guess," and the assertion that the subject is "Doubtful" yield to a similarly unorthodox ending of the fascicle's second poem, "Some things that fly there be—" (J89, Fr68). An elegantly structured poem—its three three-lined trimeter lines subliminally emphasize the trinities that are offered as "things that fly" ("Birds—Hours—the Bumblebee") and "things that stay" ("Grief—Hills—Eternity")—the poem moves along in easy triplets until the last stanza. Leaving out the "Some things," the speaker again uses threes but this time bases the trinity on alliterative sound: "*r*esting," "*r*ise," and, the scariest, "*R*iddle."

When the speaker asks the answer to the oxymoronic question of resurrection—how the "resting" can "rise"—she also asks an epistemological question, "Can I expound the skies?" Can she, to use her dictionary, "explain, lay open to meaning, clear of obscurity, interpret" the heaven she has been handed? If she knew, as she probably did, Emerson's "Brahma's" advice to "Find me, and turn thy back on heaven," she must have found congenial the exhortation to resist the handed-down assumptions about an afterlife involving spiritual polarizations such as heaven and hell. Just as she knew that "Parting is all we know of heaven / And all we need of hell" (J1732, Fr1773), she knew that Paradise is also here on earth; separation from this earth produced a grief she could not answer away by expounding the skies, at least not in *this*, the third fascicle.

Not one but two puns punctuate this second poem of Fascicle 3: "How still the Riddle lies!" That on "lies" has been noted (see, for example, Porter 1961, 80); less discussed—and never in relation to this fascicle, I believe—is the play on "still." Does she mean "how quiet" or "how long unanswered" the Riddle "rests in our minds" or "conveys untruths"? That we cannot know answers to the most central question of human existence and that it is always just a hand's reach away seem the purport of the third poem, nestled just below the riddle. Similar to those impatient poems of Fascicle 14, "Within my reach!" (J90, Fr69) conveys a kind of agonized frustration.

The fourth and fifth poems of the fascicle face the second and third; both echo and anticipate the concerns of other poems in the fascicle. The violet of the fourth ("So bashful when I spied her!" [J91, Fr70]) is wrenched like

Emerson's "Rhodora" from its secret place. When, later in the fascicle, the speaker says she "hides herself within her flower," she repeats the keyword, "hide," and she iterates the not telling ("I shall never tell") of the first and second poems. The wrenched violet merges into a mortal bird with a barbed tongue ("My friend must be a Bird—" (J92, Fr71). As with the natural characters of the first four poems, this one, too, concerns not knowing: "Ah, curious friend!" says the speaker, "Thou puzzlest me." Riddles and puzzles: These are not the concerns of Fascicle 40, in which a poem placed here and changed little appears. Context *does* affect interpretation.

A thud of disappointment also ends the next (seventh) poem, "Went Up a year this evening!" (J93, Fr72). The speaker of this little story, a spectator at a death,[7] goes through a number of stages, of which "wonder" is one, but the speaker ends the otherwise buoyant poem with this: "A Difference—A Daisy— / Is all the rest I knew!" As with "lies" and "still" in earlier poems, the "rest" resonates here, and the reader recognizes the frustration of the not knowing. Just so, the two poems that face this story, both of which might be read as cheerful nature poems,[8] nevertheless have their own disquieting thuds. "Angels, in the early morning" (J94, Fr73) "parched" flowers, an image E. Miller Budick also finds disturbing (1985, 69–70). And the "nosegay" and "Captive" of the next (eighth) poem have their own unsettling resonances. The reader of the fascicles—and only the reader of the fascicle—will notice one of Dickinson's tricks on the bottom of the opened page, though what to make of it, I confess, I'm not sure. Could she just be having fun by placing across from each other these lines: from "Went out a year": "The *wondrous* nearer drew— / Hands bustled at the moorings— / The crowd respectful grew—" and, on the right, from "My nosegays": "To such, if they sh'd whisper / Of mornings and the moors / They bear no other errand. . . ." Mooring the poems together this way cannot have been a complete accident. In all of the 1,775 poems Dickinson uses some form of "moor" or "mooring" only seven times.

Way leads on to way within Fascicle 3. Turning the page from Angels and nosegays, the reader discovers another graveyard scene, one reflecting simple acceptance, perhaps, of the death of a loved one to whom the flower and bird (both, to repeat, metonymies for poems) provide directions—and they are better than the directions of "Cato."[9] Below that, "Sexton! My Master's sleeping here" (J96, Fr75) is a reminder of the limits of knowledge, as is "The rainbow never tells me" (J97, Fr76), the ninth and tenth poems of Fascicle 3.

In spite of the limits of knowledge—or because of it—"Angels," the fascicle's seventh poem, seems to be a poem of faith. The common meter "Angels" might just as well fit Fascicle 40, but it is followed by a poem that, because of the verb in the first line, reminds us of the fascicle's opening ("Delayed till she had ceased to know"); it is "One dignity delays for all—" (J98, Fr77). This rather long poem, too, seems devotional but for that problematic verb and its dark observation that death is inevitable for all. There's a "meek escutcheon" on the crowned dead, reminding the fascicle reader of the "meek appareled thing," the dead in the fascicle's first poem, and looking toward the nineteenth poem, "The morns are meeker than they were—" (J12, Fr32).

Meanwhile, Dickinson has other (it seems to me intentional) surprises in store. Following the relative orthodoxy (if we ignore the Cato reference) of the twelfth poem, she situates the speaker of the thirteenth, "As by the dead we love to sit" (J88, Fr78), by a bedside or graveyard, grappling with the tension between knowing and believing. The grappling has to do with the mathematics of loss, a notion that is followed in the next poem by the mathematics of gain: "New feet within my garden go—" (J99, Fr79) with its itemization of things "new," which cannot make up for the sadness of the end, "And still [that pun again] the pensive Spring returns— / And still the punctual snow!"

These are the poems that prepare for and all but hide the poem that Dickinson considered important enough to place in two fascicles. The speaker (or speakers) of these graveside poets, having "grappled" with death for thirteen poems, says

> I hide myself within my flower
> That wearing on your breast—
> You—unsuspecting, wear me too—
> And Angels know the rest! (J903, Fr80)

As with other repeated poems, this one seems both centrally located and pivotal in terms of language and idea. As are earlier and subsequent poems in the fascicle, it is about knowing; the poem (the fascicle?) contains what the poet knows and conveys to the listener/the reader/the wearer of the verse. What she does not know, what only the angels (there are several in this fascicle) know is "the rest," that simple word, which has already appeared three times in the fascicle. Both the Johnson and the Franklin variorum editions note that the poem in one of its versions seems to have accompanied a literal flower. Regardless of whether this is true, it does not belie whatever meaning she attached to it when she selected it for placement here.

After declaring that she "hides [her]self," she includes four poems in a row that begin with the first-person singular. We know that the "I" of her poetry may be a "supposed person," but the almost hammered-out use of the pronoun and the tone of the poems suggest that maybe she *was* both hiding and revealing herself in this fascicle. "I never told the buried gold" (J11, Fr38), the fifteenth in the series, begins this string of poems. In it, the speaker declares lightheartedly that she wants to join forces with the plunderer (of the sunset), a kind of Captain Kidd, and will earn the right to share the "booty" she has greedily watched him hide. Comic relief it may be, but it also reminds us of the mathematics of gain and loss, the tension between knowing and not knowing and between telling and not telling. And there's another surprise in the last verse: It faces the little poem (the fourteenth, which is repeated in Fascicle 40) in which the speaker "hides" herself: There the speaker wonders "Whether to keep the secret— / Whether to reveal— / Whether as I ponder / 'Kidd' will sudden sail—"

There's a seriousness to this fun: Fascicle 3 moves to the next poem, potentially one of her fiercest assaults on orthodox belief. To anticipate that, perhaps, Dickinson the editor copied the last verse of "I never told" at the top of the page. The lines form almost an introduction to "I never lost as much but twice" (J49, Fr39): at the end of the fifteenth poem, the one that hints at the larceny of Captain Kidd—and the urge to larceny by the speaker for the "buried gold," the speaker wonders "Could a shrewd advise me / We might e'en divide— / Should a shrewd betray me— / Atropos decide!" The Atropos reference, a quotation from Shakespeare directly related to the death poems[10] but so different from the reference to Kidd in the same poem, is only a little less puzzling than the object of the verb "decide." Barton Levi St. Armand explains "the shrewd" as the reader or viewer; the treasure as the transformed beauty of the landscape—the work of the artist, whose work becomes "the spoils of aesthetic adventure" (1984, 267). Yes, that works: this is a fascicle in which the artist hides him- or herself (his or her skill) in the flower (poem about the sunset). The question of what is to be decided can only be guessed by the proximate poems and then only through a suggestion that we might again liken to that hypogrammatic shadow.

Below the unfinished thought in "Could a shrewd decide" is the poem that might indeed be the fiercest in the fascicle—though it has been called funny (Budick 1985, 126) and "far from rebellious" (Rapin 1973). Following a number of crowded pages, this poem, introduced by the "shrewd" verse, is set off with plenty of space above and below it as though its author/editor wants it to be clear:

> I never lost as much but twice—
> And that was in the sod—
> Twice have I stood a beggar
> Before the throne of God!
>
> Angels—twice descending
> Reimbursed my store—
> Burglar! Banker—Father!
> I am poor once more! (J49, Fr39)

To the reader who began this little collection with the sense that the riddle of resurrection "lies" "still," if you will; that birds have barbs; and that whatever treasure or "buried gold" may be swept away—whether that be the power to write of sunsets or simply the disappearance of beauty—the lines seem highly charged. What this says about the philosophy or theology or state of mind that Dickinson had "hidden" in her work is, of course, as open to interpretive possibilities, as the views of Budick and Rapin suggest. Three women, two of whom knew Dickinson, weigh in this way. Sue, Emily's most intimate friend, told Daniel Chester French that "Emily remained a docile child of God and a rebellious heir of his kingdom" (Bianchi 1932, 57); her daughter Martha Bianchi said something rather different: "Though Emily took liberties with her Puritan vernacular and dogma when venting her baffled patience with the inscrutable, these impish flashes were no more to the underlying God-consciousness than one gargoyle on the roof is to the heart of the cathedral within" (ibid., 55). "Rebellious heir" or "God-conscious" with "impish flashes": Neither seems quite sufficient to describe the effect of that sharp "Burglar! Banker—Father!"

Speaking of "The Daughter and the Awful Father of Love" in her *When a Writer Is a Daughter* (1982), Barbara Mossberg lingers on this poem as a reflection of "the earth-bound Emily-Edward relationship": "At first glance this is a dutiful daughter poem. . . . But instead of regarding God as the rightful owner whose authority and judgment in matters of life and death must be accepted on faith, Dickinson purports to consider God a 'Burglar.' . . . Thus she challenges the legitimacy of his power" (114). Replaced in its intended sequence, the line (as the entire poem) merges with the imagery of the taunting deity who keeps conditions for knowledge and certainty just out of reach (as in the third poem). If *He* is a "robber," reducing the speaker to "a beggar" (in the fourth poem), *she* (the poet/persona) is as well, having once "robbed the Dingle" (in the fascicle's fourth poem). There was a "plunder" of sunset, and the poet wished to be an accomplice to the piracy. If He (God) is a Banker, he is "shrewd," like the one to whom the speaker appeals in the lines from "I never told the buried gold" and so forth. The poem hurls its accusation at a usurious deity who demands much too much too often and who extorts. What creates such anger and sadness? The next poem offers the suggestion that appears throughout the fascicle: Mortal separations are too painful to voice directly, as the poet says in "I haven't told my garden yet—" (J50, Fr40), the seventeenth poem in the fascicle and the third in the congruent series of poems that begin with negatives ("I never told"; "I never lost"; "I haven't told").

Other secrets hide in the fascicle's final poems. In the next poem ("I often passed the village" [J51, Fr41]) the speaker wanders through the village of the dead, remembering passing as a schoolgirl before she "knew the year . . . in which my call would come." Facing this proleptic poem are two others that may be seen as proleptic as well. The fascicle has moved from poems in which the speaker grieves for others to one in which she imagines her own death. "The morns are meeker than they were—" (J12, Fr32), though often read as a lighthearted evocation of fall, even parodic,[11] in this sequence seems a bit eerie. It rests between the notion of a still, cool, submould existence in "I often passed" and the little poem that might partly be based on a Holmes and Barber emblem (see Monteiro and St. Armand [1981]) and that here holds the word we have already met—twice—in the earlier poems: "Whether my bark went down at sea—" (J52, Fr33), in which the speaker imagines herself out upon whatever sea of eternity it is she has been contemplating all through the fascicle. "By what mystic mooring," she asks, "She [the little bark / the soul / the dead] is held today—"? As elsewhere in the fascicle, there is no answer to the question, simply a reiteration of the need to know: "This is the errand of the eye / Out upon the Bay." She returns to the examination in the fascicle's twenty-second poem, another one that might have originated in humor,[12] "Sleep is supposed to be" (J13, Fr35). Moving toward the implied assertion that morning will occur, the poem recites two views of death. First, it is a rest: "the shutting of the eye"; second, it is some kind of heavenly place: "the station grand," surrounded by witnesses, resurrection (morn). Dickinson's lineation, however, belies the orthodoxy, however parodic, of those views. Although she might as easily have lineated the poem in five verses of three lines each, she broke one line away from that structure: "Morning has not occurred!" The lines that follow, which imagine that paradisiacal day, have a conditional cast.

The last page is crowded with text. "If I should die" (J54, Fr36) imagines life without herself. Everything in the poem again is conditional except "That Commerce will continue— / And Trades as briskly fly." There is nothing in the penultimate poem to override the conclusion of the one that preceded it ("Sleep is supposed to be") that "morn" in the theological sense might not occur. However (possibly) heterodox the end of "If I should die" might be, there's a lilt in that poem in which the poet moves from bedsides and graveyards to the world of the living, and there's a lilt in the tiny poem at the end. It may, in fact, be the answer to all of the doubt hidden within the fascicle, in which the poet seeks to discover how to be moored in her own faith. It seems as grand an assertion about the enterprise of the poet as any she ever wrote:

> By chivalries as tiny,
> A Blossom, or a Book,
> The seeds of smiles are planted—
> Which blossom in the dark. (J55, Fr37)

Look at the fascicle. This little poem is in an identical position and is identical in length and nearly so in meter to the little poem, "I hide myself," the one she pulled out to copy, some six years later, into Fascicle 40.

Fascicle 40, as Dorothy Oberhaus has shown us, is devotional.[13] There is a stillness, a certainty, far from a bland placidity, not found in earlier fascicles in the one we believe to be her last book. Nothing shows that quieter mood better than to contrast it with Fascicle 3. Here I differ from both Shurr and Oberhaus, who, in their very different readings, find a serial story from Fascicle 1 to 40. In Fascicle 3, as we have seen, the Dickinson persona spurns Cato and stamps her foot at the "Burglar!—Banker—Father!" who leaves her "poor once more." She imbeds the quatrain "I hide myself" between a cemetery poem and a reverie on how much larceny the poet is allowed (compared to Kidd's). And she ends with a celebration of mortal life and the role of the poet in that life (to live on in the "Chivalries so tiny" and make those who follow, those who inhabit the world of trade and commerce and everydayness, smile).

In Fascicle 40, however, the speaker looks with "compound vision," backward and forward, on moments of reverse and advance, claiming the power over her material ("I make his Crescent fill or lack") even as she moves beyond her own "Color—Caste—Denomination," beyond "locality." In this last fascicle there is a stillness even in the eerie sadness that hovers over what I take to be an elegy for the war dead ("Midsummer, was it when they died—" [J962, Fr822]).[14] There is a perfection in these death (and life) poems quite literally. The word "perfect" itself, in fact, is iterated three times, appearing more frequently here than in any other fascicle. Not prominent in the Oberhaus study is the fact that in the very middle (again) of this fascicle—so different from the third in tone and image clusters—on the west side of the opened volume (again) Dickinson inscribed the little poem that otherwise astute readers (citing the earlier version) call "banal" and "precious" (Griffith 1964, 153–56). To fit the new context Dickinson altered "I hide myself" (J903, Fr80) more radically than either of the two variorum editions (Johnson's and Franklin's) indicates, though not, certainly, as radically as she had the "Alabaster Chambers" of Fascicles 6 and 10. The changes call us to attention.

In this version the four lines, reworded, appear as seven:

> I hide myself—within
> My flower,
> That fading from your
> Vase—
> You—unsuspecting—feel for
> Me—
> Almost a loneliness—

Lineation is no small matter. Martha Nell Smith (whose website makes it visible) has said that Dickinson's careful holographs with their jokes and significant flourishes reveal her "performance script." She cites Susan Howe's response as a poet: "Try to copy Dickinson's calligraphy; retrace one sweeping s, a, or c, and you will know how sure her touch was / is. . . . Messages are delivered by marks" (Smith 1992, 62–63). Here "My flower," "Vase," and "Me" stand out, almost as if in apposition to each other or at least calling the reader to consider the connections among the three: The flower she so often equated with poetry, the vase that her dictionary reminds us has not only domestic but also sacred uses as a vessel for sacrifices (Oberhaus expands this [113]), and herself as source and object of feeling are joined in ways available only to the reader of the poem in its fascicle place.

Along with the lineation, the words present the poem in a new light. The concern with angels and with knowing in the last line of the earlier version ("and angels know the rest") are transformed into the loneliness of this fascicle, in which the signs of the physical world—flowers, bees, trade, and commerce—are largely replaced by the language of an almost abstract vastness: "immortality" ("The only News I know" [J827, Fr820, the first in the series]; the "ungracious country" [J961, Fr821, the second]; the "nearness to Tremendousness" and "Illocality" [J963, Fr824, the fifth]). This fascicle has none of the exasperation (or the playfulness) of Fascicle 3, in which the speakers variously doubted, raged, or quoted (parodically) from scripture. In Fascicle 40 the universe the poet reflects has room in its paradise for those who seek to "Occupy My [probably Christ's] House" ("Unto me," J964, Fr825, the sixth in the series).

Just as there was almost a mate or a second verse, perhaps, to the earlier version of this poem ("By Chivalries so tiny), so there is to the version in Fascicle 40. It, too, occupies physically a place that underscores its connectedness. The eleventh poem of Fascicle 40 is the only one (other than the repeated poem) in *this* fascicle about flowers:

> Between my country
> And the Others—
> There is a Sea—
> But Flowers—negotiate
> Between us—
> As Ministry. (J905, Fr829)

Chivalries so tiny—flowers, poems, and poems that become new in fascicles, those bundled leaves of grass Dickinson left to intrigue—no, awe—the rest of us: This is the Ministry of Emily Dickinson. Whatever else we do with the poems Dickinson left for sister Vinnie to find, whatever other ways we (as her early editors and as most scholars still do) group her poems, we must also read and teach Dickinson through her own context. She cared about context.

Nothing shows what Robyn Bell calls the "passionate certainty" (1988, 353) of the craftsmanship of the fascicles better than the final pages of the project. Much as in Frost's "Oven Bird," who "knows in singing not to sing" of the "diminished thing," Dickinson does not so much explain as inscribe in the writing itself what she acknowledges to be "Unfulfilled" and "Incomplete." It is in the way the last poem speaks to the first on the opened book. Dickinson speaks of "a Revolution / In Locality," which itself revolves visually to the "Bulletins of Immortality." She speaks of "Suns [that] Extinguish" in order that a "New Horizon" be "Embellish[ed]." She implies that the other sun of the new horizon is what illuminates "The only Show" worth seeing: Immortality. In the end, the fascicle says (again) with Hamlet, in effect, that "the rest is silence." But the silence is not dreadful, any more than is the darkness.

The last words of Dickinson's fascicles might seem like a drop into nihilism: "Fronting us—with Night," but this is a fascicle (and in many ways a project) that has provided "Compound vision— / Light—Enabling Light" and the night fronts—palpably fronts as one looks at the open book— "Bulletins from Immortality." The Bulletins, then, are the last word. The poet promises, "If other News there be— / Or Admirabler Show— / I'll tell it you—." Telling it was always the burden of her poetry. Inferring is our burden—and joy.

CHAPTER 7

"Only [Our] Inferences Therefrom!"

> As if some little Arctic flower
> Opon the polar hem—
> Went wandering down the Latitudes
> Until it puzzled came
> To continents of summer—
> To firmaments of sun—
> To strange, bright crowds of flowers—
> And birds, of foreign tongue!
> I say, as if this little flower
> To Eden, wandered in—
> What then? Why nothing,
> Only your inference therefrom!
> J180, Fr177, F8

Dickinson requires two things of her readers: their delight in her work ("her flowers" [J868, Fr908]) and an intelligence in "inferring." So she suggests in that slantwise admonition to meet her and work with her. Recall that she closed Fascicle 8—the one in which the diction surrounds the idea of power, magic, and transport—with the tale of the "little Arctic flower" that "Went wandering down the Latitudes / Until it puzzled came / To continents of summer— / to firmaments of sun." Should she return,[1] she would be astonished at the reach of those latitudes in which she is read. The little flower—the poems, if you will—are the puzzlers, requiring our attention, our intelligent inferences:

> I say, As if this little flower
> To Eden, wandered in—
> What then? Why nothing,
> Only, your *inference* therefrom! (J180, Fr177)

Hundreds of readers through the years have relished the inference game. With Amy Lowell, we say that we would "somersault all day" with Dickinson. Most have played, leaped, and turned cartwheels with Dickinson's words much longer than "all day." For only the last score of years could we do so in their fascicle contexts as Amy Lowell could not. This is the way Dickinson left them for us. Some six hundred of the poems—about a third of the *opus*,[2] appeared in another context—the letters—and that is a study that scholars such as Martha Nell Smith and Erika Scheurer and others pursue with persuasive energy. Remarkably understudied, however, are these forty books, books representing what one might consider "an authoritative text"—if one could use such a term for a poet so resistant to closure. I use it as Jerome McGann discusses it: "[T]he author is taken to be—for editorial and critical purposes—the ultimate locus of a text's authority" (1983, 81). Dickinson's work has been studied exhaustively but almost always in ways that ignore her own context, her own authority, if you will.

Admitting that "manuscript study can be a foundation; but it cannot provide the entire architecture for reading and understanding Dickinson," as Shira Wolosky says (1999, 93),[3] it is nevertheless much more intriguing and revealing than many have allowed. One reason for resistance to study of the fascicles, quite fairly, is that there are too many questions about the how and why of those forty small volumes, questions that are, of course, unanswerable. Sharon Cameron ends an essay on the fascicles with a series of questions: "What is a subject? How is it bounded? What are the boundaries around what something is?" and so forth (1998, 157). Insisting, as I have been, that ultimately all of the readings of intentionality regarding the fascicles—and to a lesser degree the certainty of the order of the fascicles themselves—is speculative, Cameron nevertheless declares "that Dickinson ordered her poems" (ibid., 141).

Whether or not she literally spread herself and her poems over the floor of her Amherst bedroom as do so many of the fifteen poet-editors about whom I wrote in chapter 5, we do not know, but we know she *chose*. What she wrote about the single word must have been even more complex as she selected individual lyrics for the books so that, wandering down the latitudes to us, they exist to provide a particular frisson. What Alicia Ostriker, Linda Pastan, and their contemporary sisters tell us about their process in gathering work for a new volume seems to be what Dickinson describes:

> Shall I take thee, the Poet said
> To the propounded word?
> Be stationed with the Candidates
> Till I have finer tried— (J1126, Fr1243)

As though I had asked a stupid question, almost every one of the fifteen poets to whom I turned for help for chapter 5 said "of course" to my query about their care in choosing the first and last poems, for example, in a given sequence. Most of them admitted to caring about much more than that as they approach collections of chapbook length or longer. Sharon Bryon is one of several who explained the importance of ordering poems in dialogue with each other.[4]

Dialogue is a keyword in describing Dickinson's collections. Hyatt Waggoner does not include the fascicles in his excellent Emersonian-based discussion of Dickinson (1984), but one might note that what he says about her work as a whole is particularly true of her fascicle groupings:

> One might think of Dickinson's poems as a record of a continuous dialogue between parts of herself, aspects of her mind, segments of her complex heritage; except that there are not just the two speakers required by dialogue, but always a third, a watcher and listener, amused or dismayed, aware of the limitations of what can be conveyed by words, superior to all dialogue. (ibid., 202)

Such dialogues occur throughout the fascicles. One of the simpler but quite telling ones is in Fascicle 3, where, on the left-hand side facing one long poem with which the three poems are also in dialogue (the long one being "I never told the buried gold" (J11, Fr38), are three short poems, written apparently at different times up to 1858 but gathered here for a conversation. At the top of the page is a poem she also wrote to the Hollands (L204), "As by the dead we love to sit." The dead, she says, are "wondrous dear," the "dear" being a word she plays with in its quantification sense. The persona speaks of the "broken mathematics" with which "We estimate our prize / Vast in the fading ratio / To our penurious eyes" (J88, Fr78). Loss and gain are also the subtext of the poem that follows, separated only by a thin line—not accidentally I surmise— under the word "penurious": "New feet within my garden go, / New fingers stir the sod—" (J99, Fr76). And this poem is followed on the page with "I hide myself within my flower / That wearing on your breast— / You unsuspecting wear me too— / And Angels know the rest" (J903, Fr80).

Only by looking at the fascicle can one observe the pattern on the page of these three poems: "As by the dead" with its grim if not bitter deathbed or graveside setting of the recently bereaved; "New Feet within my garden," with its resigned vision of the inevitable patterns of life and death; and "I hide myself," the four lines of which embody the image of poet and lover as knower and conveyer of these certitudes, as Whitman, in mystical union with cycles. Each of these also sets off a parallel set of images in the longer poem that faces it. These poems, as so many others in the fascicles, appear to be not only "in dialogue," as Waggoner and others put it, but also in a complicated conversation with each other.

One wishes Waggoner had had the opportunity to read the fascicles. He appreciates the complexity of arrangements of Wallace Stevens, for example, using language that is easily parallel to groupings of Dickinson as he describes how "Girl in a Nightgown" and "Connoisseur of Chaos" are on facing pages in *Parts of a World*, offering "thesis and counter thesis" of Stevens's explorations of experience and reality. Waggoner also appreciates the poets' care in openings and closings—as he did an individual lyric: "Just as Frost placed last in his final volume 'In winter in the Woods Alone,' which echoes and comments on 'Into My Own,' the first poem in his *Complete Poems*, so Stevens gave final position to 'Not Ideas about the thing but the thing itself'" (441).

A rage toward order, some kind of structure at least, seems a goal for poets of all times, including our own. Alicia Ostriker, for example, says that she wants "to achieve some kind of structure. . . . It has to feel 'right' as a sequence." This rage for order (however wild and idiosyncratic) harks back to Vergil and Ovid as Neil Fraistat's collection of essays demonstrates (1986). How intentional those structures were is illustrated by Petrarch, who, says Fraistat, "rearranged *Canzoniere* nine times" (6). Fraistat points out that Petrarch "visualized the *Canzoniere* as an elastic form: one allowing him to shape and reshape all of the shorter poems he wished to acknowledge publicly within an overarching if continually refocused vision" (ibid., 6). The essays in Fraistat's *Poems in Their Places* collection point to the intentionality of Dickinson's predecessors in ordering individual poems into ordered wholes and of what George Bornstein (speaking of Browning's *Dramatic Lyrics*) calls "considerable architectonic skill" (273). Bornstein notes, for example, Browning's "deployment of paired poems punctuated by individual freestanding ones" (ibid., 273). Joseph Anthony Wittreich Jr. discusses a different grouping with respect for the intentionality of Milton's choices and the appropriate alert response such choices should create in the reader:

> The juxtaposition of these poems and the ensuing dialogue [that word again] between them suggest that they are not autonomous but dependent upon one another for their meaning. Milton's poems are always a plurality of other texts that help to unravel their meaning; their intertextuality, whether overt or covert, provides access to their meaning. (1986, 164)

The "intertextuality" Wittreich notes between "Paradise Regained" and "Samson Agonistes" placed together by Milton three centuries ago provides keys to meanings beyond what they have separately. Speaking of John Donne's collections, John Shawcross says, "At least one can say that the poems read together in their place in 1633, 1635, and the manuscripts . . . will lead to this kind of reader-response, that is, will produce a reader in the poems who is different from the reader in the same poems differently arranged" (1986, 150). Vincent Carretta on Alexander Pope (195–233), Earl Miner on Herbert (18–43), Stuart Curran on Wordsworth (1986, 234–53) are equally vigorous about the importance of reading "poems in their places." Why then, this writer wonders, has the question of Dickinson's intentionality and the response that such intentionality requires from a reader been as sharply contested as I have shown it to be in earlier chapters?

Although the obvious answer is that Dickinson left conflicting comments on publication, it may be that arrangements such as those of the English poets covered by the essays in Fraistat's *Poems in Their Places* are somewhat easier to describe than Dickinson's. One poet, Hong Kong professor Andrew Parkin, responding to my inquiry, spoke of his pattern as something other than "linear" but more like "porcelain fragments"; there is order, but it is one that the reader needs to discover and needs to put together, "as one would the slivered pieces of a known whole." This image, similar to that of Solensten and of Debra Kang Dean (iron filings pulling toward a center or prism shards), might be a starting place for describing Dickinson's. The pieces may be rearranged as well, when the poet selects an almost identical poem for another setting. Just as so many of Dickinson's poems have the second (or third) context of inclusion in a letter, most of the poems in this volume have other origins. Dickinson replaced certain poems in new places to make new poems, new because of the pressure of the surrounding poems. Poets do that, and I have found it revelatory to compare the effect of such repetitions in this book.

Why should we think that Dickinson forgot (implied by Franklin's remark that she "failed to destroy a worksheet" 1981, xv–xvi) she had copied some poems into more than one setting? She knew what she was about.[5]

And we will have greater insight into what she was about by reading Dickinson's work in the several contexts she provided. This book has urged that we meet her on her own pages, reading the poems as she herself arranged them. Unlike David Porter, Ralph Franklin, and others I have quoted earlier who are so skeptical about the practice of reading the fascicles as self-conscious wholes, I believe that these are consciously crafted artifacts no less than are the poems that compose them and no less than are those of most of the poets who answered my questions about their own process. Without anything more than her metaphors for her labor and craft—so many of them of the spider weaving all night—we must *infer* what her process might have been. The contemporary poets whom I asked to infer, to guess, based on their reading of Dickinson and their own practices, suspect that the brain behind the individual lyric did not put those books together haphazardly: "I think she was a fastidious thinker, writer, person. I think she probably planned everything . . . certainly much more than I, who tend to trust more to chance," says Betty Adcock.[6]

However—and on this I strongly agree—not one of the responding poets infers (believes in?) a narrative of all of the forty fascicles. John Solensten points out that "It's the sheer volume of Dickinson's poetry—the infinite variety—that seems to resist focusing the unitary in her editing for me." Ostriker expands, imagining that Dickinson "put the fascicles together the way she put each poem together," partly to make (thematic or other) sense, partly to skirt the edge of nonsense, partly to play delightfully, partly to chart a process of exploration." Solensten adds another term for the editing process: "retrieval." He says, "In a larger sense [than the unitary] I think Emily was a melancholist who, having lost so much, worked at retrieving the lost (moment in life, nature) and incorporating it, making it part of her physical body itself—all in a system of vast retrieval." As early chapters of this study indicate, I believe some fascicles reflect retrievals of something quite different from moments of melancholy and loss—Fascicle 3, for example, is quite merry, but Solensten's point contributes to the discussion with a word that is more psychological and more plastic than "editing." Solensten continues, "And, of course, this process was a means of her demonstrating her superior imagination and intelligence. For she saw beyond sight, she did. But to edit that????"

Solensten has asked the question that causes so many Dickinsonians to balk at the thesis of this book. Sandra Gilbert warns against definitive answers. "'A spider sewed at night'," Gilbert reminds us, "but how, why, when, and for whom? Simply to speculate on these questions is to be driven into such tangles of theatrical darkness that I fear I might never extricate myself!" I do not ask readers to drive themselves into such tangles, but to try reading—playing with—somersaulting with Dickinson on the pages that I believe she constructed with the care of these other writers. No two fascicles are alike, nor will any two readers of one fascicle come to the same conclusions. Mine have simply been examples of possible readings.

The shape of Fascicle 1, for example, seems to me largely determined by the interlocking diction of seasonal progression, whereas the shape of Fascicle 14, which contains a "repeated" poem, is marked by more apparently deliberate efforts to pair poems in mirrored confrontations. In Fascicle 1 Dickinson linked the lyrics through similarities in imagery and tone, even in exact length and page arrangement ("There is a morn by men unseen" [J24, Fr13] and "Morns like these—we parted" [J27, Fr18]). In Fascicle 14, however, she has no fewer than six double pages of poems that mirror each other. The mirroring is evident even in the placement of the duplicate "The feet of people" (J7, Fr16): Apparently inserted exactly between two double sheets, it creates a remarkable symmetry within the fascicle.

Reading Dickinson in her own context can illuminate if not completely clarify as strange a poem as "A Toad Can die of Light—" (J583, Fr419, F14) as it acts as an answer to the loss of the "far treasure" of the previous poem. The "Toad" poem points to another of the pleasures, the delight, of reading Dickinson on her own pages. Unlike in its usual print version, we see that stark "Bare Rhine" on its own line—almost pounded on a table. On the previous page of the fascicle we saw three slant parallel lines crossing three "t's" opposite to the straight line above the "Toad" poem. Dickinson's poetry anticipates, when we look at it in this way, that of someone as modern and idiosyncratic as e.e. cummings. About his devices another poet explains:

> per
> haps ee knewhat
> was best,
> to slow you down
> andmakeyoulook and
> not justread but
> *think* the book.[7]

Linking Dickinson to cummings is not as strange as it might seem. Hyatt Waggoner insists on Dickinson as a conduit of the past (Bradstreet, Emerson) and a harbinger of the future: "If one were forced to choose just one poet to illuminate the nature and quality of American poetry as a whole, to define its continuing preoccupations, its characteristic themes and images, its diction and its style . . . one ought to choose Dickinson" (1984, 212–13). So it is not out of line to ask contemporary poets to talk of ways their work process, as well as their themes, might be echoes of Dickinson. To these poets, as, we might guess, to Dickinson, crawling on the floor in pursuit of order, agonizing over choices and patterning matters, it matters not because it creates a kind of neoclassic peace but because it invigorates the modernity, the wildness, the power. In the linked, echoing, reverberating, fluid (no metaphor is sufficient) structure of the fascicles, the power of every single poem that it contains is multiplied into multifoliate possibilities.

Dickinson hinted at the pleasure such work gave her in an answer to Higginson, who reported that when he asked if "she never felt the want of employment . . . never going off the place and never seeing any visitor," she told him decisively (one might say vehemently), "I never thought of conceiving that I could ever have the slightest approach to such a want in all future time. . . . I feel I have not expressed myself strongly enough" (L342a). She had her occupation; she had her company; she had her books. In the same letter Higginson speaks of Dickinson's love of them. Given books as a child, "she thought in ecstasy 'This then is a book! And there are more of them!'" Why should we resist the idea that her occupation, along with the reading, was the *making* of them—in the kind of joy, even "ecstasy"—her word (twice)—in this conversation Higginson sent back to his wife.

How can we doubt her determination to publish her own work in her own way? Not for her inclusion in books such as S. J. Hale's *Ladies Wreath,* with its prefatory bombast that "the office of poetry is to elevate, purify, and soften the human character." Not for her a softly pretty face with deep-set eyes surrounded by tendrils of curls accompanying one or two poems as in Thomas Buchanan Read's *Female Poets*. Not for her a collection of neat sonnets like that of her friend Helen Hunt Jackson. What she created—on her own, the spider weaving at night—had far more power as surely because of the choices she made in ordering them as in the craft and openness with which she composed them.

Robyn Bell wittily remarks that Dickinson's project was "bookmaking" in two ways. As she folded sheets of stationery, selected and copied her scraps, and arranged their wild chirography on the thin pages with wet ink, and as she sewed the results together, she was literally making the books we call the fascicles. It was also, in the other meaning of the word, a gamble—a gambol, too. Indeed, "This *was* a Poet," refusing to be "still" or stilled. "The poets light but / Lamps" (J883, Fr930); the rest, she tells us, is up to us.

Appendix A: Contemporary Poets Consulted

Adcock, Betty
> *Beholdings* (1988)
> *The Difficult Wheel* (1995)
> *Intervale: New and Selected Poems* (2001)
> *Nettles* (1983)
> *Walking Out* (1975)

Bryan, Sharon
> *Flying Blind* (1996)
> *Objects of Affection* (1987)
> *Salt Air* (1983)

Dean, Debra Kang
> *Back to Back* (1997)
> *News of Home* (1998)

Fay, Julie
> *Portraits of Women* (1991)
> *The Woman behind You* (1998)

Finch, Annie
> *Catching the Mermother* (1996)
> *The Encyclopedia of Scotland* (1982)
> *Eve* (1997)
> *An Exaltation of Forms* (with coeditor Kathrine Varnes, 2002)
> *A Formal Feeling Comes: Poems in Form by Contemporary Women* (ed., 1994)
> *The Ghost of Meter* (1993)
> *Marie Moving* (2002)

Gilbert, Sandra
> *Blood Pressure* (1988)
> *Emily's Bread* (1984)
> *Ghost Volcano* (1995)

In the Fourth World (1979)
Inventions of Farewell: A Book of Elegies (2001)
Kissing the Bread: New and Selected Poems 1969–2000 (2000)
The Madwoman in the Attic: The Woman Writer in the Nineteenth Century (withcoauthor Susan Gubar, (1979)
Shakespeare's Sisters: Feminist Essays on Women Poets (with coeditor Susan Gilbert, (1979)
The Summer Kitchen (1983)
Wrongful Death: A Memoir (1995)

Nelson, Marilyn
The Fields of Praise (1997)
For the Body (1978)
The Homeplace (1990)
Magnificat (1994)
Mama's Promises (1985)
Partial Truth (limited edition, chapbook, 1992)

Ostriker, Alicia
The Crack in Everything (1996)
A Dream of Springtime: Poems (1970–1978 1979)
Green Age (1989)
The Imaginary Lover (1986)
The Little Space: Poems Selected and New (1998)
The Mother/Child Papers (1980)
The Nakedness of the Fathers: Biblical Visions and Revisions (1994)
Once More Out of Darkness (1974, 1976)
Songs: A Book of Poems (1969)
Stealing the Language: The Emergence of Women's Poetry in America (criticism, 1986)
A Woman under the Surface (1982)
Writing Like a Woman (criticism, 1983)

Pastan, Linda
Aspects of Eve (1975)
Carnival Evening: New and Selected Poems: 1968–1998 (1998)
An Early Afterlife (1995)
The Five Stages of Grief (1978)
A Fraction of Darkness (1985)
Heroes in Disguise (1991)
The Imperfect Paradise (1988)
The Last Uncle (2002)

A Perfect Circle of Sun (1971)
PM/AM: New and Selected Poetry (1982)
Waiting for My Life (1981)

Saje, Natasha
"Dynamic Design," an unpublished essay on "the dynamics of reading a book of poetry"
Red under the Skin (1994)

Solensten, John
The Boys of War (1992)
Building Oahe (1997)
Curmudgeon (1998)
Good Thunder (1983)
The Heron Dancer (1984)
Mowing the Cemetery (1989)
There's Talk in Town (1988)

Wilbur, Richard
Advice to a Prophet and Other Poems (1961)
The Beautiful Changes and Other Poems (1947)
Bone Key (1998)
Ceremony and Other Poems (1950)
The Mind Reader: New Poems (1976)
New and Collected Poems (1988)
The Poems of Richard Wilbur (1984)
Responses: Prose Pieces (1953–1976) (includes "Sumptuous Destitution," 1976, 1999)
Things of This World (1956)
Walking to Sleep (1969)
Many translations, including those of Molière and Voltaire

Wright, Charles
Appalachia (1998)
Black Zodiac (1997, 1998)
Bloodlines (1975)
China Trace (1977)
Country Music (1982)
The Grave of the Right Hand (1970)
Hard Freight (1973)
The Other Side of the River (1984)
The Southern Cross (1981)

The World of Ten Thousand Things (1990)
Xionia (1990)
Zone Journals (1988)

While I was in Hong Kong as a Fulbright Senior Scholar at Hong Kong University, this project took another branch that does not appear in the essay but yielded important insights on the tantalizing question of collaboration. Two Hong Kong poets of considerable reputation in Canada and Hong Kong helped with the project, sharing insights on what happens when poets edit together. Their work is written in two languages (English and Chinese), then printed with translation in a volume arranged as one work.

Wong, Laurence, and Andrew Parkin
  Hong Kong Poems (1997)

Appendix B: Duplicate Poems

Position in fascicle and length of poems included in more than one

F	J	Fr	Position in Fascicle	No. of Lines
1	7	16	11th of 22	24
3	903	80	14th of 24	4
6	216	124	12th of 17	11
8	174	172	11th of 20	7
9	269	240	4th of 29	10
10	185	202	9th of 22	4
10	216	124	18th of 22	10
11	240	262	11th of 20	17
12	185	202	7th of 27	4
13	259	322	12th of 19	12
14	240	262	3rd of 18+**	17
14	7	16	9th of 18+**	24
18	343	375	14th of 17	12
21	174	172	12th of 17	7
24	343	375	16th of 20	12
36	269	240	3rd of 22	10
36	259	322	7th of 22	12
40	903	80	9th of 21	4

*   Represents fascicles included in this study.
** Fascicle 14 is incomplete; Franklin supplies multiple position choices: "ED may have removed the second leaf after copying onto the first, but it would have been extraordinary for her to have done so. The leaf may have become separated and lost before 1891. . . . Or the leaf, like others in fascicle 2, may have been deliberately removed by another person. The poem or poems on the leaf are not known"(Manuscript Books, 284).

J	Fr	Title	Fascicles
J7	Fr16	The feet of people walking home	Fascicles 1 and 14
J903	Fr80	I hide myself within my flower	Fascicles 3 and 40
J216	Fr124	Safe in their alabaster chambers	Fascicles 6 and 10
J174	Fr172	At last to be identified	Fascicles 8 and 21
J269	Fr240	Bound a trouble	Fascicles 9 and 36
J185	Fr202	Faith is a fine invention	Fascicles 10 and 12
J240	Fr262	Ah, moon and star	Fascicles 11 and 14
J259	Fr322	Good night! Which put the candle out	Fascicles 13 and 36
J343	Fr375	My reward for being was this	Fascicles 18 and 24

Notes

Notes to Introduction

1. Throughout this book the poems have two or three designations: "J" refers to the numbered designation in the older variorum of Thomas Johnson; "Fr" refers to the number in the newest variorum of Ralph Franklin. When the poem appears in a fascicle, it is designated as "F," followed by a number from 1 to 40, referring to the collection in which the poem appears. All of the poems quoted from fascicles use the lineation therein. This little quatrain, of course, refers to flowers, among Dickinson's constant metonymies for poems.

2. Especially in chapters 1 and 5 I quote from the distinguished scholars who have voiced serious reservations about fascicle studies that have preceded this. Indeed, I share those reservations when the reader insists on a single biographical interpretation of particular fascicles, even more of the entire body of forty books.

Notes to Chapter 1

1. According to Thomas Johnson's variorum edition, "They shut me up in Prose—" first appeared in Bianchi and Hampson's *Unpublished Poems,* 1935; "This was a Poet" in Todd's *Further Poems,* 1929; and in Bianchi and Hampson's *Centenary Edition.*

2. Throughout this book, as I have said, I cite all of the poems by both Johnson's and Franklin's numbers. Those that Dickinson entered into fascicles I also cite by "F" (fascicle number) unless the discussion is clearly limited to one fascicle. When the poem differs in lineation or in any other respect in the two sources, I use the fascicle form. Even such changes cannot convey the effect of reading the manuscripts themselves, however. Along with the substantial difference between chirography and printed letters is the important difference in punctuation, particularly the use of the dash. Along with consulting the *Manuscript Books* if possible, see the studies of Brita Lindberg-Seyersted and Paul Crumbley on the possible significance of Dickinson's apparently idiosyncratic punctuation.

3. Obviously not limited to a specific person, the referent to the "This" in J448, Fr446 nevertheless invites speculation. Barrett Browning, about whom Dickinson had written other poems and who died in June 1861, is generally associated with the poem; however, the Emersonian language of the poem invites consideration also of Thoreau, who died in May 1862, the year in which this poem was probably written.

4. In all three of the published versions of his essay, Emerson spoke of the poet as one who "distills." Dickinson, who prized her volume of Emerson, "a little Granite Book you can lean upon" (L481), elsewhere—as in this poem—reflects his description, too, as one who stands "out of our low limitations, like a Chimborazo" and as the "sayer, the namer . . . a sovereign [who] stands on the centre," as one who "unlocks our chains and admits us to a new scene," and so forth.

5. The two-volume Webster's 1828 *American Dictionary of the English Language* (New York: S. Converse; printed by Hezekiah Howe) is that to which I refer. According

to Carlton Lowenberg, it was among the textbooks of Dickinson, and according to J. Willis Buckingham (1977), it was among those Dickinson used as a textbook. Another choice would be the 1841 single-volume edition. See the work of Cynthia Hallen.

6. See, for example, the works of Martha Nell Smith, Paul Crumbley, and Marta Werner.

7. Amy Lowell, "The Sisters" in *What's O'Clock* (reprinted in *The Complete Works of Amy Lowell* 1955, 460). Lowell's poem about Elizabeth Barrett Browning and Dickinson begins, "Taking us by and large, we're a queer lot / We women who write Poetry" (459). Lowell's leap into Dickinson is more appropriate than she could have known. The onion-skin-thin pages of Dickinson's fascicles, rarely seen directly by readers, live in manilla folders in a vault entered through the Amy Lowell Room at Harvard's Houghton Library.

8. Three volumes edited by Mabel Loomis Todd and T. W. Higginson in 1890, 1891, and 1896, of course, represented the poems in altered form, as did the two that Martha Dickinson Bianchi and Alfred Leete Hampson edited in 1929 and 1942 and the "New Poems" in *Bolts of Melody*, edited by Mabel Loomis Todd and Millicent Todd Bingham. Even the variorum, the first edited by Thomas H. Johnson, published in the 1950s, the latest, that of Ralph Franklin, presents many poems altered in lineation from that of the fascicles.

9. Even before the corrected collection became available, Ruth Miller had pioneered the voyage of discovery, calling the fascicles, as she knew them, "long-link poems" (1968, 249). Warning readers not to find a chronology, not to find meaning keys in possible recipients, and not to find any single event or subject reflected by any one fascicle, she concluded nevertheless that each fascicle has a range of feelings and subjects and that single fascicles have "polar feelings" (ibid., 248). Although Miller recanted some of her early views (at the 1986 Folger Conference), a growing number of readers have followed her interest in exploring the fascicles. Almost as soon as they were published, for example, Katherine Zadravec and Martha O'Keefe (Zadravec is a poet; O'Keefe, an English teacher) undertook a study by placing all of the poems in a fascicle on a single sheet so that the interconnections among them became more immediately visible. O'Keefe later self-published what might be considered the first formal study of the fascicles, part of which she presented at the 1986 Folger Centennial Conference.

10. In the same issue Weisbuch was even more scathing about Shurr's "sensational discovery," which he calls "something akin to a Harlequin Romance" (88), and seems impatient about all of the "attempts to ignore Franklin's careful admonitions against forcing upon the sequences an undue, definitive import" (87). Such early work and reactions to them create a challenge for the subsequent fascicle reader, even one *not* interested in "forcing" upon the books any single reading.

11. See, for example, issues of *Antioch Review, Arizona Quarterly, Early American Literature, Emerson Society Quarterly, Forum, Georgia Review, Iowa Poetry, Literary Review, Midwest Quarterly, Prairie Schooner, Poetry, Southern Humanities Review, Studies in the American Renaissance,* or even, surprisingly, *Yale Review*. During that decade, by contrast, there were a number of reviews on *Mabel and Austin* and on the *Master Letters*. The *Georgia Review*, in fact, devoted two pages of its centennial issue to the *Master Letters*, but nothing to Franklin's work.

12. These two continuing discussions may be found in virtually every major Dickinson biography. In relation to the fascicles, see the privately published two-volume study by Martha Lindblom O'Keefe (1986) in relation to Dickinson's religious life and reading, which likens "This Edifice" (the fascicles) to the meditations of St. John of the Cross. On the other hand, another study by Diane Gabrielsen Scholl (1990) places Dickinson back in the Protestant camp by (anticipating Oberhaus in a way) likening the fascicles to stages in a conversion narrative. Although throughout her article Scholl speaks

of the fascicles as though they are narrated by a single character, a character as much focused on the mechanics of unbelief as of belief, Scholl says that they fit "the pattern of calvinist conversion" (202) in the "pattern" of "anticipation and climactic transformation . . . preceded by the memory of rapture experienced in the past and now lost" (207).

13. I find Riffaterre's *Semiotics of Poetry* (similar to William Doreski's study of Fascicle 27) appropriate to describe the plastic, permeable, and complex designs of the fascicles and the "retroactive reading" we are challenged to bring to both the grouping and the individual lyric. I discuss the particular applicability of the term to Dickinson in chapter 4.

14. As I pointed out at the beginning of this chapter, this is the description of Dickinson's niece and editor, Martha Dickinson Bianchi, who elaborates on the "slender packages" (1924, 86). Maryanne Garbowsky calls the chest a "cherry" bureau and asks us to imagine Lavinia's surprise when she beheld "the production of her sister's lifetime (1989, 76). Even the extent of Lavinia's surprise is questionable. As Elizabeth Phillips has pointed out, Lavinia, who knew her sister to be a "genius," who probably ordered all of her supplies and who may have shared a room with her at times, can hardly have been completely stunned. Martha Nell Smith points out, too, that Sue, who received at least four hundred poems, letters, and letter-poems and who may have been the recipient of some of the fascicles as she was of individual poems, was probably the least surprised (1992, chapters 4 and 5).

15. For example, Stephanie Tingley comes close to using Franklin's words, calling the fascicle books "a personal repository for her work in progress. . . . Her purpose was not only to collect her poetry into manageable bundles, but also to develop an orderly and efficient workshop in which to house her unfinished lyrics" (1987, 203).

16. Among the synonyms in Dickinson's dictionary are the five senses, apprehension, discernment, sensibility, acuteness, understanding, opinion, notion, judgment, moral sense, and, not least, a sense of words.

17. To name just a few in addition to Stonum and Sewall, who have pursued the Emerson influence: Charles Anderson, Robert Gelpi, Roland Hagenbuchle, Martha Nell Smith, and Robert Weisbuch.

18. Alfred Habegger's biography includes a tantalizing note: that Kate Turner (Anthon) and Susan Gilbert had signed the same copy of Kames's *Elements of Criticism* at Utica Seminary (373). Habegger makes no further comment, nor does he mention the effect Kames's theories might have had on Dickinson through her study in Amherst.

19. See the studies of Kamesian influences by Vincent Bevilacqua, Loomis Caryl Irish, Sandra Darlene Kamusikiri, David Gordon Goodwin, and particularly that of Melinda Mowry Ponder on Kames's influence on Hawthorne.

20. Page references are not from the 1830, 1847 edition that Sue owned or from the textbook Dickinson used, but from a gathering of Kamesian thought arranged in 1855, the "American edition" of James R. Boyd, republished in 1883.

21. Bingham quotes a critic (Higginson?) speaking of "the fragmentary richness . . . like a shaft of light sunk instantaneously into the dark abysm" in the *Atlantic* (1945, 95); Whicher quotes Mrs. Ford's comparison of Dickinson's poems to "orchids, air-plants that have no roots in earth" (1957, 121). Even Sharon Cameron, who later wrote a seminal book on the fascicles, called Dickinson's lyric voice "solitary" and "speak[ing] out of a single moment in time" (1979, 23).

Notes to Chapter 2

1. The accusation is part of R. P. Blackmur's famous 1937 "Notes on Prejudice and Fact," a review that itself embodies the "wars" Dickinson "laid away in books." Note his use of "business" in this passage:

I think it is a fact that the failure and success of Emily Dickinson's poetry were uniformly accidental largely because of the private and eccentric nature of her relation to the business of poetry. She was neither a professional poet nor an amateur; she was a private poet who wrote indefatigably as some women cook or knit. Her gift for words and the cultural predicament of her time drove her to poetry instead of antimacassars. (Blake and Wells 1964, 223)

2. See, for example, "The Grace that I—was chose" ("The Day that I was crowned" [J356, Fr613, F29]); "At last—the Grace in sight" ("I cross till I am weary" [J550, Fr666, F30]); "that New Grace" ("I cannot live with You—" [J640, Fr706, F33]); and "Oh what a Grace is this" (J1615). Grace in its problematic theological context is also, in Dickinson's rebellious voice, "Niggard" ("What would I give to see his face?" [J247, Fr266, F11]). Among the many who have discussed the nature of Dickinson's Puritanism are Diane Gabrielsen Scholl and Rowena Revis Jones, both, appropriately, in *Studies in Puritan American Spirituality* (1990), and Jane Eberwein in "Emily Dickinson and the Calvinist Sacramental Tradition" (1987; reprinted in Farr's collection [1996]).

3. Dickinson's dictionary includes only the flower, but the *OED* notes another meaning that Dickinson, widely read in science, may have known: Herschel's "violet-coloured glass [that] stops 955 rays of light . . . described in 1803 scientific journals." The word was also a synonym for amethyst, which Patterson linked to Dickinson's imagery of passion (1979, 131).

4. See, for example, Joanne Dobson's *Strategies* (1989, 91), Rebecca Patterson's *Imagery* (1979, 34, 47), and David Porter's *Modern Idiom* (1981, 288), all of which place the little poem in other intriguing contexts.

5. Eberwein believes Dickinson "identified vicariously with other gothic victims" (1985, 121); Ruth Miller cites a Northampton accident in 1850 resulting in the death of a boy (1968, 403). Another source, if a literal one were needed, might have been the accounts of the 1860 fire in the Pemberton Mill in Lawrence, Massachusetts, which burned alive 88 of the 750 trapped girls.

6. I use the term because the even hymn meter pulses through the poem even though in the manuscript it is eighteen lines, appearing less regular; in the Higginson/Todd version it appears in three quatrains as it does in the Johnson variorum.

7. Keats's lines, themselves in quotation marks—"'Beauty is truth, truth beauty,'— That is all / Ye know on earth, and all / Ye need to know," rephrase those in the "Negative Capability" letter to Bailey of 1817: "I am certain of nothing but the Heart's affections and the truth of Imagination—What the imagination seizes as Beauty must be truth—whether it existed before or not—for I have the same idea of all our Passions as of Love: they are all in their sublime, creative of essential Beauty" (Bush 1966, 58).
Among the many who discuss the Keats link are Gelpi (1965, 106), Capps (1966, 83), Sewall (1980, 716), and Stonum (1990, 45). Another link is to Browning's "A Vision of Poets."

8. See Buckingham's *Reception* (1989, 41–42, 75–76, 288, 412) for comments of Howells, Stoddard, and others, and see Porter's *Modern Idiom* (1981, 21–22).

9. A particular woman poet, the prolific Lydia Sigourney, in fact, said much the same thing. Elizabeth Day discovered an 1837 Sigourney poem that prefigures Dickinson's: "Oh dreams are dear to those whom waking life / Has surfeited with dull monotony" (1992).

10. Dickinson's phrase, "The Star's Whole Secret," incidentally, becomes the title of a poem by Mary Jo Bang (published in 1997 in the *New Yorker*), a poem that seems to depend upon knowing Dickinson for full understanding of its import.

11. Patterson (1979, 192) and Orzeck (1989, 135).

12. Poems that Johnson dates from prior to J616, Fr454 that were not included in a known fascicle include numbers 1, 2, 3 (Johnson's and Franklin's numbers), "I have a Bird in Spring" (J5, Fr4), "I would distill a cup" (J16 but excluded from Franklin's edition), "Whose cheek is this?" (J82, Fr48), and "Mute thy Coronation" (J151, Fr133); Franklin notes that "Mute" and at least twelve others were copied in such a way as for preparation for a fascicle. Several of those are clearly occasional verse, such as a little ode to Kate Anthon, "When Katie Walks" (J222, Fr49), and that enclosed in a letter to Sue on Ned's birth, "Is it true, dear Sue" (J218, Fr189); however, at least two are tiny and delightful—"The Juggler's Hat her country is" (J330, Fr186) and "White Asters" (J331, Fr374)—and would have been an ideal size for placing at the end of "Love thou art high," but their mood and imagery do not fit, so Dickinson, who knew the value of "poems in their places," did not use them.

13. See Patterson on Barrett Browning, Emerson, Longfellow, and the scientist Humboldt (1979, 168, 221n. 56; Farr on travel literature and *Antony and Cleopatra* (1992, 30, 170–76); and Monteiro and St. Armand on emblems (1981, 223). Shurr (1983) links the poem to the marriage poems—fourth stage of his drama. At a Society for the Study of American Women Writers (SSAWW) conference in 2001 Paula Bennett made a large point of the racial bigotry that the second half of the poem implies.

14. Melinda Mowry Ponder quotes Anne Radcliffe's use of Kames as Radcliffe's Emily looks to "the neighborhood where Valancourt was . . . and her imagination, piercing the veil of distance, brought that home to her eyes in all its interesting and romantic beauty" (1987, 77).

15. See, for example, Porter, *Modern Idiom* (1981, 199), and Kher (1974, 251).

Notes to Chapter 3

1. Pollak points us toward a particularly relevant passage in L56, in which Dickinson challenges her future sister-in-law to harness the power she feels; her words alert us to a generative time for that prose/poetry discussion she will copy into Fascicle 21 eleven years after the 1851 letter to Sue, who is teaching in Baltimore:

> "for our sakes dear Susie," she says after a long literary review of Ik Marvel and Longfellow, "who please ourselves with the fancy that we are the only poets, and everyone else is prose, let us hope they will yet be willing to share our humble world." She advises her dearest friend to live with vigor: "Susie— have all the fun wh' you possibly can—and laugh as often and sing, for tears are plentier than smiles in this little world of our's." (1984, 144)

2. See comments in Buckingham's collection of reviews (1989, 544, 518) and a more recent Louise Bernikow extension of the remark that Dickinson "spoke in tongues and she spoke against authority" (1974, 41).

3. This is a tricky number. Nine poems appear in two different fascicles, but some fascicles have more than one doubling. The number seven refers only to poems that are fairly identical and that show up in two fascicles. In this fascicle (8) we encounter another strange duplication in "Pictures / Portraits are to Daily Faces" (J170, Fr174).

4. In addition to the *Harper's* source (my find) and the *Emblem* book (Monteiro and St. Armand's), another traditional source for the wounded deer image may seem obvious: Christian typology (Moses' rock of Horeb as the type for Christ's crucifixion). As she so often does, however, Dickinson has used the image for her own purposes. Two separate articles in Miner's collection on the *Literary Uses of Typology* (1977) cite this poem as evidence that Dickinson, however influenced by traditional Puritan typology, was not ortho-

dox in using that tradition. Keller's conclusion, that in poems such as "A Wounded Deer" Dickinson parodies the typological method and that she "scoffs at the typological solution and has one, more playful, of her own" (1977, 308), seems almost beside the fact in the context of Fascicle 8. In the same volume Landow locates Dickinson's image of the wounded deer in the context of hymns such as "Guide me O Thou Great Jehovah" and "Rock of Ages," but he, too, says that in her last stanza Dickinson has "emptied" the image of its "Christological meaning, using it only for powerful emphasis" (1977, 338–39). Without attributing all of these sources, Alfred Habegger builds on the typological attribution but also compares the poem to Blake's "The Tyger" (2001, 392).

5. Admittedly Paglia also wittily, but not necessarily helpfully to this poem, says that "we're dealing with a woman who spent a lot of time with the help in the kitchen, so if any personal experience backs this poem, it's probably the evisceration of chickens!" (636). Other interesting readings of this vivid poem are the sexual reading of John Cody (1971, 425) and the mythic one of Wendy Barker (1987, 110).

6. The dashes in the manuscript lean upward so steeply that they appear almost as exclamation points. See Paul Crumbley (1996) for his manner of dealing with these marks that transcribe so poorly in a printed page.

7. This by no means exhausts the list of possible influences. Jane Eberwein, for example, cites three more candidates: Desdemona's last words in *Othello;* an article by Charles Mackay in the *Springfield Republican,* and, most likely of all, says Eberwein, Homer's "Noman" (1985, 62). Alicia Ostriker (1986, 40) posits another candidate: "[T]he split persona in this duplicitous poem," she says, relates to Shakespeare's *Coriolanus* and the self-banishment of the title character ("banish" being the variant of "advertise"). The notion of a split character in this well-known poem was made vivid at the 1998 Emily Dickinson International Society (EDIS) conference in Boulder when Gudrun Grabher and her sister Peggy dramatized a tour de force of the poem, creating dialogues between self and self, single woman and married woman, analyst and patient.

8. Sewall (270) and Bell (80) have noted a possible source for "I cautious, scanned my little life—" in George Herbert. Lindberg-Seyersted has commented on the Anglo-Saxonism of its language (1968, 64). Keller (1977, 285) and Budick (146–47) explore its theological/philosophical implications, Keller calling the poem evidence that Dickinson is "more honest than Whitman" in her approach to the universe (ibid.). And Jane Eberwein notes that this "strategy" of Dickinson is one that "offer[s] no protection against anything but exaggerated hopes" (1985, 66).

9. See "She staked her Feathers" (J798, Fr853, F38), "Better—than Music!" (J503, Fr378, F18), "The Leaves like Women interchange" (J987, Fr1098), and "Who were 'the Father and the Son'" (J1258, Fr1280).

Notes to Chapter 4

1. See, for example, Johnson (1960, 151–55), Franklin (1998, 159–64), Leyda (1960, 42–43), Sewall (1980, 201, 550), Keller (1979, 190–193), Tingley (1987, 55–56), and Smith, whose study of the Sue-Emily relationship appears in her dissertation, "Rowing" (1985, 127–224), in her 1992 *Rowing,* particularly chapter 5, and in her hypertext media project available at the Dickinson Electronic Archives at http://www.jefferson.village.virginia.edu/dickinson.

2. In fact, the publishing history of "Safe" is almost dizzying in its multiplicity and variety. Let's begin with the 1859 version of Fascicle 6, about which the end of this chapter revolves, the originating impulse for which is irrecoverable. That would be publication

#1; that was the version sent to Sue first and to Bowles, who published it in the *Springfield Republican* with the title, endline, and date (1861), which do not, of course, appear in the 1859 fascicle. Would we then be up to #2 or #3 of the publishing project? Then there is the revised poem sent to Sue across the hedge in April 1861 but presumably written after that published later (in June); it is the version that ends up in Fascicle 10, collected the previous year. Shall we call that one, the revision that begins "Grand go the years" and to which an even "frostier" verse is appended (or offered as a variant) #4? Although Sue's advice was to leave the first verse to stand alone, Emily thought well enough of the "Grand" version to publish it with two variants (a problematic term for the two "Frost" stanzas) in Fascicle 10 and then to send a truncated version of that to Higginson in the famous first exchange with him; that would be publications #5 and #6 (at least). Although his response was famously tepid in that 1862 exchange, he thought well enough of it in that version (and seemed deaf to its potential heterodox qualities) to publish it in the *Christian Union* essay of 1890, bringing the number of versions printed up to at least seven. The poem appeared in early editions as three stanzas, "Light laughs" being second and "Grand go" being third. Obviously, we are closest to Dickinson's own intentions for the poems in the two fascicles in which she so differently inscribed them.

3. "Ale and cakes" cheered Henry VIII; hock gave its name to a day noted in Dickinson's lexicon, "Hockday," or "High day; a day of feasting and mirth, formerly held in England . . . to commemorate the destruction of the Danes."

4. See "All these my banners be" (J22, Fr291, F1): "Of all the Sounds dispatched / abroad" (J321, Fr334, F12); and the bee poem, "His Feet are shod / with Gauze" (J916, Fr979, Set 7), for example, for similar settings of a "chant."

5. Robert Weisbuch's interesting discussion of "Tho' I get home how late" likens the narrator's tone to Dickinson's account (in L97 to Sue) of a lost cat. Positing also and more seriously that the "myself/itself" exchange in the poem might refer to daughter and stern father Dickinson (1972, 44), Weisbuch notes that for all of its drama "'Tho' I get home' is deeply analogic." To Weisbuch the poem implies that "the divine is achieved only by death . . . that the poet can only prophesy [her] delayed postmortem victory" (ibid., 163). Without noting its specific fascicle setting (his book, after all, was published in 1975), Weisbuch demonstrates that "Dickinson constructs surrounding contexts which implicitly explain the meaning of images most exhaustively" (ibid., 45). He is talking about cat linkages and Eden linkages, but to the fascicle reader his words make even more sense. In the fascicle, the "surrounding context" for this drama of "postmortem victory" is its place in the fascicle following the poem in which the speaker declares that, although she is neither divine nor damask, she will "bloom eternally." Triumph is "brewed from decades of Agony," as oil is made from "phosphoric toil" (two poems back) or as the cup from which the bee and the speaker drink (the fascicle's first poem) is one of both suffering and blessing.

6. Capps (1966) does not list any works by Poe as part of the surviving Dickinson library, and in fact, almost twenty years after she compiled Fascicle 10, she told Higginson (to whom she often lied) that "Of Poe, I know too little to think" (L622). However, Sewall, among others, believes that she had received a collection of Poe from her friend Henry Vaughan Emmons in 1854 (1980, 413). St. Armand (among others) finds many traces of Poe (1984, see particularly 326, fn. 28). To my knowledge no one has noted the possible influence evident in "With thee's" reference. My source for the poem is the 1829 version from Lauter's *Heath Anthology* (1994, 1423).

7. Jane Eberwein says the poem reveals linguistic subtexts for the overt "strategy for appeasing her rich reserves of appetite" (1989, 59), and Heather Kirk Thomas, citing the work of Vivian Pollak and Barbara Mossberg, finds it evidence of an illness (1990, 208), but that reference to Napoleon is not specifically discussed. Certainly Napoleon stories

were ubiquitous. If Dickinson did not have access to Hazlitt's three-volume *Life* (1843) or a similar text, she most certainly could read a long account by John S. Abbott of the tactics, politics, coronation, marriages, and death of Napoleon, which ran for five issues of the 1854 *Harper's* (volumes 6–10). Napoleon was also the subject of an Emerson speech and thus a cultural commonplace. To my ear even the physical references seem almost comical references to the emperor: There's that "not portly—mind"; the "fame petite," and "a brief campaign of sting and sweet," not to mention the image of exile away from shore at the end of the poem.

8. James Conolly calls "Come slowly" a death wish; Christof Wegelin, a "Liebestod." Both are quoted by Anne Brown O'Meara, whose dissertation on the reception of Dickinson says that "it is pointless to deny the sexual nature of the imagery," although she also says that "non-erotic readings in some sense are the only 'news' for publication after Anderson and Johnson" (1989, 327–28). She is right; for varying emphases, all of them erotic, see, for example, Patterson (1979, 35); Keller (1979, 26, 273); Juhasz (1983, 103–4); and Bennett (1990, 166), among others.

9. See the discussion of the early public printing of this poem in Bingham (1945, 56).

10. Among the many excellent discussions of this poem are those of Martha Nell Smith, who devotes most of chapter 5 of *Rowing* (1992) to the poem as it fits the relationship between Sue and Emily; Jane Eberwein (1985, 44, 130–33); Karl Keller (his interpretation of the Sue/Emily relationship differs from Smith's; 1979, 192–93); Vivian Pollak (1984, 223–24); Wolff (1986, 317–20); and, of course, Sewall in their critical biographies (1974/1980). Habegger's biography discusses the poem in the context of Dickinson's encounters with death and her relationship with Sue (2001). In all of the helpful discussion, only Smith notes the fascicle setting, but the detail of the surrounding poems in each one of those settings was not her focus.

11. Of course, selecting any statements among the hundreds she made on the subject of what happens after we die is dangerous. We recall, for example, her letter to cousins after her mother's death: "We don't know where she is, though so many tell us. / I believe we shall in some manner be cherished by our Maker—the One who gave us this remarkable earth has the power still farther to surprise that which He has caused. Beyond that all is silence . . ." (L785). The next year, when Gilbert died, she spoke of his "Rendezvous of Light, / Pangless except for us—" (L868). And what are we to make of the letter to Clara Newman Turner (L926) comparing the bounty of Christ through the clergyman to an invitation to love Santa Claus?

12. The pun possibility is one she tried out and enclosed in a letter to Higginson: "Longing is like the *Seed* / That wrestles in the Ground, / Believing if it intercede / It shall at length be found" (J1255, Fr1298).

13. Among those who discuss this reference in terms of sexual power relationships are Rebecca Patterson (1979, 202–7), Vivian Pollak (1984, 166), and Paula Bennett (1990, 160). Patterson links the spaniel image to a line in *Midsummer's Night's Dream*. Dickinson's own dictionary makes the reference even worse than some of these commentaries would have it, defining "spaniel" not only as "a dog . . . remarkable for his sagacity and obedience" but also as "a mean, cringing, fawning person."

14. In, respectively, "Nature—the Gentlest Mother is" (J790, Fr741, F36); "By my Window have I for Scenery" (J797, Fr849, F38); "I'll tell you how the Sun rose—" (J318, Fr204, F10); and "Doom is the House without the Door—" (J475, Fr204, F33).

15. In "I robbed the Woods—" (J41, Fr57, F2); "A curious Cloud surprised the Sky" (J1710, Fr509, F24); "The Past is such a curious Creature" (J1203, Fr1273); "My period had come for Prayer—" (J564, Fr525, F28); and "I had been hungry, all the Years—" (J579, Fr439, F15), respectively.

16. To my knowledge, no one has discovered this possible source. Even though I find it one more indication of the way Dickinson absorbed and transformed relics of her own culture, I am well aware of the many other possible sources for such imagery: the emblem book that Monteiro and St. Armand show so well as vivid pictorial influences on many poems, including this one (258); an allusion to the benefits of the veiled in a world that "looks staringly" in *David Copperfield*, from which, as Martha Nell Smith reminds us, Dickinson quoted in a letter to Sue (1985, 115–16). See, too, Walker's *Nightingale's Burden* (111–12).

17. The journeys of Francisco Pizarro, sixteenth-century Spanish conqueror of Peru and, with Balboa, discoverer of the Pacific Ocean, were available to English readers through William H. Prescott's *History of the Conquest of Peru* in 1844.

Notes to Chapter 5

1. The line "Whatever it is—she has tried it," which begins J1204, Fr1200, apparently interrogates what is beyond this life. Its last two lines seem relevant, however, to the completion of this study: "Give her for her Transgression / License to think of us." The notion of a transgressive, bold poet who left ways for us to converse with her, to play with her, as Amy Lowell implied in that poem with which I began this study, is helpful.

2. Jerome McGann's *Romantic Ideology*, which, unlike his excellent study on Dickinson's manuscripts, "Visible Language," does not mention Dickinson, seems particularly useful as a way to describe the breadth (put another way: the contradictions) in Dickinson scholarship. Reactions to Dickinson's many moods and voices in the fascicles as in individual lyrics may be described as he describes the general range of criticism. Calling for "a radically revisionary reading of Romanticism," McGann cites three interpretive communities: those (Abrams School) "clearly drawn from a Wordsworthian and, more generally, a Christian (Protestant) model"; those (Mellor School), who stress "the element of Romantic skepticism [but] only to the point where such skepticism does not turn from celebration to desperation"; and those (Kierkegaard/Praz School), who find a "dark, sinister" voice in the poems (1983, 22–26). Dickinson's poems inspire readings, sometimes readings of the same poem, which follow each of these models. What is remarkable about this comparison is that McGann notes a dozen authors in his study, some privileged by one school, some by another. Dickinson is only one "small" woman, but the range of her poems is so large as to admit readers of all three schools—and more.

3. Arlo Sletto in 1975; Paul Gallipeo in 1984; Robyn Bell in 1988; and Eleanor Heginbotham in 1992.

4. Franklin has many followers in his skepticism. As I noted in the first chapter, Porter and, perhaps most sharply, Robert Weisbuch in his 1983 review for *ALS* of "Whitman and Dickinson" also warn against readings such as those in early fascicle studies, citing Franklin's own conclusions. On an "emweb" discussion of Franklin, another fascicle scholar, Bruce Clary, wrote:

> My study of ED's bookmaking practices has led me to believe that Franklin is fundamentally correct: ED did not systematically [an important word in this sentence] exploit the fascicles as artistically unified poetic sequences. Nevertheless, I also believe Franklin's judgments have been too sweeping, too indiscriminate. He correctly minimizes the probabilities for comprehensive, sequential structures, but with less justification, discourages exploration for alternative structures. In other words, yes, the fascicles are a "workshop" where ED recorded and occasionally refined individual poems . . . but they

are also a testing ground or playground [another well-chosen word] where she improvised many ways to group poems meaningfully together. This comment was posted on the "emweb," begun at the University of Utah, where Cynthia Hallen is organizing her "Lexicon" project (see Hallen entry). More recently the chatline moved to a site supervised from the University of Toronto; I have listed it under Hallen's name in the bibliography.

5. A recent addition to those who look skeptically at the study of manuscripts is Domhnall Mitchell, who challenges, for example, McGann's *Black Riders: The Visible Language of Modernism,* along with others who privilege the study of Dickinson's manuscripts. Mitchell sets up McGann's arguments (with those of Smith, Hart, Howe, and others) as possibly "misrepresenting" (1998, 731) Dickinson by imposing an interest in "modernist experiments with the medium of print . . . [into] a premodernist body of writing" (730). See, too, the review of Oberhaus's book by John Gerlach (1996) and those of Cameron's book by Martha Nell Smith (1994) and Randy Blythe (1994).

6. Dickinson signed herself "Your Gnome" to Higginson (L280, for example); she implied the comparison in poems such as "Alone, I cannot be" (P298, F12) and "A Spider sewed at Night" (P1138), a poem important in exploring the self-referentiality of the poems for its line that the spider in weaving its web (its "shroud of Gnome") "Himself himself inform." The poem ends with these three lines: "Of Immortality / His strategy / Was Physiognomy."

7. To "ransack" is (along with its violent and less applicable meanings) "to search or examine thoroughly." Ransacking in that sense is exactly what Riffaterre describes as "literary competence." According to Riffaterre—and is he so different from "New Criticism" in this?—literary competence involves "the reader's familiarity with the descriptive systems [of prosody], with themes, with his society's mythologies, and above all with other texts" (1984). It also involves the ability to fill in gaps in "incomplete descriptions, or allusions, or quotations" (ibid., 5).

8. Neither adjective—"private" or "unedited"—is appropriate to Dickinson as we now know. In "New Poetry" (1840–1843) Emerson spoke of "verses of society, or those effusions which in persons of a happy nature are the easy and unpremeditated translation of their thoughts and feelings into rhyme" (1912, 137–38).

9. Most readers will know that the source of this famous quotation is the "Prologue," a series of aphorisms in which the poet—who was actually well respected in her own time—mocks her Puritan patriarchy with "A poet's pen all scorn I should thus wrong, / For such despite they cast on female wits: / If what I do prove well, it won't advance, / They'll say it's stol'n, or else it was by chance" (16). See the excellent Adrianne Rich introduction to a volume of Bradstreet's work (1967), edited by Jeannine Hensley.

10. Much of this paragraph comes from an email conversation with Smith, though the bottom line of her argument appears in her published material as well.

11. All of the citations from poets in this section are drawn from letters of response to a series of written questions I posed to these writers in 1998 and 1999.

Notes to Chapter 6

1. The eighth in the series, "There is a morn by men unseen—" (J24, Fr13); the ninth, "As if I asked a common Alms—" (J323, Fr14); the thirteenth, "Morns like these— we parted—" (J27, Fr18); and the one that is repeated in Fascicle 14, the eleventh in this series, "The feet of people walking home" (J7, Fr16).

2. Kenneth Stocks, for example, finds this "the existential response" to "some intense subjective experience . . . with a supreme reality" (1987, 62).

3. Johnson explains: "Saxon" might mean no English with which to express herself.

4. Almost alone in discussing it, David Porter calls the little "Sleep" poem "simple," allegorizing it in this way: The speaker, he says, is nature; the submerged seed, the awakening of spring (1961, 32, 94). Porter could not have read it in its fascicle setting in 1961.

5. Heginbotham, 1992a, chapter 2.

6. Jane Eberwein, for example, links the story in "Delayed" to Irving's "The Pride of the Village" in that the longed-for news arrives too late (1985, 117), and Shurr confidently places it in the *Leibestod* tradition (1983, 54).

7. Maryann Garbowsky's dissertation on Dickinson's literary community solidly roots both the sixth and seventh poems of Fascicle 3 in Dickinson's reading ("Went up a year this evening" [J93, Fr72]) to an elegy in the newspaper (1979, 58) and "Angels in the Early Morning" (J94, Fr73) to a Lydia Maria Child passage in Child's 1850 *The Rebels*, wherein "the wild flowers might be the alphabet of the angels" (ibid., 55).

8. "Delayed till she had ceased to know" appears in the 1890 collection under "Time and Eternity" and "Angels in the early morning" under "Nature." "My nosegays" serves as an epigraph in the 1891 second series, appearing just before the gathering Higginson and Todd called "Life." Categorizing poems outside of the gatherings in which Dickinson placed them may distort them.

9. This in itself trips the reader up. When one reads elsewhere, "Great Caesar! Condescend / The Daisy to receive, / Gathered by Cato's Daughter / With your majestic leave!" (J102, Fr149, F7), the apparently innocent lighthearted line ("What Cato couldn't prove me") reminds us of what Cato could mean to lawyer Dickinson's daughter. Her lexicon describes Cato this way: "Catonian: Pertaining to or resembling Cato, the Roman, who was remarkable for his severity of manners: grave, severe, inflexible." When Dickinson says Cato cannot tell her as much as flowers and birds (poetry), she may be subtly overturning the hierarchy.

10. Probably Dickinson, who told Sue that Shakespeare taught her more than anyone (Sue came next), was remembering the line at the end of a speech in ? Henry IV (II, iv). "Come Atropos I say," says Pistol to Bardolphe as they stagger out to duel. Pistol's speech is part of the play in which Shakespeare "utters the finest of many Elizabethan apostrophes to sleep" (Harrison 1948, 656). "What?" says Pistol, "Shall we have incision? Shall we embrue? / Then Death rock me asleep, abridge my doleful days! / Why then let grievous, ghastly, gaping wounds untwine the Sisters Three [the three sisters of destiny in Greek mythology, of whom Atropos was one]. Come Atropos, I say." Pistol claims death as repose, rest, sleep from the burdens of life, which is the hope, but not the certainty, in the death poems of Fascicle 3.

11. See the summaries in Duchac (1979) and also Paul Anderson's 1966 article on Dickinson's "metaphysical mirth" (93). Anderson's take on the poem as parody differs from the early one of Arlo Bates, who said of "The Morns are Meeker" that it shows "how near she could come at times to a bit of good workmanship, and how inevitably, she spoiled it" (Buckingham 1989, 30).

12. Thomas Johnson tells us that another copy of this went to Sue, introduced by a note to her father to thank him for allowing her to work through the early morning hours. He adds the word on Martha Dickinson Bianchi that the lines were sent to Sue "in fun."

13. Oberhaus devoted her 1995 book to this, the last fascicle, concluding that it is "a work of great sophistication and artistic complexity" (10); that it "treats the Bible typologically" (12); that it is "a simple conversion narrative" (19); that it is "a meditation" (22);

and that it ends with "poems of faith" (143). Although readers might differ on the possible readings of individual poems, I must agree—and I worked hard on this fascicle without having read Oberhaus's book. Her book, of course, does not note the very different tone of the fascicle (3) in which she had earlier imbedded "I hide myself."

14. Oberhaus calls it "a pseudo-elegy of two stanzas whose mortuary and seasonal tropes are mostly from Jesus' two 'corn' parables," parables from John and Mark, which she cites (1995, 41–42).

Notes to Chapter 7

1. Garrison Keillor has her return to his show quite often, and she makes her appearance in dozens of fictional representations as well as in the many literary studies that my bibliography (1992b) only begins to encompass.

2. The number comes from the dissertation by Stephanie Tingley (1987), a study of the human relationships behind the letters, one to read along with the studies of Erika Scheurer on the rhetorical voice of the letters (1995) and of Martha Nell Smith on feminist and textual issues raised particularly by the correspondence with Sue (1985; 1992). Ralph Franklin begins his variorum with the simple statement that Dickinson sent "hundreds of copies" of poems to friends (1998); in an appendix (ibid., 1547–57) he lists those friends and the poems enclosed in letters. Along with articles on the letters in the Dickinson *Encyclopedia* and others and that by Agnieszka Salska in the *Handbook* (1998), see Erika Scheurer's "'Near but Remote'" (1995) and Sarah Wider's "Corresponding Worlds" (1992).

3. Wolosky's argument is set in the context of returning the poems to their fullest context: that in letters, in history, and in the artistic development of Dickinson. I am not aware that anyone engaged in manuscript studies would elevate them to "the entire architecture for reading and understanding Dickinson." Indeed, who would think that Dickinson's poems are "only pages of script," divorced from "cultural representations, rhetorical fields, spiritual contests, personal expressions, aesthetic compositions," and all of the rest that Wolosky lists at the end of her article (1999, 96)?

4. With few exceptions, the poets consulted do *not* write with the preordained shape of the book in mind. One exception is Julie Fay, who says that in her first book she "knew" what she would put in the volume "as they are connected poems" and adds that she usually does not "intend a unity" within a book. On the other hand, Sandra Gilbert reflects on her "inner drive toward coherence," saying "Yes, I do care which poems face each other. And I DO change poems because of considerations having to do with the unity of the book." Changing poems, filling gaps, and writing new poems to create a story: All of these are questions on which the fifteen attempted to explain their own practices. Sharon Bryan, for example, speaks of writing some of the poems in *Flying Blind* as "based on an emerging order and where I could see gaps in it." She says she has "revised poems when I discovered ways they were in dialogue with one another. I think more in terms of groups and books than of single poems."

5. Two short examples from others may serve to illustrate the importance of reading the poems in Dickinson's own form and in the sequence in which she "published" them. One is illustrated by an amusing entry by Jayne Relaford Brown in a prize-winning collection, *Visiting Emily*. The book includes some eighty poems inspired by or in parody of Dickinson, a number of them by the poets included in chapter 5. One is not a new poem; it is Dickinson's "My Life had stood—a Loaded Gun" (J754, Fr764, F34). Here, however, it is titled "Emily Dickinson attends a Writing Workshop," and the poem is surround-

ed by a thicket of arrows, numbers, and comments ("Emily—Nice language here but I end this poem feeling confused," and so forth [ibid., 8]). Such editing (making a playful point here) may be a witty extreme, but it demonstrates what can happen when others interfere with the poet's intentions on a given poem. As for the collection of many poems into books (fascicles, portfolios, chapbooks—whatever we wish to call them), Paul Crumbley, who points us to a Constance Fenimore Woolson short story, offers this example. In it an artist said of an attempt to intervene with a poet's ordering: "I amended, altered, left out, put in, pierced, condensed, lengthened. . . . I could not succeed in completing anything that satisfied me." The character, Miss Grief, decides to leave the work of the poet "just as it stood" (1996, 163–64).

6. Debra Kang Dean agrees: "[I]t would be difficult to believe that the groupings were arbitrary." Based on her own experience, Dean says that the chapbook needs "a greater sort of unity . . . the way the short poem must be tighter than a longish poem."

7. Perry J. Rablin. "TRIBUTE TO e e cummings" published on a note card for the National Council of Teachers of English 1977 convention.

Bibliography

Dickinson, Emily. 1890, 1891, 1896. *Poems by Emily Dickinson,* ed. Mabel Loomis Todd and T. W. Higginson. Boston: Roberts Brothers.

———. 1929, 1942. *Poems by Emily Dickinson,* ed. Martha Dickinson Bianchi and Alfred Leete Hampson.

———. 1945. *Bolts of Melody: New Poems of Emily Dickinson,* ed. Mabel Loomis Todd and Millicent Todd Bingham. New York: Harper & Brothers.

———. 1958. *The Letters of Emily Dickinson,* ed. Thomas H. Johnson. 3 vols. Cambridge, Mass.: Harvard University Press, Belknap Press.

———. 1960. *The Complete Poems of Emily Dickinson,* ed. Thomas H. Johnson. 3 vols. Boston: Little Brown.

———. 1981. *The Manuscript Books of Emily Dickinson,* ed. R. W. Franklin. Vols. I and II. Cambridge, Mass.: Harvard University Press, Belknap Press.

———. 1998. *The Poems of Emily Dickinson: Variorum Edition,* ed. R. W. Franklin. 3 Vols. Cambridge, Mass.: Harvard University Press, Belknap Press.

Letters from Contemporary Poets. See Appendix A.

Secondary Sources

Anderson, Charles R. 1960. *Emily Dickinson's Poetry: Stairway of Surprise.* New York: Holt, Rinehart and Winston.

Anderson, Paul W. 1966. The Metaphysical Mirth of Emily Dickinson. *Georgia Review* 20:72–83.

Barker, Wendy. 1987. *Lunacy of Light: Emily Dickinson and the Experience of Metaphor.* Carbondale: Southern Illinois University Press.

Bell, Robyn Margaret. 1988. Emily Dickinson's Bookmaking: A Companion to the Manuscript Volumes. Ph.D. diss., University of California at Santa Barbara.

Benfey, Christopher. 1986. *Emily Dickinson: Lives of a Poet.* New York: George Braziller.

Bennett, Paula. 1986. *My Life a Loaded Gun: Female Creativity and Feminist Poetics.* Boston: Beacon.

———. 1990. *Emily Dickinson: Woman Poet.* Iowa City: University of Iowa Press.

———. 1992. By a Mouth That Cannot Speak: Spectral Presence in Emily Dickinson's Letters. *The Emily Dickinson Journal* 2:76–79.

Benstock, Shari. 1988. Authorizing the Autobiographical. In *The Private Self: Theory and Practice of Women's Autobiographical Writings,* ed. Shari Benstock, 10–33. Chapel Hill: University of North Carolina Press.

Bernikow, Louise, ed. 1974. *The World Split Open: Four Centuries of Women Poets.* New York: Random House.

Bevilacqua, Vincent Michael. 1961. The Rhetorical Theory of Henry Home, Lord Kames. Ph.D. diss., University of Illinois at Urbana-Champaign.

Bianchi, Martha Dickinson. 1924. *The Life and Letters of Emily Dickinson.* Boston: Houghton Mifflin.

———. 1932. *Emily Dickinson Face to Face: Unpublished Notes and Reminiscences.* Boston: Houghton Mifflin.

Bingham, Millicent Todd. 1945. *Ancestors' Brocades: The Literary Debut of Emily Dickinson.* New York: Harper & Brothers.

Blackmur, R. P. 1937. Emily Dickinson: Notes on Prejudice and Fact. In *The Recognition of Emily Dickinson* by Caesar R. Blake and Carlton F. Wells, 201–223.

Blake, Caesar R., and Carlton F. Wells. 1964. *The Recognition of Emily Dickinson.* Ann Arbor: University of Michigan Press.

Blasing, Mutlu Konuk. 1987. *American Poetry: The Rhetoric of Its Forms.* New Haven, Conn.: Yale University Press.

Blythe, Randy. 1994. Review of *Choosing Not Choosing,* by Sharon Cameron. *South Atlantic Review* 5, no. 2:154–56.

Bogan, Louise. 1970. Emily Dickinson. In *A Poet's Alphabet: Reflections on the Literary Art and Vocation,* ed. Robert Phelps and Ruth Limmer. New York: McGraw Hill.

Bornstein, George. 1986. The Arrangement of Browning's "Dramatic Lyrics" (1842). In *Poems in Their Place,* ed. Neil Fraistat, 273–288. Chapel Hill, University of North Carolina Press.

Bradstreet, Anne. 1967. *The Works of Anne Bradstreet,* ed. Jeannine Hensley. With a foreword by Adrienne Rich. Cambridge, Mass.: Harvard University Press.

Brown, Jayne Relaford. 2000. Emily Dickinson Attends a Writing Workshop. In *Visiting Emily,* ed. Sheila Coghill and Thom Tammaro. Iowa City: Iowa University Press.

Browning, Elizabeth Barrett. [1856] 1979. *Aurora Leigh.* Chicago: Cassandra Editions, Academy Chicago.

Buckingham, Willis J. 1977. Emily Dickinson's Dictionary. *Harvard Library Bulletin* 25:489–92.

———. 1984. Review of *Manuscript Books. American Literature* 54:613–14.

———. 1989. *Emily Dickinson's Reception in the 1890s.* Pittsburgh: University of Pittsburgh Press.

Budick, E. Miller. 1985. *Emily Dickinson and the Life of Languages.* Baton Rouge: Louisiana State University Press.

Bush, Douglas. 1966. *John Keats: His Life and Writings.* New York: MacMillan.

Cady, Edwin H., and Louis J. Budd, eds. 1990. *On Dickinson: The Best from American Literature.* Durham, N.C.: Duke University Press.

Cameron, Sharon. 1978. "A Loaded Gun": Dickinson and the Dialectics of Rage. *PMLA* 93:423–37.

———. 1979. *Lyric Time: Dickinson and the Limits of Genre.* Baltimore: Johns Hopkins University Press.

———. 1992. *Choosing Not Choosing: Dickinson's Fascicles.* Chicago: University of Chicago Press.

———. 1998. Dickinson's Fascicles. In *The Emily Dickinson Handbook,* ed. Gudrun Grabher, Roland Hagenbuchle, and Cristanne Miller. Amherst: University of Massachusetts Press.

Capps, Jack L. 1966. *Emily Dickinson's Reading: 1836–1886.* Cambridge, Mass.: Harvard University Press.

Clary, Bruce W. 1998. Emily Dickinson's Menagerie: The Fascicles as Poetic Scrapbooks. Ph.D. diss., Kansas State University.

Cody, John. 1971. *After Great Pain: The Inner Life of Emily Dickinson.* Cambridge, Mass.: Harvard University Press, Belknap Press.

Crumbley, Paul. 1996. *Inflections of the Pen: Dash and Voice in Emily Dickinson.* Lexington: University Press of Kentucky.

Curran, Stuart. 1986. Multum in Parvo: Wordsworth's Poems in Two Volumes of 1807. In *Poems in Their Place: The Intertextuality and Order of Poetic Collections,* ed. Neil Fraistat, 234–53. Chapel Hill: University of North Carolina Press.

Dandurand, Karen. 1982. Another Dickinson Poem Published in Her Lifetime. *American Literature* 54:434–37.
———. 1984. New Dickinson Civil War Publications. *American Literature* 56:17–27.
Day, Elizabeth. 1992. This Comes of Writing Poetry. Ph.D. diss., University of Maryland.
Dickenson, Donna. 1985. *Emily Dickinson*. Dover, N.H.: Berg.
Dickie, Margaret. 1991. *Lyric Contingencies*. Philadelphia: University of Pennsylvania Press.
———. 1995. Dickinson in Context. *American Literary History* 7:320–33.
Diehl, Joanne Feit. 1981. *Dickinson and the Romantic Imagination*. Princeton, N.J.: Princeton University Press.
———. 1983. "Ransom in a Voice": Language as Defense in Dickinson's Poetry. In *Feminist Critics Read Emily Dickinson*, ed. Suzanne Juhasz, 156–76. Bloomington: Indiana University Press.
Ditta, Joseph M. 1984. *Natural and Conceptual Design: Radical Confusion in Literary Theory*. New York: Peter Lang.
Dobson, Joanne. 1989. *Dickinson and the Strategies of Reticence: The Woman Writer in Nineteenth-Century America*. Bloomington: Indiana University Press.
Donoghue, Denis. 1965. *Connoisseurs of Chaos: Ideas of Order in Modern American Poetry*. New York: Macmillan.
Doreski, William. 1986. "An Exchange of Territory": Dickinson's Fascicle 27. *Emerson Society Quarterly: A Journal of the American Renaissance* 32:55–67.
Duchac, Joseph. 1979. *The Poems of Emily Dickinson: Annotated Guide to Commentary Published in English 1980–1977*. Boston: G. K. Hall.
Eberwein, Jane Donahue. 1984. Doing Without: Yankee Woman Poet. In *Critical Essays on Emily Dickinson*, ed. Paul Ferlazzo. Boston: Hall.
———. 1985. *Dickinson: Strategies of Limitation*. Amherst: University of Massachusetts Press.
———. 1987. Emily Dickinson and the Calvinist Sacramental Tradition. *Emerson Society Quarterly: A Journal of the American Renaissance* 33:67–81.
———, ed. 1998. *Emily Dickinson Encyclopedia*. Westport, Conn.: Greenwood.
Emerson, Ralph Waldo. [1840–1843] 1912. New Poetry. In *Uncollected Writings*. Port Washington, N.Y.: Kennikat.
———. [1841] 1971. The Poet. *The Early Lectures of Ralph Waldo Emerson*, ed. Robert R. Spiller and Wallace E. Williams, 347–65. Vol. III. Cambridge, Mass.: Harvard University Press.
———. [1844] 1968. The Poet. In *Essays of Ralph Waldo Emerson: Second Series*, 1–40. New York: AMS.
———. [1872] 1875. Poetry and Imagination. *Letters and Social Aims*. Vol. VII. Centenary edition. Boston: Houghton Mifflin.
Farr, Judith. [1961] 1990. Dickinson and the Metaphysical Poets. In *On Dickinson: The Best from American Literature*, ed. Edwin H. Cody and Louis J. Budd, 54–68. Durham, N.C.: Duke University Press.
———. 1992. *The Passion of Emily Dickinson*. Cambridge, Mass.: Harvard University Press.
———. 1996. *Emily Dickinson: A Collection of Critical Essays*. Upper Saddle River, N.J.: Prentice Hall.
Fraistat, Neil., ed. 1986. *Poems in Their Place: The Intertextuality and Order of Poetic Collections*. Chapel Hill: University of North Carolina Press.
Franklin, Ralph W. 1967. *The Editing of Emily Dickinson: A Reconsideration*. Madison: University of Wisconsin Press.

———. 1978. The Houghton Library Dickinson Manuscript 157. *Harvard Library Bulletin* 28: 245–57.

———. 1979a. The Dickinson Packet 14 and 20, 10 and 26. *Papers of the Bibliographical Society of America* 73:348–54.

———. 1979b. Emily Dickinson's Packet 27 (and 80, 14, and 6). *Harvard Library Bulletin* 27: 341–48.

———. 1983. The Emily Dickinson Fascicles. *Studies in Bibliography* 36:1–20.

Frost, Robert. [1939] 1972. The Figure a Poem Makes. In *Robert Frost Poetry and Prose,* ed. Edward Connery Lathem and Lawrance Thompson, 393–96. New York: Holt, Rinehart and Winston.

Gallipeo, Paul Thaddeus. 1984. The Amherst Fascicles of Emily Dickinson. Ph.D. diss., SUNY Albany.

Garbowsky, Maryanne. 1979. Emily Dickinson's Literary Community. Ph.D. diss., Drew University, Madison, N.J.

———. 1989. *The House without the Door: A Study of Emily Dickinson and the Illness of Agoraphobia.* Rutherford, N.J.: Fairleigh Dickinson University Press.

Gelpi, Albert. 1965. *Emily Dickinson: The Mind of the Poet.* Cambridge, Mass.: Harvard University Press.

———. 1975. Emily Dickinson: The Self as Center. In *The Tenth Muse: The Psyche of the American Poet,* 219–99. Cambridge, Mass.: Harvard University Press.

———. 1987. Emily Dickinson's Word: Presence as Absence, Absence as Presence. *American Poetry* 4:41–45.

Gerlach, John. 1994. Reading Dickinson: Bolts, Hounds, the Variorum, and Fascicle 39. *Emily Dickinson Journal* 3, no. 2:78–99.

———. 1996. Review essay on Oberhaus's *Emily Dickinson's Fascicles: Method and Meaning. Emily Dickinson Journal* 5, no. 1:121–23.

Gilbert, Sandra. 1983. The Wayward Nun beneath the Hill: Emily Dickinson and the Mysteries of Womanhood. In *Feminist Critics Read Emily Dickinson,* ed. Suzanne Juhasz, 22–44. Bloomington: Indiana University Press.

———. 1986. The American Sexual Poetics of Walt Whitman and Emily Dickinson. In *Reconstructing American Literary History,* ed. Sacvan Bercovitch, 123–54. Cambridge, Mass.: Harvard University Press.

———., and Susan Gubar. [1979] 1984. *The Madwoman in the Attic: The Woman Writer and the Nineteenth-Century Literary Imagination.* New Haven, Conn.: Yale University Press.

Goodwin, David Gordon. 1986. The Rhetoric of British Rhetorical Handbooks (1758–1828) and Romantic Modes of English Epic Poetry. Ph.D. diss., University of Toronto.

Grabher, Gudrun, Roland Hagenbuchle, and Cristanne Miller. 1998. *The Dickinson Handbook.* Amherst: University of Massachusetts Press.

Grabher, Gudrun, and Martina Antretter. 2001. *Emily Dickinson at Home.* Trier, Austria: Wissenschaftlicher Verlag Trier.

Griffith, Clark. 1964. *The Long Shadow: Emily Dickinson's Tragic Poetry.* Princeton, N.J.: Princeton University Press.

Habegger, Alfred. 2001. *My Wars Are Laid Away in Books: The Life of Emily Dickinson.* New York: Random House.

Hagenbuchle, Roland. 1979. Sign and Process: The Concept of Language in Emerson and Dickinson. *Journal of the American Renaissance* 27:137–55.

Hallen, Cynthia L., and Lavra M. Harvey. 1993. Translation and the Emily Dickinson Lexicon. Emily Dickinson Journal 2, no. 2: 130–46 http://humanities.byu.edu/ED Lexicon/nehgrant.html

Harrison, G. B., ed. 1948. *Shakespeare: The Complete Works*. New York: Harcourt Brace.
Hart, Ellen Louise. 1994. Poetic License. *The Women's Review of Books* (January):24.
———, and Martha Nell Smith, eds. 1998. *Open Me Carefully: Emily Dickinson's Intimate Letters to Susan Huntington Dickinson*. Ashfield, Mass.: Paris.
Hartman, Geoffrey. 1970. *Beyond Formalism: Literary Essays*. New Haven, Conn.: Yale University Press.
Heginbotham, Eleanor. 1992a. Dwelling in Possibilities: The Fascicles of Emily Dickinson. Ph.D. diss., University of Maryland.
———. 1992b. "No Romance Sold": Representing Dickinson in Fiction. *EDIS Bulletin* 10, no. 1 (spring):2–3, 20–21.
———. 1993. The Poet in the Cupola: Charles Wright and Emily Dickinson. *EDIS Bulletin* 5:5–6.
———. 1996. Dickinson's "What if I say I shall not wait!" *The Explicator* 54, no. 3:154–60.
———. 2001. Contemporary Poets on Editing—and Dickinson's Fascicles. *Emily Dickinson at Home: Proceedings of the Third International Conference of the Emily Dickinson International Society in South Hadley*. Trier, Austria: Wissenschaftlicher Verlag.
Herrnstein Smith, Barbara. 1968. *Poetic Closure: A Study of How Poems End*. Chicago: University of Chicago Press.
Homans, Margaret. 1980. *Women Writers and Poetic Identity: Dorothy Wordsworth, Emily Brontë, and Emily Dickinson*. Princeton, N.J.: Princeton University Press.
Home, Henry (Lord Kames). [1761] 1855. *Elements of Criticism*, ed. James R. Boyd. New York: A. S. Barnes.
Howe, Susan. 1985. *My Emily Dickinson*. Berkeley: North Atlantic Books.
———. 1993. *The Birth-Mark: Unsettling the Wilderness in American Literary History*. Hanover, N.H.: Wesleyan University Press.
Irish, Loomis Caryl. 1961. Human Nature and the Arts: The Aesthetic Theory of Henry Home, Lord Kames. Ph.D. diss., Columbia University.
Johnson, Greg. 1985. *Perception and the Poet's Quest*. Tuscaloosa: University of Alabama Press.
Jones, Rowena Revis. 1990. Edwards, Dickinson and the Sacramentality of Nature. *Studies in Puritan American Spirituality* 1:225–53.
Juhasz, Suzanne, ed. 1983a. *Feminist Critics Read Emily Dickinson*. Bloomington: Indiana University Press.
———. 1983b. Review of *Manuscript Books*. *English Language Notes* (December):57.
———. 1983c. *The Undiscovered Content: Emily Dickinson and the Space of the Mind*. Bloomington: Indiana University Press.
Kamusikiri, Sandra Darlene. 1985. "A Building of Magnificence": Blake's Major Prophecies and Eighteenth-Century Conceptions of the Human Sublime. Ph.D. diss., University of California, Riverside.
Keller, Karl. 1977. Alephs, Zahirs, and the Triumph of Ambiguity. *Literary Uses of Typology*, ed. Earl Miner, 274–314. Princeton, N.J.: Princeton University Press.
———. 1979. *The Only Kangaroo among the Beauty*. Baltimore: Johns Hopkins University Press.
Kher, Inder Nath. 1974. *The Landscape of Absence: Emily Dickinson's Poetry*. New Haven, Conn., and London: Yale University Press.
Knapp, Bettina. 1989. *Emily Dickinson*. New York: Continuum.
Landow, George P. 1977. Moses Striking the Rock: Typological Symbolism in Victorian Poetry. In *Literary Uses of Typology*, ed. Earl Miner. 315–44. Princeton, N.J.: Princeton University Press.

Lease, Benjamin. 1990. *Emily Dickinson's Readings of Men and Books: Sacred Soundings.* New York: St. Martin's.
Leyda, Jay. 1960. *The Years and Hours of Emily Dickinson.* New Haven, Conn.: Yale University Press.
Lindberg-Seyersted, Brita. 1968. *The Voice of the Poet: Aspects of Style in the Poetry of Emily Dickinson.* Cambridge, Mass.: Harvard University Press.
———. 1976. *Emily Dickinson's Punctuation.* Oslo: American Institute of Oslo.
Longsworth, Polly. 1984. *Austin and Mabel: The Amherst Affair and Love Letters of Austin Dickinson and Mabel Loomis Todd.* New York: Holt, Rinehart and Winston.
Loving, Jerome. 1981. Whitman and Dickinson. *American Literary Scholarship,* 84–85. Durham, N.C.: Duke University Press.
———. 1983. Emily Dickinson's Workshop. *Review* 5:195–201.
Lowell, Amy. 1955. *Complete Poetical Works of Amy Lowell.* Boston: Houghton Mifflin.
Lowenberg, Carlton. 1986. *Emily Dickinson's Textbooks.* Lafayette, Calif.: Carlton Lowenberg.
McGann, Jerome J. 1983. *A Critique of Modern Textual Criticism.* Chicago: University of Chicago Press.
———. 1983. *The Romantic Ideology: A Critical Investigation.* Chicago: University of Chicago Press.
———. 1993. Emily Dickinson's Visible Language. *Emily Dickinson Journal* 2. Reprint in *Emily Dickinson: A Collection of Critical Essays,* ed. Judith Farr, 248–59. Upper Saddle River, N.J.: Prentice Hall, 1996.
Miller, Cristanne. 1983. How "Low Feet" Stagger: Disruptions of Language in Dickinson's Poetry. In *Feminist Critics Read Emily Dickinson,* ed. Suzanne Juhasz, 134–55. Bloomington: Indiana University Press.
———. 1987. *Emily Dickinson: A Poet's Grammar.* Cambridge, Mass.: Harvard University Press.
Miller, James E. 1962. Emily Dickinson: The Thunder's Tongue. *The Minnesota Review* 2:302–3. Reprint in *Quests Surd and Absurd: Essays in American Literature,* 145–58. Chicago: University of Chicago Press, 1967.
———. 1967. Emily Dickinson's Bright Orthography. In *Quests Surd and Absurd: Essays in American Literature,* 137–44. Chicago: University of Chicago Press.
Miller, Mary Cender. 1988. Emily Dickinson's Oriental Heresies. In *After a Hundred Years,* ed. Tamaaki Yamakaweka, 143–58. Kyoto: Emily Dickinson Society of Japan.
Miller, Ruth. 1968. *The Poetry of Emily Dickinson.* Middletown, Conn.: Wesleyan University Press.
Miner, Earl, ed. 1977. *Literary Uses of Typology.* Princeton, N.J.: Princeton University Press.
———. 1986. Some Issues for the Study of Integrated Collections. In *Poems in Their Places: The Intertextuality and Order of Poetic Collections,* ed. Neil Fraistat, 18–43. Chapel Hill: University of North Carolina Press.
Mitchell, Domhnall. 1998. Revising the Script: Dickinson's Manuscripts. *American Literature* 70, no. 4:703–37.
Monteiro, George, and Barton Levi St. Armand. 1981. The Experienced Emblem: A Study of the Poetry of Emily Dickinson. *Prospects* 6:186–280.
Mossberg, Barbara. 1982. *Emily Dickinson: When a Writer Is a Daughter.* Bloomington: Indiana University Press.
Oberhaus, Dorothy Huff. 1995. *Emily Dickinson's Fascicles: Method and Meaning.* University Park: Pennsylvania State University Press.
O'Keefe, Martha Lindblom. *This Edifice: Studies in the Structure of the Fascicles of the Poetry of Emily Dickinson.* (Privately printed, 1986).

———. 1988. I hide myself within my flower. In *After a Hundred Years,* ed. Tamaaki Yamakawa, 57–66. Kyoto: Emily Dickinson Society of Japan.

O'Meara, Anne Brown. 1989. Representing Emily Dickinson: A Study of Literary Practice. Ph.D. diss., University of Minnesota.

Orsini, Daniel J. 1981. Emily Dickinson and the Romantic Use of Science. *Massachusetts Studies in English* 7/8:57–69.

Orzeck, Martin A. 1989. Emily Dickinson and the Problem of Audience. Ph.D. diss., Arizona State University.

Ostriker, Alicia. 1986. *Stealing the Language: The Emergence of Women's Poetry in America.* Boston: Beacon.

Paglia, Camille. 1991. *Sexual Personae: Art and Decadence from Nefertiti to Emily Dickinson.* New York: Vintage Books.

Patterson, Rebecca. 1956. Elizabeth Browning and Emily Dickinson. *Educational Leader:* 21–48.

———. 1979. *Emily Dickinson's Imagery.* Amherst: University of Massachusetts Press.

Pebworth, Ted, and Jay Summers. 1969. Dickinson's "The feet of people walking home." *Explicator* 27: 76.

Phillips, Elizabeth. 1988. *Emily Dickinson: Personae and Performance.* University Park: Pennsylvania State University Press.

Pickard, John B. 1967. *Emily Dickinson: An Introduction and Interpretation.* American Authors and Critics Series. New York: Holt.

Poe, Edgar Allan. 1829. Sonnet—To Science. Rpt. 1994. *Heath Anthology of American Literature.* Vol. 1. 2d ed. Ed. Paul Lauter. Lexington, Mass.: D.C. Heath and Co.

Pollak, Vivian. 1984. *Dickinson: The Anxiety of Gender.* Ithaca, N.Y.: Cornell University Press.

———. 1988. *A Poet's Parents.* Chapel Hill: University of North Carolina Press.

Ponder, Melinda Mowry. 1987. The Role of Eighteenth-Century Anglo-Scottish Theorists in Hawthorne's Aesthetic Education and Literary Creation of the Early Tales. Ph.D. diss., Boston College.

———. 1990. *Hawthorne's Early Narrative Art.* Lewiston: Edwin Mellen.

Porter, David. 1961. *The Art of Emily Dickinson's Early Poetry.* Cambridge, Mass.: Harvard University Press.

———. 1981. *Dickinson: The Modern Idiom.* Cambridge, Mass.: Harvard University Press.

———. 1983. Review of *Manuscript Books. Papers of the Bibliographical Society of America* 77:84–86.

———. 1984. Dickinson's Readers. *New England Quarterly* 57:106–7.

———. 1996. Dickinsons Unrevised Poems. In *Dickinson and Audience,* ed. Martin Orzeck and Robert Weisbuch, 11–29. Ann Arbor: University of Michigan Press.

Rapin, Rene. 1973. Dickinson's "I never lost as much but twice." *Explicator* 31, no. 7:52.

Rich, Adrienne. 1995. Reissue. Vesuvius at Home: The Power of Emily Dickinson. In *On Lies, Secrets, and Silence: Selected Prose 1966–1978,* 157–83. New York: Norton, 1979.

Riffaterre, Michael. 1984. *Semiotics of Poetry.* Bloomington: Indiana University Press.

———. 1983. Semantics of the Poem. In *Text Production,* 26–42. Trans. Terese Lyons. New York: Columbia University Press.

Rosenbaum, S. P. 1964. *A Concordance to the Poems of Emily Dickinson.* Ithaca, N.Y.: Cornell University Press.

Rosenthal, M. L. 1982. Poems by the Packet. *Times Literary Supplement* (March 26):357.

Rosenthal, Macha L., and Sally Gall. 1983. *The Modern Poetic Sequence.* Oxford: Oxford University Press.

Ross, Christine. 2001. Uncommon Meters: Emily Dickinson's Subversive Prosody. *Emily Dickinson Journal* 10, no. 1:70–98.
St. Armand, Barton Levi. 1984. *Emily Dickinson and Her Culture*. Cambridge, Mass.: Harvard University Press.
———. 1988. Heavenly Rewards of Merit: Recontextualizing Emily Dickinson's "Checks." In *After a Hundred Years: Essays on Emily Dickinson,* ed. Tamaaki Yamakawa, 219–38. Kyoto: Emily Dickinson Society of Japan.
Salska, Agnieszka. 1998. Dickinson's Letters. In *An Emily Dickinson Handbook,* ed. Gudrun Grabher, Roland Hagenbuchle, and Cristanne Miller, 163–80. Amherst: University of Massachusetts Press.
Schenck, Celeste. 1988. All of a Piece: Women's Poetry and Autobiography. In *Life/Lines: Theorizing Women's Autobiography,* ed. Bella Brodzki and Celeste Schenck, 281–305. Ithaca, N.Y.: Cornell University Press.
Scheurer, Erika. 1995. "Near but Remote": Emily Dickinson's Epistolary Voice. *Emily Dickinson Journal* 4, no. 1:86–107.
Scholl, Diane Gabrielsen. 1990. Emily Dickinson's Conversion Narratives: A Study of the Fascicles. *Studies in Puritan American Spirituality* 1 (December):202–24.
Sewall, Richard B. 1980. *The Life of Emily Dickinson*. 2 vols. New York: Farrar, Straus and Giroux.
Shawcross, John T. The Arrangement and Order of John Donne's Poems. In *Poems in Their Place: The Intertextuality and Order of Poetic Collections,* ed. Neil Fraistat, 119–63. Chapel Hill: University of North Carolina Press, 1986.
Shurr, William H. 1983. *The Marriage of Emily Dickinson*. Lexington: University Press of Kentucky.
Sletto, Arlo Duane. 1975. Emily Dickinson's Poetry: The Fascicles. Ph.D. diss., University of New Mexico, Albuquerque.
Small, Judy Jo. 1990. *Positive as Sound: Emily Dickinson's Rhyme*. Athens: University of Georgia Press.
Smith, Martha Nell. Emily Dickinson Hypermedia Archive. http://jefferson.village.virginia.edu/dickinson.
———. 1985. "Rowing in Eden": Gender and the Poetics of Emily Dickinson. Ph.D. diss., Rutgers University.
———. 1992. *Rowing in Eden: Re-Reading Dickinson*. Austin and London: University of Texas Press.
———. 1994. Review essay of Sharon Cameron's *Choosing Not Choosing. Emily Dickinson Journal* 3, no. 1:107–9.
Stocks, Kenneth. 1987. *Emily Dickinson and the Modern Consciousness*. New York: St. Martin's.
Stonum, Gary Lee. 1990. *The Dickinson Sublime*. Madison: University of Wisconsin Press.
Tate, Allen. 1932. New England Culture and Emily Dickinson. Rpt. 1964. In *The Recognition of Emily Dickinson,* ed. Caesar Blake and Carlton Wells, 153–67. Ann Arbor: University of Michigan Press.
Thomas, Heather Kirk. 1988. "Renunciation" and Anorexia Nervosa. Reprint in *On Dickinson: The Best from American Literature,* ed. Edwin H. Cady and Louis J. Budd, 191–211. Durham, N.C.: Duke University Press, 1990.
Thorpe, B. J. 1858. *Harper's* 17:619.
Tingley, Stephanie Ann. 1987. "My Friends Are Very Few": The Influence of Emily Dickinson's Select Contemporary Audience on Her Poetry. Ph.D. diss., University of Illinois at Urbana-Champaign.
Waggoner, Hyatt H. 1984. *American Poets: From the Puritans to the Present,* rev. ed. Baton Rouge, La.: Louisiana State University Press.

Walker, Cheryl. 1987. *The Nightingale's Burden: Women Poets and American Culture before 1900*. Bloomington: Indiana University Press.
Webster, Noah. [1828] 1847. *American Dictionary of the English Language*. New York: Converse.
Weisbuch, Robert. 1972. *Emily Dickinson's Poetry.* Chicago: University of Chicago Press.
———. 1982. Review *American Literary Scholarship: An Annual*.
———. 1983. Whitman and Dickinson. *American Literary Scholarship: An Annual*.
Werner, Marta L. 1995. *Emily Dickinson's Open Folios: Scenes of Reading, Surfaces of Writing*. Ann Arbor: University of Michigan Press.
———. 1996. Review of *Emily Dickinson's Fascicles: Method and Meaning. New England Quarterly Book Review*.
Whicher, George. 1957. *This Was a Poet*. Ann Arbor: University of Michigan Press.
White, William. 1983. Review of *Manuscript Books. Dickinson Studies* 45:3–6.
Wider, Sarah. 1992. Corresponding Worlds: The Art of Emily Dickinson's Letters. *Emily Dickinson Journal* 1, no. 1:19–38.
Wilbur, Richard. 1960. Sumptuous Destitution. Rpt. 1996. In *Emily Dickinson: A Collection of Critical Essays,* ed. Judith Farr, 53–61. Upper Saddle River, N.J.: Prentice-Hall.
———. 1997. Riddles. In *The Catbird's Song: Prose Pieces, 1963–1965*. New York: Harcourt Brace.
Wittreich, Joseph Anthony Jr. 1986. "Strange Text!" Paradise Regain'd . . . to which is added Samson Agonistes. In *Poems in Their Place: The Intertextuality and Order of Poetic Collections,* ed. Neil Fraistat, 164–94. Chapel Hill: University of North Carolina Press.
Wolff, Cynthia Griffin. 1986. *Emily Dickinson*. New York: Alfred A. Knopf.
Wolosky, Shira. 1999. Emily Dickinson's Manuscript Body: History/Textuality/Gender. *Emily Dickinson Journal* 8, no. 2:87–99.
Wylder, Edith. 1971. *The Last Face: Emily Dickinson's Manuscripts*. Albuquerque: University of New Mexico Press.
Yamakawa, Tamaaki, ed. 1988. *After a Hundred Years: Essays on Emily Dickinson*. Kyoto: Emily Dickinson Society of Japan.

Index

Index to Names and Subjects

Adcock, Betty, 113, 147, 151
Anderson, Charles, 158n. 17, 167n. 11
Anthon, Kate (Kate Anthon Turner), 75, 158n. 18

Barker, Wendy, 27, 31, 64, 83, 92, 161n. 5
Bates, Arlo, 167n. 11
Bell, Robyn, xi, 6, 49, 142, 150, 161n. 8, 164n. 3
Benfey, Christopher, 48
Bennett, Paula, 12, 150n. 13, 163n. 8, 164n. 13
Bentstock, Shari, 106
Bernikow, Louise, 161n. 3
Bianchi, Martha Dickinson, ix, x, 8, 138, 158n. 14, 163n. 9
biblical/religious references, 26, 87, 132–35, 138
Bingham, Millicent Todd, x, 8, 158n. 21
Blackmur, R. P., 43, 159n. 1
Blake, William, 16
Blasing, Mutlu Konuk, 65
Blythe, Randy, x, 165n. 5
Bogan, Louise, xiii
Bornstein, George 146
Bowles, Samuel, 1, 72, 75, 79, 80, 95, 102, 130, 162n. 2
Bradstreet, Anne, 107
Bray, Robert, 105
Brontë, Emily, 110
Brown, Jayne Relaford, 168n. 5
Browning, Elizabeth Barrett, 6, 43, 75, 108, 110, 156n. 3
Browning, Robert, 34, 84, 146
Bryon, Sharon, 145, 151
Buckingham, Willis, 9, 14, 82, 160n. 8, 161n. 2, 167n.11
Budick, E. Miller, 135, 137, 138, 161n. 8

Cameron, Sharon, x, xi, 10, 12, 13, 28, 43, 47, 90, 105, 144, 158n. 21
Capps, Jack, 34, 95, 101, 162n. 6
Cato, 135, 140, 166n. 9
Clary, Bruce, 165n. 4
Cody, John, 63, 161n. 5
common meter, 30
contextual poetics, 47–48, 74, 104–7; support for and challenges to contextual readings (manuscript readings): 9–10, 12–15, 39, 104–5, 111–15
Copland, Aaron, 99
Crumbley, Paul, 12, 105, 131, 161n. 6, 168n. 5
cummings, ee, 149, 168n. 7
Curran, Stuart, 22
Danderand, Karen, 111
Day, Elizabeth, 160n. 9
Dean, Debra Kang, 115, 147, 151, 168n. 6
Dickenson, Donna, 39
Dickie, Margaret, 12
Dickinson, Austin, ix,13, 14,
Dickinson, Edward, 26, 75, 108, 138
Dickinson, Emily: attitude to publication, 10–11; preparation/ambition 107–12, 123–26
Dickinson, Lavinia, x, 13, 142
Dickinson, Susan Gilbert, xii, 13, 16, 64, 71, 72–73, 75, 110, 138, 158n. 18, 160n. 1, 162n. 1, 162n. 2, 162n. 5, 163n. 10, 167n. 12, 167n. 2
Diehl, Joanne Feit, 121, 131
Dobson, Joanne, 159n. 4
Donoghue, Denis, 21, 50, 51
Doreski, William, xi, 22, 43, 74
duplicate poems, xi–xii, 48–49

Eberwein, Jane Donahue, 61, 100, 120, 127, 159n. 2, 159n. 5, 161n. 7, 161n. 8, 163n. 7, 163n. 10, 166n. 6
Emerson, Ralph Waldo, 7, 18, 19, 38, 42, 52, 68, 97, 107, 109, 134, 156–57n. 4, 165n. 8

179

Farr, Judith, 159n. 2, 160n. 13
fascicles: appearance of, x; discovery of, 8; term ("portfolio," "book"), 8, 106–9
Fay, Julie, 114, 167n. 4
Finch, Annie, 113, 151
Fish, Stanley, 11
Fraistat, Neil, xi, 5, 15, 22, 43, 47, 115, 146
Franklin, Ralph, viii, ix, xi, 5, 9–10, 11, 14, 47, 48, 72, 104–5, 127, 130, 147, 162n. 1, 167n. 2
Freeman, Margaret, x, 42
Frost, Robert, xiii, 16, 85, 146

Gallipeo, Paul, xi, 12, 164n. 3
Garbowsky, Maryanne, 6, 9, 158n. 14, 166n. 7
Gelpi, Albert, 38, 84, 158n. 17
Gerlach, John, xi, 165n. 5
Gilbert, Sandra, 51, 63, 95, 112, 114, 148, 151, 167–68n. 4
Grabher, Gudrun, 161n. 7; and Martina Antretter, 112
Griffith, Clark, 140

Habegger, Alfred, 11, 158n. 18, 161n. 4, 163n. 10
Hagenbuchle, Roland, 158n. 17
Harper's Monthly, 49, 101, 161n. 4, 163n. 7
Hart, Ellen Louise, xiii, 12
Hartman, Geoffrey, 36
Hawthorne, Nathaniel, 17, 20, 31, 32, 108, 158n. 19
Herrnstein Smith, Barbara, 47, 74
Higginson, Thomas Wentworth, 10–11, 12, 17, 72, 75, 81, 85, 107, 110, 115, 123, 125, 128, 133, 149, 162n. 2, 163n. 12
Holmes and Barber, *Book of Emblems*, 49
Homans, Margaret, 46, 110
Home, Henry (Lord Kames), 19–20, 31, 42, 158n. 18, 158n. 19, 158n. 20
Howe, Susan, 12, 141
hymns: "Amazing Grace," 17; "Guide me O Thou Great Jehovah," 161n. 4; "Rock of Ages," 50, 161n. 4

Jackson, Helen Hunt, 108, 150

James, Henry, 21, 34
Jenkins, MacGregor, 52
Johnson, Greg, 83, 120
Johnson, Thomas, xiii, 13, 72–73, 102, 162n. 1, 167n. 12
Jones, Rowena Revis, 159n. 2
Juhasz, Suzanne, viii, 128, 163n. 8

Kames, Lord. *See* Home, Henry
Keats, John, 17, 30, 34, 42, 52, 95, 159n. 7
Keller, Karl, 6, 61, 69, 79, 129, 161n. 4, 161n. 8, 162n. 1, 163n. 8, 163n. 10
Kher, Inder Nath, 28, 32, 132, 160n. 15
Knapp, Bettina, 51

Landow, George P., 161n. 4
Lease, Benjamin, 96
Leyda, Jay, 71, 75, 162n. 1
Lindberg-Seyersted, Brita, 62, 75, 161n. 8
Longfellow, Henry Wadsworth, 98
Longsworth, Polly, 13
Lord, Judge Otis, 85
Loving, Jerome, 9
Lowell, Amy, 9, 20, 157n. 8
Lowenberg, Carlton, 19
Lyon, Mary, 11, 26

McGann, Jerome J., xii, 12, 104, 110, 144, 164n. 2, 165n. 5
Miller, Cristanne, 43, 62, 134
Miller, James, 12
Miller, Mary Cender, 32
Miller, Ruth, 13, 79, 104, 157n. 9, 159n. 5
Miner, Earl, 43, 161n. 4
Mitchell, Domhnall, 165n. 5
Monteiro, George, and Barton Levi St. Armand, 49, 160n. 13, 161n. 4, 164n. 16
Mossberg, Barbara, 92, 138, 163n. 7

Napoleon, 163n. 7
Nelson, Marilyn, 112, 152

Oberhaus, Dorothy, xi, 10, 11, 104, 132, 133, 140, 141, 158n. 12, 165n. 5, 167nn. 13–15
O'Keefe, Martha Lindblom, xi, 10, 104,

157n. 9, 158n. 12
O'Meara, Anne Brown, 163n. 8
Orsini, Daniel J., 85
Ostriker, Alicia, 106, 112, 114, 144, 146, 148, 152, 161n. 7

Paglia, Camille, 51, 65, 161n. 5
Parkin, Andrew, 147, 154
Pastan, Linda, 115, 144, 152
Patterson, Rebecca, 159n. 4, 160n. 11, 160n. 13, 164n. 13
Pebworth, Ted-Larry, and Jay Claude Summers, 120, 127
Phillips, Elizabeth, 158n. 14
Pickard, John, 62
Poe, Edgar Allan, 80–81, 162–63n. 6
Pollak, Vivian, 45, 51, 79, 108, 109, 160n. 1, 163n. 7, 163n. 10, 164n. 13
Ponder, Melinda Mowry, 20, 31, 158n. 19, 160n. 14
Porter, David, ix, 10, 11, 14, 48, 127, 134, 147, 159n. 4, 160n. 8, 160n. 15, 166n. 4

Rapin, Rene, 137–38
Rich, Adrienne, 62, 165n. 9
Riffaterre, Michael, xii, 13, 43, 45, 74, 133, 158n. 13, 165n. 7
Rosenbaum, S. P., 33
Rosenthal, M. J., and Sally Gall, 9, 10 12, 104
Ross, Christine, 19

St. Armand, Barton Levi, 49, 51, 52, 90, 108, 137
Sands, Marget, 105
Saje, Natasha, 114, 115, 152
Schenck, Celeste, 106
Scheurer, Erika, xii, 144, 167n. 2
Scholl, Diane Gabrielsen, 15, 158n. 12, 159n. 2
Sewall, Richard, xii, 6, 9, 51, 84, 95, 108, 161n. 8, 163n. 6, 163n. 10
Sewell, Maryann, 99
Shakespeare, William, 30, 127, 130, 137, 142, 161n. 7, 164n. 13, 166n. 8
Shurr, William, 10, 11, 27, 79, 104, 106, 157n. 10
Sigourney, Lydia, 34, 108, 160n. 9

Small, Judy Jo, 64, 69
Smith, Martha Nell, xiii, 9, 12, 13, 43, 47, 72, 73, 74, 98, 105, 110, 111, 123, 125, 141, 144, 158n. 14, 158n. 17, 162n. 1, 164n. 16, 166n. 10, 167n. 2
Solensten, John, 115, 147–48, 153
Stearns, Frazer, 130
Stocks, Kenneth, 166n. 2
Stonum, Gary Lee, 7, 18, 28, 37, 40, 125

Tate, Allen, 46
Thoreau, Henry David, 32, 34, 51, 156n. 3
Thorpe, B. T., 49
Tingley, Stephanie Ann, 108, 158n. 15, 167n. 2
Todd, Mabel Loomis, x, 8, 13, 14, 83, 128

Wadsworth, Charles, 10, 75
Waggoner, Hyatt, 145, 149
Walker, Cheryl, 164n. 16
Webster, *Dictionaries,* 13, 7, 24, 25, 32, 35–36, 39, 42, 51, 52, 64, 66, 67, 68, 69, 76–77, 86, 97, 141, 157n. 5, 158n. 16, 164n. 13
Weisbuch, Robert, 10, 11, 12, 34, 48, 81, 83, 106, 157n. 10, 158n. 17, 162n. 5
Whitman, Walt, 7, 8, 16, 111, 145
Wider, Sarah, 167n. 2
Wilbur, Richard, 112, 114, 153
Wittreick, Joseph, 146
Wolff, Cynthia Griffin, 17, 30, 38, 76, 86, 120, 127, 132, 163n. 10
Wolosky, Shira, 144, 167n. 3
Wordsworth, William, 22, 90
Wong, Laurence, 154
Wright, Charles, 112–13, 114, 153
Wylder, Edith, 43

Index to Poems and Letters

Poems

A clock stopped (J287, Fr259, F11), 101
A fuzzy fellow without feet (J173, Fr171, F8), 61
A great Hope fell" (J1123, Fr187, ?), 50
A Lady red—amid the Hill (J74, Fr137, F6), 70, 91
A little Bread—a crust (J159, Fr 135, F10), 70, 77, 82, 84
A nearness to Tremendousness— (J963, Fr824, F40), 119, 141
A poor—torn heart— (J78, Fr125, F6), 70, 98
A Shady friend—for Torrid days— (J278, Fr306, F14), 117, 128
A solemn thing—it was / I said— (J271, Fr307, F14), 128
A Toad, can die of Light (J583, Fr419, F14), 117, 130, 148
A transport one cannot contain (J184, Fr203, F10 and 12), 70, 81
A word is dead (J1212, Fr278), 115
A *Wounded* deer—leaps highest— (J165, Fr181, F8), 49, 63
Adrift! A little boat adrift! (J30, Fr6, F1), 124
Ah Moon—and Star! (J240, Fr262, F11 and 14), 48, 127
Ah! Necromancy Sweet! (J177, Fr168, F8), 65
All these my banners be— (J22, Fr29, F1), 116, 120, 121
Angels in the Early Morning (J94, Fr73, F3), 166n. 6
An awful Tempest mashed the air— (J198, Fr224), 37
Artists wrestled here! (J110, Fr111), 71
As by the dead we love to sit (J88, Fr78, F3), 118, 136, 145
As Children bid the guest (J133, Fr127, F6), 70, 98
As if I asked a common alms (J323, Fr14, F1), 122
As if some little Arctic flower (J180, Fr177, F8), 21, 68, 143
At last—to be identified— (J174, Fr172, F8 and 21), 23, 32–34, 35, 39, 42, 44, 46–47, 48, 62

Besides the Autumn poets (J131, Fr123, F6), 70, 93, 95
Between my country / And the Others (J905, Fr829, F40), 119, 141
Bound—a Trouble (J269, Fr240, F9 and 36), 48
Bring me the sunset in a cup (J128, Fr140, F6), 70, 90

Circumference thou Bride of Awe (J1620, Fr 1636), 37
Cocoon above! (J129, Fr142, F6), 70, 92
Come slowly—Eden! (J211, Fr205, F10), 83
Could—I do more—for Thee— (J447, Fr443, F21), 27–28

Delayed till she had ceased to know (J58, Fr67, F40), 133, 166n. 6
Did Our Best Moments last— (J393, Fr560, F27), 109
Distrustful of the Gentian (J20, Fr26, F1), 121, 123
Dreams are well—but / Waking's better— (J450, Fr449, F21), 30–31, 33
Dust is the only Secret— (J153, Fr166, F8), 44, 52, 64

Essential Oils—are wrung— (J675, Fr772, F34), 17, 78
Except to Heaven, she is nought (J154, Fr173, F8), 44, 52
Exultation is the going (J76, Fr143, F6) 70, 92

Faith is a fine invention (J185, Fr202, F10), 70, 80
Frequently the woods are pink— (J6, Fr24, F1), 120, 121, 122

Garlands for Queens (J34, Fr10, F1), 116, 124
Give little Anguish (J310, Fr422, F14), 117, 129
God permits industrious Angels— (J231,

Fr245, F10), 70, 77
Going to Heaven! (J79, Fr128, F6), 70, 99
Good to hide, and hear 'em hunt! (J842, Fr945), 21

He touched me, so I live to know (J506, Fr349), 37
Heaven—is what I cannot / reach! (J239, Fr310, F14), 117, 129
'Houses'—so the Wise Men tell me (J127, Fr139, F6), 70, 90
I breathed enough to take / the trick (J272, Fr308, F14), 117, 128
I bring an unaccustomed (J132, Fr126, F6), 70, 98
I cautious, scanned my little life (J178, Fr175, F8), 24, 67, 68, 99, 107
I cried at Pity—not at Pain— (J588, Fr394, F19), 100
I died for Beauty—but was scarce (J449, Fr448, F21), 30
I dwell in Possibility— (J657, Fr466, F22), 6
I have never seen 'Volcanoes'— (J175, Fr165, F8), 44, 62–63
I haven't told my garden yet— (J50, Fr40, F3).118, 138
I hide myself (J903, Fr80, F3 and 40), 48, 118, 136, 145
I'm the little 'Heart's Ease' (J176, Fr167, F8), 65, 66
I met a King this afternoon! (J166, Fr183, F8), 44, 52
I never hear the word (J77, Fr144, F6), 70
I never lost as much but twice (J49, Fr39, F3), 40, 118, 137
I never told the buried gold (J11, Fr38, F3), 118, 136, 145
I often passed the village (J51, Fr41, F3), 118, 138
I see thee better—in the Dark (J611, Fr442), 26, 29–30
I rose—because He sank— (J616, Fr454, F21), 23, 38–40
I think just how my shape / will rise

(J237, Fr252, F10), 70, 87
I—Years had been—from / Home— (J609, Fr440, F21), 23–24, 40
If *He dissolve*—then—there is *nothing—more* (J236, Fr251, F10), 70, 86–89
If I could bribe them by a Rose (J179, Fr176, F8), 24, 67, 68
If I should die (J54, Fr35, F3), 118, 139
If the foolish call them *"flowers"* (J168, Fr179, F8), 44, 54, 56
I'll tell you how the Sun rose (J318, Fr204, F10), 70. 81
In falling Timbers buried— (J614, Fr447, F21), 23, 29–30
In Ebon Box, when years have flown (J169, Fr180, F8), xiv, 40, 54–55, 57, 67
Inconceivably solemn! (J582, Fr414, F14), 117, 128
It ceased to hurt me, though / so slow (J584, Fr421, F14), 117, 130
It was given to me by / the Gods— (J454, Fr551, F21), 23, 24, 39, 41–42, 71, 109
It would have starved a Gnat— (J612, Fr444, F21), 28, 29, 41
It's all I have to bring today— (J26, Fr17, F1), 116, 124
I've nothing else—to bring, You know— (J224, Fr254, F10), xiv, 70, 86, 89

Just lost, when I was saved! (J160, Fr132, F10), 70, 82

Kill your Balm—and it's / Odors bless you— (J238, Fr309, F14), 117, 128

Least Rivers—docile to some sea (J212, Fr206, F10), 70, 83
Love—thou art high— (J453, Fr452, F21), 23, 33, 35–36
Low at my problem bending (J69, Fr99), 71, 114
Luck is not chance— / it's toil (J1350, Fr1360), vii, 71

Midsummer was it when they died (J962, Fr822), 119, 140

More Life—went out –when / He went
  (J422, Fr415, F14), 117, 128
Morns like these—we parted (J27, Fr18,
  F1), 116, 120, 148
My friend must be a Bird— (J92, Fr71,
  F3), 135
My life closed twice before its close—
  (J1732, Fr1773), 134
My Life had stood—a Loaded Gun (J754,
  Fr764, F34
My Wars are laid away in Books (J1549,
  Fr1579), 13

New feet within my garden go— (J99,
  Fr79, F3), 118, 136, 145
Nobody knows this little Rose— (J35,
  Fr1, F1), 124–25

One dignity delays for all— (J98, Fr77,
  F3), 118, 136
One life of so much / Consequence! (J270,
  Fr248, F10), 83–84
Our journey had advanced— (J615,
  Fr453, F21), 23, 36–37, 40
Our lives are Swiss (J80, Fr129, F6), 70,
  100

Perhaps I asked too large— (J352, Fr368,
  F17), xiv, 224
Portraits / Pictures are to daily faces
  (J170, Fr174, F8), 51, 59, 66
Proud of my broken heart, since thou
  didst break it (J1736, Fr1760), 76
Publication is the Auction (J709, Fr788,
  F37), 11

Rehearsal to Ourselves (J379, Fr664,
  F30), 50
Removed from Accident of Loss (J424,
  Fr417, F14), 117, 129

Safe in their Alabaster Chambers— (J216,
  Fr124, F6 and 10), 70, 71–102
Sexton! My Master's sleeping here (J96,
  Fr75, F3), 135
Shall I take thee, the Poet said (J1126,
  Fr1243), 144
She died at play (J75, Fr141, F6), 70, 91
She slept beneath a tree (J25, Fr15, F1),
  116, 124
Sleep is supposed to be (J13, Fr35, F3),
  118, 139, 166n. 4, 167n. 12
So bashful when I spied her! (J91, Fr70,
  F3), 135
Some things that fly (J89, Fr68, F3), 6,
  133, 134
Superiority to Fate (J1081, Fr1043), 72

Tell all the Truth but tell it slant—
  (J1129, Fr1263)
The Brain is Wider than the / Sky (J632,
  Fr358, F17), 18, 19
The Clock strikes one that just struck
  two— (J1569, Fr1598), 79
The Court is far away (J235, Fr250, F10),
  77
The feet of people walking home (J7,
  Fr16, F1 and 14), 104, 116, 120, 121,
  125, 127–32, 148
The Gentian weaves her fringes— (J18,
  Fr21, F1)
The Lamp burns sure—within— (J233,
  Fr247, F10), 70, 78, 83
The maddest [nearest] dream—recedes—
  (J319, Fr304, F1), 126
The Maylay—took the Pearl— (J452,
  Fr451, F21), 34–35, 40
The morns are meeker than they were—
  (J12, Fr32, F3), 118, 136, 139
The Only News I know (J827, Fr820,
  F40), 119, 132, 141
The Outer—from the Inner (J451, Fr450,
  F21), 23, 31, 39
The Poets light but / Lamps— (J883,
  Fr930, Set 5), 78, 102
The rainbow never tells me (J97, Fr76,
  F3), 118, 135
The Rose did caper on her cheek— (J208,
  Fr200, F10), 70, 79–80
The *Sun—just touched* the / Morning
  (J232, Fr246, F10), 70, 77–78
The Sun kept stooping—stooping low!
  (J152, Fr182, F8), 44, 51
The thought beneath so slight a film—
  (J210, Fr203, F10), 70, 80–81
There came a Day at Summer's Full
  (J322, Fr325, F13), 11
There are two Ripenings (J332, Fr420,

F14), 117, 129, 130
There is a morn by men unseen– (J24, Fr13, F1), 116, 120, 121, 124
These are my Letters to the World (J441, Fr519, F24), 8
These are the days (J130, Fr122, F6), 70, 92
They ask but our Delight— (J868, Fr908), viii, 143
They shut me up in Prose—, (J613, Fr445, F21), 2, 5–7, 16–22, 40, 84
This was a Poet— (J448, Fr446, F21), 2, 5–7, 16–22, 40, 84, 124
Tho' I get home how late— / how late (J207, Fr199, F10), 70, 79
Tho' my destiny be Fustian— (J163, Fr131, F10), 70, 78–79
'Tis anguish grander than Delight (J984, Fr192,), 50
'Tis so much joy! (J172, Fr170, F8), 60–61
To fight aloud is very brave— (J126, Fr138, F6), 70, 91
To learn the Transport by the Pain (J167, Fr178, F8), 53
Trust in the Unexpected (J555, Fr561, F27), 16

'Unto Me?' I do not know you— (J964, Fr825, F40), 119, 141

Wait till the majesty of Death (J171, Fr169, F8), 55, 59, 60, 61
We—Bee and I—live / by the quaffing— (J230, Fr244, F10), 76
We lose—because we win— (J21, Fr28, F1), 121
Went up a year this evening! (J93, Fr72, F3), 135, 166n. 7
What if I say I shall / not wait (J277, Fr305), 127
Whatever it is—she has tried it— (J1129, Fr1263), 103

When I was small, a / Woman died (J596, Fr518, F24), 90
Whether my bark went down at sea (J52, Fr33, F3), 118, 139
Who never lost (J73, Fr136, F6), 70, 102
With thee, in the Desert— (J209, Fr201, F10), 70, 80

You're right—'the way *is* /Narrow'— (J234, Fr249, F10), 84–85

Letters

L6, 109
L105, 107
L110, 109
L225, 75
L238, 109
L255, 130
L256, 130
L260, 126
L261, 8, 125–26
L265, 111, 123, 126
L268, 12
L271, 10
L342, 18
L342a, 19, 149
L444a, 8
L470, 131
L750, 86
L785, 163n. 11
L805, 79
L868, 163n. 11
L902, 79
L926, 163n. 11
L937a, 8
L979, vii
L1034, vii
L902, 79
L926, 163n. 11
L937a, 8
L979, vii
L1034, vii

www.ingramcontent.com/pod-product-compliance
Lightning Source LLC
Chambersburg PA
CBHW021215240426
43672CB00026B/177